# The
# POWER of
# PASSION

# About the Author

JUSTIN LANGER OPENS THE BATTING for Australia in Test match cricket. He had a slow start to his career after surviving a baptism of fire in his first Test against the West Indies in 1993. Having overcome many adversities and setbacks, he is now an admired and respected member of one of the most powerful Australian teams in cricket history.

He was chosen in the Western Australian Team of the Century and was one of only four members of the Australian Test team to play in every one of the phenomenal world record run of 16 consecutive Test match victories. He has played in 51 Tests going into the summer of 2002-2003 and scored 12 Test centuries, forming a formidable opening partnership with Matthew Hayden. Statistically, this partnership is comparable to that of the great opening partnership of West Indies greats Greenidge and Haynes in the 1980s.

He is happily married to his childhood sweetheart Sue and is the proud father of three daughters, Jessica, Ali-Rose and Sophie. If he has his way he will be adding to this list of children in the future, although Sue may have something to say about that.

Justin comes from a very close family and credits his success on the cricket field to his backyard Test match experience with his brothers Adam and Jonathon and his sister Jemma. His parents Colin and Joy-Anne are his greatest supporters who have been his best mentors throughout his life.

Apart from being a devoted family man, Justin is the Patron of the Children's Leukaemia and Cancer Research Foundation in Western Australia, as well as a member of the Australia Day Council of Western Australia. He is a very patriotic Australian who likes nothing more than spending time with his family and friends.

Justin is also a keen writer who is a regular contributor to websites, newspapers and magazines.

# JUSTIN LANGER

# The
# POWER of
# PASSION

Edited by Arthur Stanley

SWAN
SPORT

Published by:

Swan Sport Pty. Ltd., P.O. Box 80, Isle of Capri QLD 4217  Australia

Fax: (07) 5531 7986  E-mail: swan.sport@bigpond.com

ISBN 1-877082-25-2

Edited by Arthur Stanley

Text design by Eli Nacson

Cover design by Eli and Rhett Nacson

Front and back cover images by Jack Atley - www.jackatley.com

Printed and Bound in Australia by Griffin Press

1 3 5 7 9 8 6 4 2

*I dedicate this book to my four angels,*

*Sue, Jessica, Ali-Rose & Sophie.*

*And to absent friends.*

# Acknowledgements

I would like to sincerely thank Arthur Stanley for turning my words into a book - he has done a great job. Eli Nacson for his patience and expertise in turning this book into a product of which I can be proud of. Austin Robertson for backing the project. Noddy Holder and Justin Hogan for their support and opinion. Mum and Dad for giving me the power of passion.

# Contents

Foreword  *xi*

Preface  *xiii*

Introduction  *xvii*

1. Goals with Wings  *1*
*Why The Baggy Green Cap Means So Much To Australian Cricketers*

2. Champions and Characters  *23*

3. Best of the Best  *45*
*Secrets Behind The Success Of The Australian Test XI*

4. Courage, Discipline and Matty Hayden  *75*

5. The Battler  *93*

6. The Pain of Disappointment  *103*

7. Tackling Inner Demons  *117*

8. Fighting Back  *123*

9. The Joys of Touring  *133*

10. He Who Endures Wins in the End  *147*

11. The Power of Positive Thoughts  *155*

12. The Smiling Assassin  *163*

13. Laughter is Inner Jogging  *175*

14. Backing Yourself Takes Guts  *183*

15. Mind Power and Creating Your Dreams  *217*

16. Mentors  *243*

17. Keeping Life in Perspective  *273*

# Foreword

## By Stephen Waugh

IF EVER THERE'S BEEN A CRICKETER I've played alongside who is ideally suited to writing a book about life's lessons, to pass on his wisdom and perspective on different issues and situations, it is Justin Langer. Like most people who communicate well, Lang is a great listener and learner. These two qualities are very often undervalued. The ability to listen and learn enables people to move forward in their lives and deal with what is presented to them. Of course, you must also be pro-active in what you do and believe in what you want to achieve, in order to realise your dreams and ambitions.

Quite often on tour, Lang and I will discuss our thoughts on the "meaning of life" and why things turn out a certain way. We agree that you decide your own destiny and that you are in charge of the direction you want to go. Being fortunate enough to have toured the world for many years as professional cricket players, we have met many varied and interesting people, tasted other cultures and been exposed to events we could never have imagined.

While many people have also had these privileged opportunities, not all make use of the ingredients required to make life's recipe a lot easier to assemble. Like a good recipe, everyone has the basic ingredients to make the end result, but it's the way you use them and the little extra bits of knowledge that make the final product.

Treating people with compassion, knowing the difference between right and wrong, being a leader, setting the right example to younger people, and taking time for other's needs are just some of the qualities I see in Justin. But, as always, he is continually looking to better himself. I'd be lying if I said he hasn't got some faults. I'm sure his wife could name a few, but to me, Lang's greatest strength is his resilience and inner strength. Coming back from being dropped as the No.3 batsman on the 2001 Ashes tour to become a record-breaking opening batsman is one of modern day's great sporting stories.

For a time, Lang was a languisher, feeling sorry for himself, but once his mind conquered this obstacle, he bounced back a better, more rounded cricketer and a person everyone now looks up to. To me he is always an inspiration and someone to "chew the fat over" because he always has a way of knowing what to say and how to say it. His message always seems to make sense. He has a gift of insightfulness and a manner that makes for peaceful resolutions, and I for one can't wait to read his book, to continue life's learning process.

*– Steve Waugh*

# Preface

*"Be bold – and mighty forces will come to your aid"*

**BASIL KING**

I WAS ENCOURAGED TO ATTEMPT this story because I believe that certain aspects of our society promote limitations. Why limit yourself to being average? If you have a talent, make the most of it. If you have a dream, why not go after it?

It is my belief that anyone who achieves their ambitions has taken giant steps toward throwing off those limitations so easily placed upon us by our society. How many times have you heard, "It's impossible", "You'll never be able to do that", "You/him/her - no way", "Why would you want to do that?", "It's too risky", "You're not good enough", and so the list of cliches that infest our cultural vocabulary goes on.

To believe in this way of thinking is insane, and I have to say, I just don't believe in the trap of this attitude or thinking. It is as simple as that.

You can read example after example of people who have beaten all odds to achieve greatness. There are thousands of books and stories about famous people who have achieved greatness in their chosen field. Greatness is relative of course, but what may seem the smallest act of achievement can be an act of greatness to you. There is nothing more inspiring than seeing people achieving their ambitions. Reaching a goal takes courage and determination: it takes desire and the strength to follow a dream, it takes commitment and discipline, and it takes a willingness to say no to those people or attitudes that say it can't be done.

A friend once told me that critics or doubters are "either jealous, or they wouldn't really know". With this in mind, why worry about the critics or the cynics? Why let others steal your power and rob you of the one thing in life that is truly yours? Your dreams and ambitions should be cherished and under no circumstances given to or taken away by anyone. This is easier said than done, but the challenge is to go forward towards your dream. Find the courage to live the lifestyle that you truly desire, not one that you feel is simply the right thing to do.

I have not achieved greatness in my chosen profession of cricket, but I can say that I am giving it a go. The worst thing that can happen in doing something we are truly passionate about is that we can fail. Believe it or not, the more times you fail at something the closer you are to getting it right. In most cases you can learn more from failing than you do from succeeding.

Throughout my cricket career I have felt the pain of disappointment and failure many times. In the big picture, I wouldn't be the player or person I am today if I hadn't been through these times.

If we are truly willing to follow our ambitions with commitment and passion then the chances of us not achieving our targets are pretty remote. Along the way we may fail a few times, maybe many times, but this makes us stronger and stronger and leaves the final rewards tasting even sweeter.

By sharing my experiences and the lessons I have learned, I hope you may be able to find new focus in your own life. Many of the people written about in this book have been inspirations to me and I hope the lessons I have learned from them will also be of help to you.

*– JL*

# Introduction

## I am Justin Langer

*I am a professional cricket player who has been fortunate to be part of a great Australian cricket team.*

*I feel like I could run through a brick wall when I am wearing the baggy green cap.*

*I have learned my best life lessons in times of adversity and disappointment.*

*I am glad now that I have fought through these tough times in my life.*

*I struggle coming to terms with other people's poverty and sickness.*

*I admire anyone who gives 100 per cent and leads by example.*

*I believe loyalty is worth more than any money in the world.*

*I know living in a comfort zone is dangerous and unfruitful.*

*I believe in respect, discipline, love, passion and hard work.*

*I am a happily married father of three beautiful daughters.*

*I know life is worth living for these four heavenly angels.*

*I know that self-belief is the essence of personal progress.*

*I am convinced your family is your most important asset.*

*I have many good friends and a few best ones.*

*I don't like ignorance, quitters or disrespect.*

*I know single-minded pursuit is rewarding.*

*I believe in the power and mystery of God.*

*I often think about the meaning of life.*

*I love kids and the freedom of youth.*

*I think flexibility in life is important.*

*I love watching the sun rise and set.*

*I believe in the power of dreaming.*

*I enjoy being part of a team.*

**I am Justin Langer**

\* \* \*

THIS BOOK IS MORE THAN JUST a cricket book. It is true that I do play cricket for a living, but I hope the chapters you are about to read will reflect more than just a cricketer's story. The beliefs, values and lessons I have learned in my life as a sportsman, a son, a brother, a husband, a father, and a true-blue Australian, have helped mould who I am today. *The Power of Passion* is a tribute to the many people who have influenced my development. They have taught me many valuable lessons. I want to share them with you.

# CHAPTER 1

# Goals with Wings

## WHY THE BAGGY GREEN CAP MEANS SO MUCH TO AUSTRALIAN CRICKETERS

**SHOT OF INSPIRATION # 1:**
*Dream and don't be afraid to dream BIG. No matter what, don't let anyone steal your dreams from you.*

*"A person can be as great as they want to be. If you believe in yourself and have the courage, the determination, the dedication, the competitive drive - and if you are willing to sacrifice the little things in life and pay the price for the things that are worthwhile — it can be done. Once a person has made a commitment to a way of life, they put the greatest strength in the world behind them. It's something we call heart power. Once a person has made this commitment, nothing will stop them short of success."*

VINCE LOMBARDI - **NFL coach and general manager**

## THE BAGGY GREEN CAP

I F YOU ASK ME, everything starts with a dream. When I was boy I wanted to be like the incomparable Sir Donald Bradman. If he could do it, then why can't I? If it wasn't The Don, then it was Allan Border and his 11,174 Test runs. On other occasions I would say, if Kim Hughes can play a cover drive on one knee, then surely I can too! These men were my heroes, but more than that, they were a part of my dream. They were like actors in the fantasy world of my dreams. Some day, some how, I wanted to wear the baggy green cap and be just like them.

To appreciate this book you need to understand that the baggy green cap means absolutely everything to me. It has been part of my life since I was a very young boy. If it weren't for the baggy green cap I wouldn't be who I am today, because the journey towards my dream has taken me to all parts of the emotional and physical spectrum.

It has been a dream that has kept me hungry: hungry to become the best I can be; hungry for success; hungry for constant improvement; hungry for more victories and triumphs; hungry to overcome adversity; hungry to be a winner; hungry for a commitment to excellence.

The same dream has been instrumental in teaching me the value of determination, discipline, desire, passion, commitment and honesty. Without these values I would never have achieved my dream of wearing the baggy green cap of the Australian cricket team. Without the dream I wouldn't be the person that I am today. Thanks to my dream I have experienced an incredible life journey that has taught me many lessons. When I first gained selection in the Australian cricket team it felt like I had reached the summit of my own personal Mt Everest.

The phone call came as the eggs boiled on the stove in front of me.

*"JL, it is Tony Mann (cricket manager at the WACA), here. I am calling to give you the wonderful news that you have been selected to play for Australia."*

Knowing that the Fourth Test was starting the following morning in Adelaide, I presumed this must have been a hoax call from one of my mates.

*"What do you mean I am playing for Australia? The Test starts tomorrow doesn't it?*

*"Yes, that is right but Damien (Martyn) has been poked in the eye at training this morning and will miss the Test. You have to be at the airport in an hour's time or they will find someone else to play."*

At a time like this it is almost impossible to describe the emotions. For years I had dreamed, planned, hoped and prayed for this moment. Now, it was here. At first my face went white because all of the blood in my body poured from my head into my pumping heart. Then, when the realisation hit me between the eyes, I ran around the house jumping up and down like I had just won the lottery.

Grabbing my younger brother Jonathon by the ear, I scampered up the stairs and picked up my favourite bat and softest pair of batting gloves. We ran out into the backyard and he threw me a few balls to prepare me for my Test debut that was only 24 hours away.

Although my brother isn't exactly in the same mould as the West Indian bowlers – he is five foot seven and throws left handed – I felt in good form and ready to take on the West Indies the following morning.

The enormity of the moment didn't hit me until I was sitting on the plane to Adelaide.

On my 21st birthday a friend of mine, Don Lee, told me that a short time after my sixth birthday I proclaimed to him, and anyone who would listen, that when I grew up I was going to play cricket for Australia. Having played a few good innings in the Sheffield Shield competition, I think Don was using this reminder to re-assure himself that I was on the way to keeping my childhood promise. He loves cricket and I knew he would be very proud if the day came when I wore the baggy green cap.

The Lee family were our next-door neighbours at the first house we ever lived in. Every Saturday morning Don would roll the lawn mower about a kilometre around the corner to the local park. When we arrived he mowed out a brand new cricket pitch, and all of the kids in the neighbourhood would come along for a "Test Match". After two teams had been selected, the Test Match would begin with gusto.

To this day, the smell of freshly cut morning grass reminds me of those magical Test matches. I would pretend to be Don Bradman, Viv Richards, Allan Border, Kim Hughes or Graeme Wood, while one of the other kids would look like Joel Garner, Andy Roberts or Michael Holding in my imagination.

I obviously can't remember telling the world that I wanted to play cricket for Australia, but I do remember those great Test matches at the local park. Even then I hated getting out, and because I was a pretty small kid, there was no way I was going to let the big kids get the better of me.

This attitude hasn't changed.

Sitting on the plane that day in January 1993, I began to understand how my childhood dreams and boasted ambitions back then were the catalysts to where I was that day. Daydreaming in the classroom, under a tree or at the local park helped me form a blueprint for my life. Obviously I had no idea what I had to do to play cricket for my country, but I did know that is what I most wanted in my life. Albert Einstein once said: "Imagination is more important than knowledge." How true.

As a kid I had absolutely no knowledge of the necessary pathways to playing cricket for my country, but I did have a wild imagination that re-assured me that my dream was possible.

I am a dreamer. I believe that without dreams it is hard to achieve anything. Unless you have an idea of what you know, or at least think, will make you happy and content, then it is going to be very tough achieving anything in this life.

Like most young people I admitted hundreds of times to having no idea what I wanted to do when I left school. I think the majority of people have been through this panic. Some adults still have no idea what they want to do when they leave school, even though school finished for them years ago. I went to university for a year and started an arts degree, basically because I had no idea what else to do. I liked writing, but how on earth was an arts degree going to help me get a job in the future? I didn't really want to be a journalist, an English teacher or an artist, or did I? To be honest I wasn't really sure.

During school I had contemplated being a physical education teacher. I thought teaching sport all day would be fun. I think the novelty of teaching wore off after 12 years of a school classroom, so I thought about becoming a chef. This ambition was put to rest quickly when a big, fat, grumpy young chef made my life misery during a week of work experience at school. Cooking for a living was not for me, so I finally decided that I would work hard in my final year of school, get enough marks and study physiotherapy at university. Unfortunately, this didn't work out either because I didn't get enough marks in my exams. As disappointed as I was at the time, I wonder now how different my life would have been had I become a physiotherapist.

Hindsight is a wonderful thing and I occasionally wonder where I would be today if I had chosen a different fork in the road?

Among all my pubescent doubts and insecurities was one constantly shining light - the baggy green cap.

When the captain of the flight announced our arrival into Adelaide, I knew I was only an hour away from touching the soft, woollen fabric of the baggy green cap. Everything I had dreamed about was about to become reality. The moment couldn't come fast enough.

After bumbling my way through a short press conference at the Adelaide airport, I finally arrived at the Hindley Park Royal. I will never forget arriving at the hotel.

Picture the moment: walking through the double doors of the hotel entrance I looked over my left shoulder to the raised piano bar area. Sitting at the bar, waiting to go out for a meal, were Allan Border, Ian Healy, David Boon, Mervyn Hughes and Tony Dodemaide. Having met these guys only once or twice before as opposition players, I was extremely shy as to what to say or do. While they were on to me like a shot, shaking hands and congratulating me, I was all at sea. These guys were my heroes rather than my new teammates, and I was speechless and uneasy.

Fortunately, this attitude changed when the concierge guided me to my hotel room. Luckily my roommate Ian Healy was downstairs, because the next few minutes turned into something of a frenzy. Skipping into the room, the first thing I saw was a large, cardboard box with a gold insignia written on the top saying: JUSTIN LANGER – AUSTRALIAN TEST CRICKETER. Wow!

Ripping off the wrapping tape, I dived headfirst into the box.

When you play for Australia, it is like Christmas. You are given shirts, tracksuits, helmets, shorts, bike pants and sweaters. These are nice, but I had eyes for one thing only. Throwing these extras recklessly over my right shoulder, I had to wait until I reached the bottom of the box before I found what I was looking for. There, at the base of the pile, was my dream, my summit, my life and even today, my most treasured possession. Shining out like a beacon in the sea was my baggy green cap. No longer "a" baggy green cap or "the" baggy green cap, but MY BAGGY GREEN CAP.

For many people that is all it is - an unusual looking baggy green cap - but for me it was everything. I felt like a gold prospector who had spent his life searching for a gold nugget. After years of prospecting, hunting and exploring, I finally came across a massive gold lump that looked more beautiful than anything I had ever seen before. My baggy green was like the gold nugget to the prospector; the masters degree to the student; the first baby to a parent; the premiership trophy to the coach; the Olympic medal to the athlete; the black belt to a martial artist; the first yacht to a sailor. In other words, it was the destination that I had dreamt about since I was a six-year-old boy. Regardless of what happened from that day forth, I had worked hard for my target and no one could ever take it away from me. Besides the birth of my three beautiful daughters, I can't remember a prouder moment in my life.

Like my babies, the first few moments were totally consumed by staring. I couldn't believe it was really mine. I wanted to cherish every single bit of the moment. When I finally mustered up the courage to pick it up and place it on my head, the smile beaming from my face was priceless. As I mentioned, I am glad Ian Healy wasn't in the room, because I was prancing around watching every single move in the mirror. I felt like the only person in the world, as I hopped, skipped and swaggered around like I was the king of the world. For a while I felt untouchable as I reminisced on my journey to this point.

This indestructibility was reasonably short-lived because within a few minutes it dawned upon me that reaching my dream was one thing, doing something with it was another. The fact was that in less than 24 hours I would be in the centre of the Adelaide Oval facing the mighty West Indies fast bowlers. This prospect shakes you into reality at the best of times, let alone when you have never done it before.

## BATTING NO.3 FOR AUSTRALIA

After a sleepless night I arrived with my new teammates to the magnificent Adelaide Oval. At the practice nets before the game a short, stocky bloke came up to me and said, "JL, what do you think about batting at No.3 for Australia today?"

"No worries AB, I would love to."

I mean, here I was calling Allan Border AB, and he was calling me JL. Basically, life couldn't get much better than that. I really had made it. The great Allan Border, my childhood hero, was calling me by my nickname and I was calling him by his. How much better can this dream get?

History shows that we won the toss that day and sent the West Indies into bat. In an incredible day's play, we bowled out the West Indians cheaply and had to bat for 45 minutes before stumps. Because we fielded first I had an opportunity to calm the nerves a little and get into the pace of Test match cricket. In all honesty, even five hours fielding in the baggy green cap could never have prepared me for what was to come later that afternoon.

With dark clouds forming over the horizon, David Boon and Mark Taylor, two of the most experienced campaigners in Australian cricket history, walked out to open the batting against one of the fiercest bowling attacks in the game. The presence of these two outstanding veterans was a very comforting feeling for me. I figured their experience would see us through the day, allowing me to relax, have a good night's sleep and prepare myself for my first bat in Test cricket the following day.

This wish couldn't have been further from what actually happened.

While I was strapping on my right pad, a huge appeal and a disappointed roar from the crowd echoed through the home team changing rooms. Mark Taylor was out first ball of the innings. I couldn't believe it. It was like one of those bad dreams when you miss your alarm, or lose all of your clothes in the middle of the classroom. Panic set in, as the image of being the first player timed out in a game of Test cricket flooded my mind. I didn't even have my second pad on when Mark Taylor was halfway back to the changing room.

Frenzied, I slapped on my left pad, before attempting to stand up on my legs that felt like wobbly jelly. The nerves were suffocating me as I pushed my protective box and thigh pad into place. From there, I grabbed my brand new Australian helmet lying next to Mark Taylor, who was already sitting on the changing room bench. Time felt like it was speeding like light as I tripped over my own feet on my way out onto the ground. A couple of PK chewies brought a sense of familiarity to the scene as I eventually walked out of the rooms to the best wishes of my teammates.

This was the moment of truth. The moment I'd been waiting for all my life.

Walking down the race there were plenty of best wishes coming from the crowd, although I can remember a couple of comments from die-hard South Australian supporters, suggesting Darren Lehmann or Greg Blewett would have been far better choices by the selectors. If there wasn't enough pressure already, the moment was intensifying with every passing second.

## FIRST BALL IN TEST CRICKET

If my legs felt like jelly in the changing rooms, they had been reduced to liquid when I took guard for the first ball of my Test career. I will never forget it. A man by the name of Ian Bishop was pushing off the Adelaide Oval sightscreen. For those who don't know Ian Bishop, he is a massive man, with a physique like Adonis. Unfortunately, the straight boundaries in Adelaide are the longest in the world, so from where I was standing, this Adonis-like giant from Antigua looked more like a tiny stick figure. This is a frightening feeling, because although he may look like a stick figure one minute, a few seconds into his bowling approach you know that he transforms into something resembling a fire-breathing dragon.

Before the stick figure, turned giant, had bowled a ball at me, great West Indian opening batsman Desmond Haynes, who was fielding under the helmet at short leg, was shouting, "Come on Bishy . . . he's scared Bishy, he's scared."

At the same time, Keith Arthurton, who was always the most immaculately groomed cricket player in the world, was dancing around at point like he was practising for the nightclub later that night. Smiling and singing, he transferred similar sentiments to Ian Bishop who was scratching at the end of his bowling mark like an angry, ferocious bull. Arthurton was suggesting that, "This boy should be at high school Bishy . . . not playing Test cricket Bishy . . . send him back to dee schoolyard Bishy."

When I looked around for support, the wicketkeeper and slips were standing near the sightscreen at the opposite end to the bowler. Seeing the fieldsmen so far back behind the stumps is never a pleasant experience. Brian Lara was kissing his teeth and grinning like a Cheshire cat, while Richie Richardson and Carl Hooper were standing around, looking as relaxed as they would during a game of Caribbean beach cricket. This whole scene was classic stuff, but it did nothing to ease my nerves. The pressure felt like it was about to swallow me whole.

Unfortunately, there is nowhere to hide in the middle of a Test match, so I had to rely on the mantra that I still use today. As Ian Bishop came roaring in to bowl that first ball, I kept saying, "Watch the ball, watch the ball, watch the ball." This I did, because as it whistled past my nose at about 150km/h, I am sure I saw the shiny Kookaburra emblem on the ball laughing at me. Smiling, I thought to myself that although I was under the pump, I had survived one ball in Test cricket.

History goes on to write that the third ball of my Test debut was marginally different than the first. While the process may have been identical, the result was very different. Again, "Dessie" Haynes and Keith Arthurton were encouraging their fired-up teammate, and again I relied on my pre-ball routine and mantra. The difference this time was that I didn't execute my plan of watching the ball because on this occasion the laughing Kookaburra turned into a guided missile that rocketed into the back of my helmet. At that instant I felt like I had been struck on the back of the head by a sledgehammer.

Right at this defining moment I was in something of a predicament. I knew that Richie Benaud and Bill Lawry were up in the commentary box. I knew that my mum and dad were watching me from the grandstand. I knew there was a capacity Adelaide Oval crowd cheering for Australia and I knew the West Indians thought that I would retire hurt and wimp out of the contest. I also knew that although it would have been easy to walk off and retire hurt, I was playing cricket for my country and batting with another childhood hero, all-round tough man David Boon. There was no way I was going to let down Boony, my team, my family, friends and the supporters, by quitting this challenge.

Unfortunately, tough man Boon didn't exactly offer me the support or advice I was expecting. Walking down the pitch, as only the staunch David Boon could, he took me away from the huddle that had gathered around me, and whispered, "JL, there are no heroes in Test cricket, I suggest you retire hurt." Looking at him in disbelief, I quickly explained my predicament. I would be too embarrassed to walk off now, as I would be admitting that I was a bit of a weakling and I certainly didn't want this to be the perception after only three balls in Test cricket. I had worked too hard for this moment and although the bang on the back of my head had shaken me, there is no way that I was going to retire hurt.

After translating these feelings to Boony, he simply nodded, frowned and said, "Well young man, it is your choice, but I just want you to remember, there are no heroes in Test cricket." With this, he turned and walked back to his position at the non-striker's end.

With my eyes refocused and my brain resettled, I took guard for the fourth ball in my Test career. The scenario was no different than previously, in that Bishop was running in like a steam train, the West Indian fieldsmen were keyed up and I was telling myself to watch the ball. The problem was that one Antiguan stick figure, rapidly turning into a fire-breathing dragon, became three Antiguan stick figures come fire-breathing dragons. The knock to the head was obviously taking its toll.

Now, I know that in Rocky III, brother-in-law Paulie tells Rocky to hit the one in the middle when Rocky describes seeing three Apollo Creeds in front of him, but I'm afraid I was not willing to take that risk. Instead of gambling on one of the three Ian Bishops, I pulled away, stumbled a little, and felt like I was about to go down for the count. This was a very strange feeling, and again the fear of embarrassment entered my world. For the second time in as many minutes, David Boon waddled up to me, put his arm around my shoulder and suggested in no uncertain terms that, "I've told you once, I don't want to tell you again, there are no heroes in Test cricket - retire hurt." By this time the doctor had run out on to the field and he was giving me the same advice. "You don't have to be a hero. There are no heroes in Test cricket, you should come off the ground with me, so that I can take a better look at you."

With stars flying around in front of my eyes, I will admit that this advice a second time around was more tempting than the first time, but again I turned them both down. I didn't want to be seen as a wimp in the Australian colours. Telling Boony this, he shook his head, rather than nod it, frowned, turned and left me to face the music.

As luck would have it, dark clouds and fading light saved me from much more misery on that first night. When the umpires offered me the light, I couldn't get off the ground quick enough, even though I was having the time of my life. In seven overs, I'd been hit on the body about five times, my batting partner had told me to wimp out, and the West Indians were convinced I wasn't ready for Test cricket. Although I thought I was in the form of my life having hit a few balls in the middle of my bat with my brother the morning before, I had all night to contemplate being 0 not out after one of the toughest ordeals of my life.

## FACING UP TO CURTLY AMBROSE

After consecutive sleepless nights, the first ball of the following day couldn't come quick enough. Although I felt a little punch-drunk walking out to the middle with my childhood hero, I was desperate to make amends for the night before. I was ready to take on these West Indian bullies and show them I wouldn't be intimidated. As it turned out, I was standing at the non-striker's end when Curtly Ambrose came in to bowl the first over of the second day's play.

Boony, with his characteristic look of determination and fight etched across his face, was enough to inspire anybody, let alone me in my first Test match. As the nuggety, tough, right-hander faced up to the third ball from the bounding Ambrose, I was pinching myself that this wasn't just a dream.   Unfortunately, a half volley from Ambrose that bounced a little higher than expected, hit my Tasmanian teammate flush on the end of his left elbow.  This was an instant reminder that this was definitely reality.  I knew this had really hurt Boony, because it was very unusual to see the great David Boon hopping and grimacing his way out to square leg, rather than staring back at the bowler as if to say, "You'll have to hit me harder than that."  I knew how my mate was feeling.

After a few seconds, and ever the opportunist, I couldn't pass up this moment.  Running over to David, who was clutching his left arm like he'd been shot by a rifle, I put my arm around my hero and whispered, "Boony, there are no heroes in this Test cricket mate - I think you should retire hurt."  With a look of defeat on his face, he glared at me, nodded his head and said, "I think you're right son", and with this he turned toward the Adelaide Oval changing room and retired hurt.

## A HAPPY FIRST TEST

My first Test match was better than I could ever imagine. Although Australia lost the match by one run, I had been involved in one of the greatest Test matches ever played.  Australia had been chasing 185 for victory in the second innings and I found myself at the crease at 1/5 after Boony had gone for a duck in his second dig. It was tough facing up to four fierce Windies pacemen – Ambrose, Bishop, Courtney Walsh and Kenny Benjamin – in my first Test. Wickets fell around me and before I knew it, we were within sight of victory with eight wickets down – just 41 runs short of our target.

When I tried to pull a short ball from Bishop, the Windies players screamed as one. I had feathered a ball to the wicketkeeper and was on my way for 54. Many cricket fans will recall this Test match – it was the one in which Craig McDermott (18) and Tim May (41no) bravely took us to the brink of victory only for McDermott to get a much-disputed touch off Ambrose. The sight of Allan Border throwing a cricket ball to the ground in the changing room, his face etched in pain and frustration, said much about how important that game was to Australia.

My debut was no fairytale as I didn't score a century (20 and 54) or hit the winning run, but I did experience the immense pride and satisfaction of achieving and living a dream. Like that Test match the journey had been no fairytale either. It had taken a great deal of hard work, discipline and passion to get there, but when I did it was worth every single bit of it.

## MORE THAN A PIECE OF CLOTH

One of the most inspirational books that I have ever read is called *Zen in the Martial Arts*. Over the years this book has acted as a reminder to me of some of the basic principles of peak performance. Regardless of the endeavour you pursue, the basic principles are fundamentally the same. Author Joe Hyams uses martial arts to highlight these principles, just as I have used cricket in *The Power of Passion* to describe the important principles of success.

One of the concepts Hyams writes about involves dreams, goal setting and the journey involved in achieving your life ambitions. In describing the physical and spiritual journey of a martial artist, Hyams says: "The beginning student in most martial arts disciplines wears a white belt that, according to tradition, signifies innocence. With the passage of time the belt becomes soiled from handling and use, so the brown belt signifies the second stage of learning. As more time passes the belt becomes darker until it is black – the black belt stage. With even more use, the black belt becomes frayed, almost white, signifying that the wearer is returning again to innocence – a Zen characteristic of human perfection."

During the recent summer I was surprised by the criticism of Steve Waugh's baggy green cap. After 17 years and 148 Test matches you would expect his cap to look a little worse for wear. The criticism surrounded the untidy and tatty appearance of the cap sitting on top of the captain's head. As far as I am concerned, these people mustn't have anything better to talk about. Like the martial arts master, Steve Waugh's cap is symbolic of everything that is great about Steve Waugh and Australian cricket. He has almost completed the full journey of his career.

Starting as a young boy, or white belt, he learnt his craft and developed his skills to the point where different levels of achievement were attained. At first he learned the basic skills of batting, just like a novice martial artist learns the basic kicks, punches and concepts of defence. By doing this he was able to move through the junior ranks until he eventually played and mastered club cricket, or the green belt. From there he moved on to first-class cricket or the brown belt. To reach this level he needed to show strength of character and an ability to fight and conquer. When this level was conquered, he earned the right to play Test cricket, or wear the black belt. With this, came respect and standing in the community. It was also here that the journey of understanding and teaching was about to begin. With each level came new challenges. Rather than getting easier, the challenges deepened. Each Test match broadened his understanding of himself and the game. Like a black belt he had to constantly improve every aspect of his life if he was to survive and triumph in the tough, cutthroat world of Test cricket. Like the martial artist's black belt, he never washed his baggy green cap. The sweat, the dust, the blood, the celebrations, the pain, the sacrifice, the effort of each encounter, simply added more character to the cloth on his head or around his waist.

If you were to ask a high-ranking martial artist why he never washes his black belt, he will tell you the same as Steve Waugh will tell you. These treasures are more than just a piece of cloth; these treasures are a symbol of everything. Everything Steve Waugh and the martial arts master believe in can be seen in their baggy green cap or their black belt. There is no way they will wash away a single ounce of the life of their cloth.

I look at Steve Waugh's tattered, torn and smelly cap and see more than just a piece of cloth. I see 17 years and around 150 Tests worth of blood, sweat and tears. In his cap I see a career of ups and downs, good times and bad, stories of many lands, stories of camaraderie and victories, lessons from adversity and triumph. I see the make-up of a champion, a character of steel. His baggy green cap tells a story of a young man who started with a dream and ended as a master. Steve Waugh's baggy green cap shouldn't be chastised or condemned, it should be admired and revered and used as a symbol of inspiration, aspiration and pride. The cap's peak might be coming apart at the seams and the green felt may be faded, but let us not forget that a masterpiece like this develops over a man's life or his career. I think it should be applauded and honoured like the Zen master's worn old belt or pure white garments.

Steve Waugh deserves to wear this priceless treasure on his head because it symbolises the man, the master, the role model, and the leader. Who has the right to question that right?

My baggy green cap, the black belt, the degree, the first job, the first child, the wedding vows, the first book, or the uniform are all symbols of a life's journey. I call these things "goals with wings". I believe it is important to have targets in your life, which will help you fly toward your life's dreams. My baggy green cap means the world to me because it tells the story of my life until now. It is more than just a reward of achievement; it is a symbol of the journey of my life. It is the reason why I leave home and my family for a greater part of the year. It is why I left the security of a 9-5 job and the reason I push myself endlessly towards my goals. I see in my baggy green cap what I see in Steve Waugh's cap or my martial arts teacher's rugged black belt. My cap may not be as worn and soiled as my captain's, but I hope mine will end up looking just as rough.  If it does, I know that I will have lived a wonderful journey of ups and downs that will make me the person I aspire to be.

* * *

*For what it's worth, my advice to you is this: have a dream and believe in your ability to achieve that dream.  Pursue your dream in a structured, prepared and relentless manner. Be tenacious and resilient. You can realise anything your imagination can conceive if you want it badly enough.*

# Champions and Characters

ONE OF THE BEST aspects of playing cricket for Australia is
that I have had the opportunity to meet some extraordinary
players along the way. These champions of the game offer pearls of
wisdom through their words or actions that inspire the rest of us.

### DENNIS LILLEE

Winding back the clock I will never forget December 26, 1981.
While the great Dennis Lillee sent the Melbourne Cricket Ground
spectators into a frenzy with his last ball of the day, this 11-year old

schoolboy was sent into a fantasy world of dreams and ambitions.

After watching my batting hero Kimberley John Hughes, with his golden hair and upright collar, score an incredible unbeaten Test century against the fierce combination of Holding, Roberts, Garner and Croft, the day only got better as I stared enchanted by the warrior Lillee and the 39,046 screaming Melbourne fans.

Watching D.K Lillee, with two wickets to his name in 3.5 overs, he placed the relatively new ball in his right hand. With the crowd chanting Li-LLEEE, Li-LLEEEE, Li-LLEEEEE, and the youngsters banging the advertising boards like they were trying to hammer holes in the metal signs, my aggressive, sweating, long-haired, pumped up, inspired and confident hero bent forward and pushed off to commence the final ball of the day. Forty four yards away, standing as still as a lighthouse, another hero, the incomparable, gum-chewing, fearless, unflappable Vivian Isaac Richards was waiting to tame anything Lillee had to offer. In the background were Rodney Marsh, Greg Chappell, Allan Border and Kimberley John, while Clive Lloyd was leaning nonchalantly on his bat at the non-striker's end.

In runs the king of pace bowling to the king of Test match batting. This is the ultimate battle. Two greats going head to head in front of a delirious, blood-thirsty Australian crowd. My eyes are glued to the television and my heart pumps like I am actually there, living the moment in the middle of the MCG. As D.K reaches the crease and jumps into the air, like only he could, he bowls a wide delivery to the externally calm Richards who swings his bat, only to inside edge the ball back onto his stumps. He is out on the last ball of Boxing Day 1981. Pumping his arm like a victorious general, Dennis ran straight past the conquered hero, towards the team changing room and throngs of stunned but delighted Melbourne fans. In the background of this insatiable drama, I stared triumphantly at Dennis's 10 teammates in baggy green caps, running around backslapping and laughing and cherishing the moment. It just doesn't get any better than that, especially for a cricket junkie like me.

I tell this story because from that day forth, I wanted to play a Boxing Day Test match for Australia. Also, because a few of the actors in that particular drama have turned out to be some of the great champions and characters that I have met over the years as a professional cricket player.

### ROD MARSH

When I was young boy I visited the WACA with my junior cricket team. Two particular images remain with me today of my first outing to the ground. The first is of Rodney Marsh jogging a warm-up lap with his teammates. Wearing a pair of running shorts and a tight T-shirt, Bacchus jogged along at the front of the pack with his chest out and his shoulders back. He looked like a prizefighter, looking fit and strong and ready to take on the world. To a young boy, he looked like a giant as he stared forward with the eye of a focussed boxer. Later in the day I watched as this prizefighter ran back to a mistimed hook shot and dived full length to take a spectacular running catch. It is funny the things a young mind remembers. Over time this champion player, ambassador and person called Rod Marsh has become a good friend and mentor of mine.

Recently, I was asked to talk on behalf of the Australian team and the Commonwealth Bank Cricket Academy, to farewell Bacchus from his position as the head coach of the academy. In a way it was like giving a eulogy because it is rare that you get the opportunity to publicly applaud a person like Rod. In my speech I thanked him for the role he had played in Australian cricket as a player, coach and icon. From the time I was a young boy, through my formative years as a player, until now, Rod has always been nothing short of a champion. When I was dropped from the Australian team in 1993, I rang Rod for some advice. All he had to say was, "Don't feel sorry for yourself, get on the next plane to Adelaide and do some bloody hard work here at the academy during the winter."

I couldn't get on the plane fast enough.

During that time he encouraged and supported me but he never gave me an easy ride. Like most champions, he is tough but very honest and fair. It was Rod in 1993 who told me that batting is about scoring runs, not occupying the crease. He roused me to back myself and play my shots and always look to score runs rather than survive. His message is the same as that of all the champions: Be bold, be aggressive and never look back, always forward.

A few years later I accepted an invitation to be a scholarship coach at the academy. To this day some of my fondest memories are of late Friday afternoons at the British Hotel in North Adelaide where I would sit with Rod, Dave Jennings, Richard Done and Jack Clark and talk cricket over a few very cold beers. Marsh, the legend, would reminisce on the past and predict the future, as we all discussed our greatest passion, the game of cricket. Then and now, I could never see my mate and my hero, the epitome of Australian cricket folklore, taking up a position as head coach of the English Cricket Academy, but then knowing Bacchus, he is doing it for the greater good of the game of cricket.

## GREG CHAPPELL

Standing next to Rod during that magnificent Boxing Day Test in 1981 was another great Australian player who has had an impact on me. Arguably the greatest modern-day player in Australian Test history, Gregory Stephen Chappell. His playing record speaks for itself. Technically he was an exceptional batsman, but now that I have met him, I understand that mentally he must have been as organised and prepared as any player ever, hence his outstanding record when he retired. Steve Waugh apart, I have never come across a person who knows the inner game of cricket as well as Greg Chappell does, or at least who can explain it as well as he is able to. On a number of occasions throughout my career, Greg has taken me aside and helped me re-organise my thinking.

Once in Adelaide when I was going through a rough patch, Greg tapped me on the shoulder and asked if he could be of any help. An hour or so later he was standing with me in the Adelaide Oval nets and talking to me about the importance of clearing my mind and focussing on the ball when I was batting. He described how he relied on one or two cues when he was batting and suggested that I might employ a similar approach to my game. Simplicity of thinking and a clear mind was his message. Just 24 hours later I scored 150 runs against South Australia, kicking off one of the most fruitful periods of my career. I am not sure Greg would offer me the same advice in Adelaide now that he is the coach of South Australia, but his encouragement and wisdom back then was invaluable.

Only last year, when I was watching the Lord's Test match against England from the sideline, Greg again asked me how I was getting along. At that stage I was fast approaching the lowest point of my career, so his words were timely. This time the champion Greg Chappell reiterated the importance of the mind, as well as talking about trusting my routines and relaxing so that I could react to anything the bowler had to dish up to me. He also told me to be sharp and ready when the next opportunity came around. He suggested I look back over all of my best innings and determine the fundamental characteristics and factors for the successes on those occasions. This I did, and I was amazed at how closely linked each success was in terms of preparation, thinking and execution.

By looking back at my past successes I not only gave myself a boost in confidence but I also gave myself a framework for which I could base the remainder of my career. Again, call it a coincidence, but when the next opportunity came in the final Test of the series I was sharp and ready and scored a Test century. I also went on to enjoy the most successful period of my Test career.

### KIM HUGHES

Statistically not as impressive, but certainly as entertaining, Kim Hughes is another champion I have had the privilege of meeting over the years. Like the images of Lillee and Marsh, I will never forget one particular shot played by Kim at the WACA ground. At the time I was only seven or eight years old, but on this day, Australia were playing New Zealand and Jeremy Coney was bowling his medium pacers. Dancing down the wicket, Kim launched into a cover drive on one knee. Admittedly this was his autograph stroke, but the image was tattooed into my brain as I vowed to learn how to play this shot if it was the last thing I ever did. Unfortunately I have never perfected such brilliance, but I still strive to play just one of these strokes before my career is over.

The first bat I ever bought with my saved up pocket money was a Kim Hughes black Slazenger bat, and the first bat I ever scored a century with was an old Kim Hughes bat that my Dad had bought at a charity auction. The memory is still strong in my mind, as this weapon was the one that helped ignite my hunger for scoring runs. Dad had purchased two bats that Kim had wielded in Test matches. Like chocolate sitting in the fridge at home, there was always the temptation to steal these bats from Dad's study and use them in our backyard Test matches. Unfortunately Dad refused to allow this to happen and instead of being put to good use, the two SS Jumbos lay sleeping in Dad's study, acting as trophies to be admired rather than weapons to be used.

Unfortunately, or fortunately depending upon whose eyes you are looking through, temptation finally got the better of me and while I resisted using the bats against wet tennis balls out in the backyard, I slipped one of the blades into my cricket bag one fateful Sunday morning. The pleasure of walking to the middle with my hero's bat in my hand, even though it was too big and far too heavy, was obviously an incredible confidence booster. If Kim Hughes could use this bat in a Test match then I wasn't going to let him down in my under-13s game for Sorrento/Duncraig Junior Cricket Club. The memory of plundering fours and sixes around the park stays solidly in my mind. That first century is as memorable as my first kiss and one that has obviously stayed with me throughout the years.

Today the pleasure of scoring runs on some of the best cricket grounds in the world is the motivation that keeps me inspired like it did as a 13-year-old.

My association with Kim Hughes today is much broader than that of a fanatical schoolboy. We are currently neighbours. Until recently he was the chairman of selectors for Western Australian cricket, he is still as passionate about the game of cricket as any-one I know, and he is a tremendous bloke and an incredibly inspir-ing person to be with. He has faced the ups and downs in life and has come through them like a true champion.

Both Dennis Lillee and Rod Marsh have told me that Kim was the most courageous batsman they have played with, as well as one of the most entertaining. He is a champion and I would say a good mate, which seems a little strange considering my earliest memo-ries of him.

In more recent times I have come across many champions in my playing days. The champions I most admire are those who simply love playing for Australia and wearing the baggy green cap. There is no doubt in my mind that everyone who has represented Australia has enjoyed their experiences, and have left satisfied with fulfilling a dream.

## THE SONG MASTERS –
## MARSH, BOON, HEALY AND PONTING

There are a few champions who really stand out. Funnily enough, four of these guys have been given the honour of leading the team song after a Test match victory. Rod Marsh handed the mantle to David Boon, who passed it on to Ian Healy, who in turn passed the privilege on to today's song master Ricky Ponting. These four characters and champions epitomise the spirit of Australian cricket. They are all as tough as nails, they love wearing their baggy green caps, they are fanatical about the well-being of Australian cricket, and they all love nothing more than sitting around sharing a beer with their mates after the job has been done. There is more to their role in the team than just being good players because they in a sense have a role in continuing the spirit and the culture of the rich history of Australian cricket.

For this reason, the man chosen to sing the team song is held in high esteem by every one of his teammates.

## MORE AUSSIE HEROES

In the bigger picture, my great heroes have included men like Sir Donald Bradman, Arthur Morris, Bill Brown, Keith Miller, Bob Simpson, Neil Harvey, Graham McKenzie, Ian Redpath, Allan Border, Mark Taylor, Stephen and Mark Waugh, Geoff Marsh, Merv Hughes, Craig McDermott, Tom Moody, Glenn McGrath, Shane Warne and Matty Hayden. I know that I have missed a few, and for this I apologise, but those who have worn and cherished the baggy green cap would know that I am talking about them as well.

In these names you see the same champion traits shining through. Apart from talent, these people are passionate about the game of cricket, particularly the Australian game of cricket. They were, or are, extremely talented and they have all worked hard to reap the rewards of their labours. They have dedicated their lives to the game of cricket and as a result they provide role models, as heroes, for the strength of the game well after they leave it. That is why they are out and out champions.

I believe this is where Australian cricket is so fortunate and ahead of many other countries in the world. We have many champions to whom our youngsters can look up to. From experience I have also found that these champions are very willing to share the secrets of their successes with anyone who wants to listen and learn.

Through the Commonwealth Bank Cricket Academy, or the streamlined Australian youth and domestic system, young people have enormous opportunity and exposure to the great players that Australian cricket has produced. This has invaluable benefits because it means our traditions, knowledge and expertise are passed on through the generations, allowing the success to continue. Our incredible pool of talent and expertise is something Australian cricket must be extremely proud of.

### MERV HUGHES

Apart from the out and out champions I have met, I am often asked who is the biggest character I have come across in my time with the Australian team. There is no doubt that one person springs to mind every time the question is asked – it is the big

Victorian, Mervyn Hughes. Not only was he a champion on the cricket field, taking 200 Test wickets and scoring 1000 Test runs, but he is also a champion person who is loved by everyone who meets him or who watched him play. Merv is a bit of a larrikin, there is no denying that, but his feats on the cricket field, where he battled injuries and criticism over his body shape were outstanding.

The one trait that Merv had that earned him most respect was his ability to give 100 per cent every time he entered the cricket arena. During the 1993 Ashes series he bowled his heart out for Australia, even though his knee was basically rubbing bone against bone. Regardless of the pain he was suffering, there was no way he was ever going to give in, and it was this contagious attitude that laid the foundation for another successful Ashes campaign. Even though I wasn't on that tour, his effort has become legendary among the senior players in the team who will never forget his contribution.

To this day, Merv regularly visits the changing room to tell a few jokes (I have never met a man who knows more jokes), or to offer a bit of encouragement or advice to anyone he thinks may need it. He is a classic bloke who embodies the spirit of the lovable Aussie larrikin who enjoyed a very successful career by giving it a red-hot go every time the opportunity presented itself.

## COLIN MILLER

Another very colourful character who I have had the privilege of playing with and against is Colin "Funky" Miller. The journeyman who played Test cricket for the first time at age 34, Funky is an excellent example of how perseverance and determination can be used to reach our goals. For Funky, the ultimate goal of playing for Australia may have taken longer than it took most people, but when he arrived on the scene of Test cricket he had an immediate impact. While he gained major publicity for his unusual hair cuts and colours, it should never be forgotten that amid all the glamour and theatre of the Colin Miller persona was a man who won the Test Player of the Year Award in the 1999/2000 Test season. His contribution to the Australian team's success over the last few years shouldn't be underestimated, especially his contribution as an off-spinner when we have toured overseas. In a way he, like Stuart MacGill, has had to live in the enormous shadow of the incomparable Shane Warne, but whenever the opportunity presented itself, he made his own mark on Test cricket.

Many years ago Dennis Lillee wrote his name into Australian cricket folklore by asking Her Majesty the Queen of England for her autograph when the team met the Queen on the hallowed turf of Lord's. Last year in England, Funky had an equally humorous meeting. My diary after the event read:

*"To break the ice, Steve Waugh only had to introduce Colin 'Funky' Miller to Her Majesty the Queen this afternoon in the Lord's committee room. Sporting dyed pink hair, Funky offered Her Majesty some sort of entertainment when he entered the room. My nerves were eased when I followed my extroverted teammate in the introduction line, because Funky's new look was too much for Her Majesty. As she started to giggle at the entry of our 37-year-old teenager, the tension was lifted from the atmosphere immediately."*

Australian cricket's version of basketball's Dennis Rodman is a character who reached the peak of his career very late, offering encouragement to anyone who has a dream, to hang in there through thick and thin until the dream is attained. Funky Miller announced his retirement from first-class cricket as I was writing this book in July, 2002. He played in 18 Test matches.

He was the hero of every sporting 30-something who lives with a dream of one day getting a call from the national selectors.

Fortunately, in Australia we boast many champion cricketers, but my admiration for great players stretches well beyond our shores. I have had the privilege of meeting many superstars from all around the world. Growing up, the West Indies was the team of the era. Boasting a fast bowling outfit that is legendary in terms of reputation and performance, the mighty West Indians set the standard for international cricket with their incredible consistency and destruction of lesser teams.

## SIR VIVIAN RICHARDS

Even now, the best batting advice anyone ever gave me was simply: "Watch the ball like a hawk." Another childhood hero of mine, Sir Vivian Richards, offered these words to me many years ago and I have adopted them as the best advice I can give to anyone trying to play successful cricket as a batsman. When I was young, World Series Cricket controversially took the cricket world by storm. My uncle Robbie was part of the World Series Cricket set-up, so I had an added interest and incentive to watch every ball bowled in coloured clothes and under the lights.

35

Although I was only a young boy at the time, my young mind stored away clear memories of the World Series days. Funnily enough most of these memories are centred on the man who probably best epitomised the spirit and freedom of one-day cricket.

The great Sir Vivian Richards was like a demi-God to me, and there are two images in particular that encapsulates the incomparable Antiguan genius. One is a photograph on the front cover of a board game called World Series Cricket. Surprisingly, the majestic Richards was playing a forward defensive shot under the big lights of one of the main stadiums in Australia. Dressed in his blood-red clothes, sweat dripping off his brow, he was watching the ball like a hawk eyes its prey. His left leg was stretched a long way forward, his bat was perfectly straight and his muscles were bulging through his sweat-drenched clothes. The lights in the background made the image more spectacular as this magnificent figure of balance, composure and concentration beamed off the cardboard cover and into my living room at home.

The second image came through information that Robbie shared with me. I will never forget him talking to my dad and telling him about his first meeting with Viv Richards. The description is still so clear in my mind. Rob told us how he had walked into the opposition changing rooms at the end of one of the games and saw Viv sitting in the corner with his shirt off. He described the size of the man and, in particular, the muscular build of an awesome athlete. The more Rob described the world's best batsman the more I built up a Gladiatorial image of my hero.

I figured that if I was to become an international cricket star in the future I would have to build myself up to become a giant figure like Rob had described. Hence, I guess, my love of physical fitness and a healthy lifestyle today.

## BRIAN LARA

Another great West Indian champion who I have admired is Brian Lara. Back in 1999 when Australia last toured the West Indies I stood in the field and witnessed three of the greatest innings that I have ever seen. Under pressure that many people couldn't possibly appreciate, Brian swaggered out onto Sabina Park in Jamaica and played one of the most amazing innings that I have ever seen. After comprehensively beating the West Indies in the First Test in Trinidad, Lara was under extreme pressure as the captain of the Test team.

The people love their cricket in the Caribbean and the calls were coming from all sectors to have Lara dropped and punished for the team's poor performance. It seemed to all that one more failure would mean the end of Lara's reign as captain. Knowing this, he came out and blasted a Test double century, while in the process setting up his team to win the Second Test. This they did and although we outplayed our rallying opponents for much of the Third Test in Barbados, B.C Lara again stood tall, leading his men to consecutive Test victories in the most unlikely of circumstances. His second innings was as brilliant a batting performance as you could ever see.

Champions have the ability to perform under pressure in varying environments against varying opponents. The 1999 tour of the

West Indies simply confirmed what a champion player Brian Lara really is. I can't remember a man being under so much scrutiny, and yet he was able trust his instincts and play with a clear mind to produce innings' of sheer brilliance. Playing golf with Brian in Darwin a few years ago, he told me that the most important thing for him is that he makes his good days, massive days. He said that people remember the big innings, and that we as batsman have so many tough days that when a good day comes along it is vital to cash in and score a very, very big score.

A trait of champions is that they back up their words with actions and I think it would be fair to say that anyone who has a first-class 500 beside their name and holds the current world record for the highest ever Test score is backing up his words with actions.

## MALCOLM MARSHALL

Having lived in Scotland for six months with a West Indian cricket player called Henderson Springer, I have always had a huge regard for the way the West Indian people love and play their cricket. The late, great Malcolm Marshall was always a fantastic person to be around, and a man who was admired and respected as one of the greatest players to have ever played the game. When I was only 18, I played against Malcolm in an invitational game in Western Australia. On the first ball of the innings I clipped the ball through mid-wicket for four runs. This shot must have been lucky, because for the next 11 balls that I faced from Malcolm, I literally did not put bat to ball. It got to the stage where I was apologising for my lack of ability to hit his outswingers, inswingers, leg-cutters and off-cutters, which were all being delivered at high pace.

Amazingly, Malcolm kept smiling at me and telling me to "hang in their young man" and "don't give up".

## OTHER WINDIES GREATS

Other Windies greats like Desmond Haynes and Gordon Greenidge had an effect on me with the way they played, and the way they forged a partnership that will always be remembered. Richie Richardson used to bat in his wide brim hat and hook the ball fearlessly off the end of his nose, like he was playing against a tennis ball on the beach in front of his beachside bar called Lashings in Antigua. Jimmy Adams and Michael Holding are two of the great gentlemen who I have met through cricket and Curtly Ambrose and Courtney Walsh were the best bowling combination that I have faced in my Test career.

## BOTHAM, GOWER AND CO.

From England, Ian Botham and David Gower were as talented as players come, and I used to enjoy watching them go about their business. While I played for Middlesex County Cricket Club, I also became friends with guys like Mike Gatting, Mark Ramprakash, Angus Fraser and Phil Tufnell; all of whom have had distinguished careers for England. Gatting was the ultimate British bulldog in the way he played the game. He was uncompromising and determined and I always enjoyed his company and spirit, while Tufnell is without doubt the funniest character that I have ever played with. If he had had the confidence in his awesome natural talent that some of the great spin bowlers possess, then I believe Tuffers could have been one of the best spinners ever produced by England. For some reason he never backed himself as much as he should have and, as a result, didn't play as much cricket for England as he perhaps could have done. But there are few people I would rather sit down with if I needed a laugh. His antics are simply hilarious, if not a little frustrating at times, especially when I took on the role as captain of the county.

## MIKE BREARLEY

Mike Brearley, who is considered by many as one of the best cricket captains of all time, is one of the most interesting people I have ever met. In his book *The Art of Captaincy*, Mike summed up the role of a leader by saying: *"What I have learnt from my own experiences of being a patient and a psychoanalyst is that whether you are in charge of people, or responsible like parents of small children or teachers, you need to have thick enough skin to receive the emotional force of the complaints, pressures, demands and anxieties that people bring to you, but a firm enough skin to keep hold of your own thinking under that kind of pressure. It is a matter of empathy. The parent kisses the baby better; with a cricket team it is something similar. If a captain is working well he is alert to people who have different states of mind, and someone may need to be treated with firmness, toughness, humour, resilience."*

When I took over the captaincy of Middlesex, I had the good fortune of spending some quality time with Mike, discussing captaincy and the way to get the best out of different characters and personalities. Our time together was invaluable as he imparted aspects of his knowledge on me through our lengthy chats. Of all the things he told me, the one he stressed most strongly was that the best leaders consider process rather than concentrate on outcome. "Process over outcome is the crucial component," he used to say.

## ALLAN DONALD

Playing county cricket gave me the opportunity to see many outstanding players from close range. One who comes to mind and who I also have played against in the international arena is White Lightening, South Africa's Allan Donald. As far as champions go, AD is right up there. What I admire most about him is that he has longevity and endurance on his side, combining international commitments with county commitments for many consecutive years. This dedication to the game of cricket is outstanding, especially considering the way he goes about his business. If looks could kill, AD would be a mass murderer of batsmen around the world. He is super competitive and always lifts his teams when they are down. Another characteristic of a great champion!

## JONTY RHODES

One of AD's South African teammates, Jonty Rhodes, is another champion in his own right. A master of the one-day game, he has all the attributes of one of the great players to have played one-day cricket for his country. Fast, fit and aggressive, Jonty turned the world of fielding upside down with his remarkable athleticism, energy and attitude in the field. Cricket skills aside, there are few better people to have played international cricket and, at the end of the day, this is more important than any trophies one may earn through skill alone. If you were choosing a one-day or Test team, Jonty would always be considered for the effect he can have on the team through his infectious attitude to the game and to life in general.

## HANSIE CRONJE

Tragically, while I was writing this book, Hansie Cronje was killed in a plane crash. His story is a tragedy in itself. Before Hansie experienced one of the biggest falls from grace in the history of sport, he was one of the most determined, committed, disciplined and respected leaders of men that international cricket has seen. His error in judgment certainly shocked the cricket world more than anyone could know, and for his offence he copped the harshest penalty of a life ban. One night in London, I listened to the ex-South African captain talk at a dinner to over 500 people. After his address I left saying that he could be Prime Minister after he retired from cricket. He recited poetry, talked of the history of the game and his views on the future of the game. In a nutshell, he spoke as well as any sports man or woman I have heard. Such was the respect he had gained, it seemed impossible that he would fall from grace like he did. Now that he has left this earth, I only hope people can remember some of the good things he did for international cricket rather than focus solely on his misdemeanours which were quite obviously crazy errors in judgment from such an educated and disciplined man.

## SACHIN TENDULKAR

From South Africa to India and there is no question in my mind that the best batsman I have played against is Sachin Tendulkar. The beauty in his batting is its pure simplicity. He has as close to a perfect technique as a man can have, while his concentration is like that of a fighter pilot. Like many champions, there is an aura about Sachin that stands him in a league of his own. The way he handles the mass hysteria of the Indian public who see him as a demi-God is quite extraordinary. Regardless of the massive expectation and pressure on his shoulders, he is still able to dominate international cricket with the grace of one of the greatest players to have ever lived. Of all the champions that I have described in this chapter, Sachin exudes all their characteristics and at times more.

## WASIM AND WAQAR

While the West Indies have had Curtly and Courtney, Pakistan have had Wasim and Waqar. This bowling combination is as deadly as any attack in the world when they are on song. Wasim is the most difficult bowler I have ever encountered. Bowling left arm fast, he has the ability to control the cricket ball like a puppeteer controls their puppet. Combine his bowling expertise with his ability to score crucial runs with the bat and Wasim is one of the best all-round players to have played the game. When he is bowling fast alongside Waqar, who swings the ball both ways, it is hardly surprising to see this partnership up with names like Lillee/Thompson, Ambrose/Walsh, Roberts/Marshall and

McGrath/Warne.  Throw Shoaib Akhtar into the trio and you have an amazing bowling line-up that will disturb the sleeping patterns of any top-order batsman before a Test match.

## MUTTIAH MURALITHARAN

Talking about bowlers, Sri Lankan wicket-taking machine Muttiah Muralitharan is the most difficult bowler I have had to face, particularly in his home conditions.  Controversies aside, he is an incredible bowler who has had an immense impact on international cricket.  If he continues taking wickets at the rate that he is, he will destroy the record for the most number of wickets taken by a bowler in international cricket.  He, like many great bowlers, is a smiling assassin.  He plays the game in tremendous spirits and leads by example for his teammates to follow.  If he is not appealing to an umpire, he is smiling and laughing and looking like he is enjoying his work.  It is a pity his career has been steeped in controversy, but with his record and attitude he must be classified as a true champion.

# CHAPTER 3

# Best of the Best

## SECRETS BEHIND THE SUCCESS OF
## THE AUSTRALIAN TEST XI

SHOT OF INSPIRATION # 3:
*Attitude is contagious – is yours worth catching?*

IN MAY 2002 THE Australian cricket team was voted the Laureus World Team of the Year. At a lavish ceremony in Monte Carlo's Grimaldi Forum, Steve Waugh, Glenn McGrath, Shane Warne and Ricky Ponting accepted the award on behalf of the exceptional Australian cricket team that I have been so privileged to be part of over the last few years. This award was an incredible honour, and while you don't necessarily play sport to receive such accolades, it was a grand reward for a very successful era in Australian cricket history.

I am often asked to speak to corporate groups about the secrets of success within the Australian cricket team. The question always asked is WHY? Why have we enjoyed so much prosperity over the last few years? While Australian cricket has enjoyed an incredible run since 1989, when the Allan Border-led team comprehensively beat England to win back the Ashes, the last few years have been phenomenal.

Since winning the last World Cup in England, and going into the 2002-2003 Australian summer, the national team had won a record-breaking 16 straight Test matches, has broken the winning streak for consecutive one-day international victories and maintained the No.1 ranking in Test cricket since the new rating system was introduced. It really has been a wonderful run of success that I hope will be admired and cherished in the future.

Throughout this book I point out that regardless of your pursuit in life, the basic principles of success are the same. It is easy to draw parallels between a successful sporting team and a successful business, because the fundamental ideologies and philosophies are no different. The foundations of the Australian cricket team's success are not really secrets, but rather a basic set of values, principles and assets that we are lucky enough to possess. These assets include talent, strong leadership, a proven game plan and a very powerful culture.

## TALENT TO BURN

First and foremost, the Australian cricket team has an enormous amount of talent. In our case, this undeniable talent adds up to a fantastic product of a skilful, experienced, dedicated and marketable group of individuals. While it may be unusual to have such an abundance of extraordinary players in one team, the fact is that many of the guys will retire as "great" players. Defining the criteria for a great player is difficult because greatness is not only relative, but also a term that should never be used lightly. The current Australian side is in the enviable position of having the Michael Jordans of basketball, the Ian Thorpes of swimming, the Michael Schumachers of Formula One and the Pete Sampras's of tennis under one roof. So many superstars in one team is incredible, but like the dominant West Indies of the 1980s, the Chicago Bulls of the 90s or the Manchester United Football team, it automatically gives us a massive advantage before a ball is bowled.

Not only does talent allow us to win games of cricket, it also acts as a marketing dream because people want to come and watch the team play. Great players provide entertainment and entertainment means bums on seats and eyes on the television. Because of this, cricket in Australia is currently in a very strong position in the market.

The great players that I am so lucky to play with include the Waugh brothers, Shane Warne, Glenn McGrath, Ricky Ponting and Adam Gilchrist.

### STEVE WAUGH

The mentally toughest player I have played with. This is proven by his outstanding consistency over the last decade, and his 9600 Test runs. He has led by example with the bat and is a revered player within and outside the team. With 148 Test matches and over 300 one-day internationals to his name, he has seen everything there is to see in international cricket. He is also a perfect role model in that he is an outstanding batsman, a strong leader, a devoted family man, an astute businessman, a proud, patriotic Australian and one hell of a good bloke to top it all off.

### SHANE WARNE

Warney is an absolute superstar who needs no introduction from me. Not only has he transformed the game of Test cricket with his leg-spin mastery, but he has also been one of the forerunners in the dominance of Australian cricket since his debut. He is his own man who stands tall in his beliefs. Like Adam Gilchrist, it is no coincidence that Shane has become a champion. When we were at the Commonwealth Bank Cricket Academy together, there was no one who worked harder at his game than Warney. There is no doubt that he has superb natural talent but he has also worked as hard as any player on mastering his skills. I have very fond memories of Warney spinning pool balls into the pockets of our resident pool table at the Alberton Hotel where we stayed during our stint at the academy. He would practice most nights at the pub, bowling leg-spinners, wrong'uns, flippers and top-spinners with the coloured pool balls. He, like the rest of the team, is a loyal Australian who takes enormous pride in his work.

### MARK WAUGH

Junior is also nicknamed Pretty for a very good reason. One of the most elegant batsmen of the modern era, there are few more pleasing players to watch than the captain's twin brother. Although Mark has a laid back, carefree style of game, he is another very tough competitor, who has a more astute cricket brain than he is often give credit for. Like all players, Junior has had his critics, but any player who has the endurance and skill to play 125 Test matches, with 20 Test centuries and an average of over 40, must qualify as a great player. Add to his batting capabilities his brilliance in the field, where he has helped inspire his teammates through regular instances of sheer genius, and you can understand why he has been an integral member in the team's success.

## GLENN McGRATH

In 1993 I captained a cricket academy team to India and Sri Lanka. On my return I predicted that this tall, skinny, country lad named Glenn McGrath would play for Australia within the year. I was right, and the big Pigeon hasn't looked back since his debut. There is no doubting Glenn's extraordinary ability with a cricket ball in his hand. He, like Warney and Dennis Lillee, is nothing less than a superstar. With 389 Test wickets, and about the same number of Test match runs, he has been crucial to the success of the team. Besides the fact that he is an absolute clown, who is undoubtedly the most annoying bloke in the team, he adds character and good spirit to the intense battle of international cricket. No-one knows their own game better than our No.1 bowler and his courage to publicly plot the demise of the best players in the opposition line-up indirectly gives his teammates confidence before a ball has been bowled. He is in the same league as the great West Indian fast bowlers who have made every batsman's life a nightmare.

### ADAM GILCHRIST

A player like Gilly makes a player like me feel sick in the stomach. He makes the game look so easy that you would think he was walking out in a Test match wearing a pair of board shorts and a T-shirt. He has been so dominant since his arrival in international cricket that he could be mistaken for playing the game with the same ease as he would play a game of beach cricket. His natural talent and co-ordination is exceptional, as is his work ethic and determination to be the best in the business. Few players work as hard on their game as Gilly does, especially behind the stumps where he is also a brilliant contributor to the team.

### RICKY PONTING

Rick is an extraordinarily talented young man who adds excitement to every cricket contest. Wielding his big, chunky Kookaburra cricket bat around like an elite swordsman, he has the ability to change the face of a game in a short space of time. He is a matchwinner as a batsman. In the field he, like his good mate Mark Waugh, is prone to displays of genius. His attitude is infectious as is his strength of character. The best compliment to give Punter is that he was asked to sing the team victory song at the end of every Test match victory. Considering the past song leaders have been Rod Marsh, David Boon and Ian Healy, Rick couldn't be held in higher esteem by his teammates. It is no surprise that he is currently captaining the one-day side.

### BRETT LEE

While my young mate has a way to go before being considered a great player, he is a classic example of the raw talent being produced through Australian cricket. To be honest, Brett hasn't really got much going for him. He is on the verge of bowling 100 miles an hour. He is young, extremely fit, blonde, good looking (so my wife tells me) and single. He is a brilliant musician that plays in a rock band. He is earning a few bob doing what he loves doing. He has a fantastic work ethic and steely determination to do well, and worst of all, he is one of the nicest young blokes you could ever come across.

Let's face it, he could at least be an average person to bring him back to the field, but this couldn't be further from the case. Binger epitomises the plethora of young talent coming through the system, ensuring Australian cricket stays at the top of the tree for a long time to come.

### AN EXTRAORDINARY TEAM

Among these guys, going into the 2002-2003 season, we had an aggregate of 568 Test matches, 26,100 Test runs and 1071 Test wickets. These statistics in themselves are a credit to the accomplishments of the players. More significant though is the impact they have on the next generation of cricketers coming through. Junior cricket today is made up of kids trying to bowl fast like Brett Lee or leg spin like Shane Warne. It is about fielding or hitting sixes like Ricky Ponting and Mark Waugh. Kids want to finish an innings off like Michael Bevan in one-day cricket or watch the ball as closely as Steve Waugh watches it. They want to bat left handed and smash 90-ball centuries like Adam Gilchrist, or appeal to the umpire like Jason Gillespie does. Kids want to dominate spinners like Matty Hayden and they want to grow up to win Test matches for Australia. We are in an extraordinary era of Australian cricket in terms of the product walking onto the park every time a final XI is selected.

Testimony to the extreme talent is the number of outstanding players sitting and knocking at the doorstep of the team door. Guys like Michael Bevan, Darren Lehmann, Stuart MacGill, Shane Watson, Greg Blewett, Jimmy Maher, Damien Fleming, Simon Katich, Brad Hodge, Brad Williams and Matthew Nicholson. It seems unimaginable that Michael Slater, who has scored 14 Test centuries at the age of 32, is currently out of the team, while players like Stuart Law, Tom Moody and Jamie Siddons hardly played Test cricket.

It is no coincidence that we are witnessing such an exceptional period. There is a very streamlined system in Australian cricket. Like companies using training to ensure that their staff are highly tuned and up to date with the latest techniques and ideas, the Australian cricket system trains their people by using and nurturing the most competitive, cut-throat domestic competition in the world. Our domestic structure is seen as a nursery for producing the toughest and most highly skilled players in the world, and judging by the results of the last three to 13 years, this approach is working well. From junior cricket to the Commonwealth Bank Cricket Academy to domestic first-class cricket and Test cricket, there is a survival of the fittest process where only the best make it to the top.

Basically every player aspiring to wear the baggy green cap understands that they have to be the best of the best if they want to earn the right to play for Australia. This may seem harsh, but it is reality in this very competitive market. Like all businesses today, competition is at fever pitch. As far as I am concerned, competition is critical to the success of any team or business. Legendary Chinese warrior Sun Tzu said: "Competition is a matter of vital importance for the general of any army. Competition determines who advances and who retreats. Who succeeds and who fails. Who profits and who loses. Who lives and who dies."

In answering the question about why the Australian team has played so consistently, I think competition has been one of the keys. In making it through the highly competitive Australian system, I have developed my philosophy using this competition to continually better my game so that I am the next cab off the rank.

When I have been out of the team I have wanted to make sure that I was the next person to be selected, or promoted, or given the opportunity when it came up. This can only happen by being the best performer, at the level below that to which you are aspiring. Invariably, opportunity has a way of popping up when it is least expected, so you have to be ready at all times to grab the opportunity when it presents itself. By preparing yourself through conscientious and disciplined effort you will perform at a level that will have you next in line.

There have been plenty of times in my cricket career when I have been in the wilderness. Even during those times my philosophy has been to dominate the level at which I was currently playing so that I was ready to step up and be promoted if the opportunity called.

When I first started playing club cricket in Australia I wanted to dominate fourth grade so that I could play third grade. From third grade, my theory was to dominate so that I could play seconds and so on until I was selected in the first team. For me personally, I was lucky that different people around the Scarborough cricket scene could see some talent, so my progress was perhaps accelerated faster than others.

When I had made it to first grade, I knew that the only way to catch the eye of the Western Australian selectors was to dominate, or at least play as well as I could, at the first grade level. Unless I did this I had no chance of gaining selection in the Western Australian team. I knew that I had to play first-class cricket to realise my dream of playing for Australia, so the choice was simple. Work hard on all facets of my game, out-perform others and do whatever was necessary to gain the edge over all of my competitors, or, stay playing first-grade cricket for the rest of my life. To be the next player in line I had to get fitter, stronger and improve my technical and mental skills so that I could consistently perform and literally get the runs on the board. I believe this attitude is the best choice to adopt and it is the same choice for every other player or person with ambitions to go forward in their life.

This type of attitude is symbolic of all the players in the Australian cricket sanctum. Every player in first-class cricket has to adopt this same attitude towards gaining selection in the

Australian first XI. All players know that unless they are performing exceptionally over a consistent period of time, then they won't even get noticed, let alone be given an opportunity with selection. The bar has been raised to such a level that anyone who wants to put their case forward to the selectors has to be out-performing others over and over again. At the same time, the players in the team know that they can never let their guard down. If they do, those hungry players knocking patiently at the door are waiting for their demise.

Having been in both camps, there are pressures as the hunter or the hunted. As the hunted you know that you have made it to the top but there is plenty of competition snapping at your heels for a chance to take your spot. In contrast, the hunter is hungry and working towards the top spot. While he isn't sitting at the top of the tree, he is doing everything in his power to get there. In the ideal world it is best to be the hunted with the attitude offered to me by my ex-West Australian teammate Mark Lavender. He told me to remember the old Indian proverb, "The wolf at the top of the hill is not as hungry as the wolf climbing the hill, but when he is hungry, the food is there!"

Either way, the intense competition ensures the men at the top are the best of the best in the Australian cricket team. While everyone would like an easy ride to the top, or at the top, the reality is that there is no such thing as an easy ride. This is true in anything in life, not only in professional sport. If you want to progress it is important to adopt an attitude of continual improvement and mastering of the level that you are currently at.

## ALL THE BIG NAME PLAYERS HAVE FOUGHT BACK

My journey towards wearing the baggy green meant that I had to spend times fighting and clawing and working out my game at levels lower. I am thankful for these times because they gave me the opportunity to improve and become as good a player as I could possibly be. Whether it was making my way through the system early in my career, or after being dropped from the top team, these times gave me the chance to monitor where I was at, and what I had to do, to make further progress. Every player in the current team has been on similar journeys to what I have. They had to work through the grades or fight back from being dropped at one stage or another to become better, tougher players. Steve Waugh, Ricky Ponting, Matty Hayden, Damien Martyn and Darren Lehmann have all been dropped, re-assessed where they were at, before coming back stronger and hungrier than before.

Most of the bowlers have faced this re-assessment period in times of injury. Every one of the current group of bowlers – as well as quality players and people like Andy Bichel and Michael Kasprowicz – has made their way back into the team through good old-fashioned hard work. Shane Warne has battled shoulder and finger injuries before fighting back and retaining his standing as the greatest ever leg-spin bowler. Brett Lee has resurrected his career after back and elbow injuries, and fast bowler Jason Gillespie has shown admirable determination on a number of occasions to fight back from injuries that may have ruined a lesser man's career. In my opinion, Gillespie has led the way in terms of professionalism, especially among the new generation, as he has had to work with every inch of conviction and tenacity to be where he is today. His constant battle to stay fit has helped him mould a character of steel, while at the same time earning himself a respect as healthy as anyone I know in the game.

I once heard Australian Rules Football legend Kevin Sheedy say, "Natural talent means bugger all, it is what you do with your natural talent that counts." The benefit Australian cricket has over some of the other countries is that while we have mountains of natural talent available, the players at the top have had to do more than just rely on their God-given ability. Everyone who plays for Australia has had to work hard, endure adversity and battle through a very tough system to make it to the top. While there will be some unfortunate players who miss an opportunity in this environment, the result is generally very healthy for producing the best of the best.

## STRONG LEADERSHIP

*"If you want to be a leader, ask yourself whether your men would fight with you in the trenches, or run through a brick wall for them if you asked them to?"*

\* \* \*

Over the last few years I have publicly declared that if Steve Waugh, the captain of the Australian cricket team, asked me to run through a brick wall for the team, I would run as hard as I could. I wouldn't do this because I am an idiot, but rather because I don't think he would ask me to run through the wall unless he honestly thought I could get through it. Because of the faith he has shown in me, he has earned a respect reserved for few.

Through his actions, and quiet but thoughtful words of wisdom, he has been a guide in helping me find my feet in Test cricket. He is the epitome of leadership in that he leads by example. He is balanced, tough but fair, has vision, strong values and principles and, as a result, he is very, very highly respected.

Two days before the Second Test match against Pakistan in 1999-2000, Stephen said a few words that helped me rise to the occasion. The media was on my back and questioning my position in the team after a disappointing tour of Sri Lanka and a failure in the first Test of the series. The pressure was mounting. Sensing this, the captain pulled me aside at breakfast and told me: "You are the best No.3 in Australia. I want you in the team, Buck (John Buchanan) wants you in the team, the selectors want you in the team, and your teammates want you in the team. I don't want you to worry about the press any more; I just want you to go out in this Test match and bat and show everyone what you are made of." This backing from the captain meant a lot. I was floating and ready to go into the match feeling pumped up and focussed to do my best.

Later that morning when training had finished, I happened to walk past the pre-match press conference just as one of the journalists asked Tugga whether he had any advice for me leading into the Test match. "Justin Langer is obviously under enormous pressure for his spot in the team. Have you as captain got any advice for him?" the journalist asked. Without blinking Steve replied,

"Yes, I have some advice for Lang leading into this Test match." Pausing and looking the journalist straight in the eye, he finished, "My advice to Justin Langer is to stop reading your rubbish."

If I was floating before, I was ready for a war now. My chest was out, my head was high and I was smiling like a Cheshire cat. The captain was backing me and I was ready to give him my best. He had privately and publicly backed me and I was ready to do anything to repay his faith in me.

As it transpired, that Test match in Hobart proved a turning point for me personally and for the team as a whole. In the first innings I scored 59, followed up by 127 and a match-winning partnership in the second innings with Adam Gilchrist. Tugga's courage in backing me publicly raised my respect for him enormously. He didn't have to do it, but he did. Just as he proclaimed to the world that Matty Hayden would finish his career averaging 50. It is no coincidence that his men rise for him when we know he is backing us to the limit. This in itself is a great lesson to any aspiring leader

Stephen first earned my respect as a leader before he became captain. Like Allan Border, and all the best leaders, he always leads by example on the cricket field. The 1993 tour of England, particularly his match-saving innings at Trentbridge, seemed to be the turning point in his rise to batting mastery. Two years later, when he stood up to the awesome Curtly Ambrose on a grassy, green pitch at Trinidad in the West Indies, we witnessed another turning point in terms of his respect as a leader. With the ball seaming and bouncing like a spitting cobra, he stood toe-to-toe, eyeball-to-eyeball, with the great Ambrose. In a classic Test match scene, West Indian captain Richie Richardson had to run from the slips and literally pull Ambrose by the arm, away from the unflinching Steve Waugh. Considering the conditions, this was the ultimate David and Goliath battle on the cricket field. Stephen's resolute and unwavering act of bravery sent shivers down the spines of his teammates sitting in the changing room searching for inspiration. The respect and admiration for the man went through the roof as he battled defiantly through the hardest session of Test cricket that I have ever seen. From that moment on, it became apparent that his teammates would stand shoulder to shoulder with him in any circumstance.

Tugga's courage in Trinidad was followed up by a double century in Jamaica a few weeks later. Partnering his younger brother, in a stand that took Australia to the brink of its first series victory against the West Indies in many years, he displayed a strong spirit and determination to set up a momentous victory. Without having a captain's title, he was establishing himself as a respected leader in the team. Over and over his batting feats have paved the way for memorable Australian victories. On the 1997 Ashes tour, Stephen's centuries in each innings of the Third Test at Old Trafford, scored with a bruised right thumb and an Ashes series to rescue, were feats of exceptional skill, determination and concentration.

In the four years between the two most recent Ashes tours he continued to dominate Test cricket as the No.1-ranked batsman in the world. His last Test innings of the 2001 Ashes tour confirmed his extraordinary strength of character and commitment as a leader of Australian cricket. Fighting back from a torn calf muscle, he defied all odds, not only to play the Test, but also to score an amazing Test century. I believe one of the motivators in that comeback innings was to lift the bar in terms of what can be achieved if you put your mind to it. I would say that 99 per cent of people would have given up all hope of playing, but leading by example, our captain proved to his players that we can all take the road less travelled if we are willing to look adversity in the eye and defy all odds.

Apart from Stephen, the team has many leaders in their own right. There is so much experience, strength of character and expertise among the list of players that leadership, like talent, is in abundance. Whether it is in feats of leadership on or off the field, the actions of each individual make a huge difference to the successful functioning of the team.

A small but significant example of an inspirational off-field action by one of our teammates happened during the recent tour of South Africa. One morning early in the tour, Adam Gilchrist circulated a message to the team. Gilly's re-invented story arrived under my door on the morning that the new Australian one-day captain was to be announced. With Steve Waugh having been left out of the one-day team, and speculation growing about the changing face of Australian cricket, Gilly felt that this message was worth having a think about. While there was no tension within the team, there seemed to be growing speculation that we were about to fall apart and lose our unity leading into the Test series. This couldn't have been further from the truth, but Gilly felt it was timely to bring everyone together.

This was Gilly's story:

*"One day a farmer's donkey called Dizzy fell down into a well. Dizzy cried piteously for hours as the farmer tried to figure out what to do.*

*Finally he decided Dizzy was old and the well needed to be covered up anyway, so it just wasn't worth retrieving the useless jackass. He invited all his neighbours to come over and help him. They all grabbed a shovel and began to shovel dirt into the well.*

*At first, Dizzy realised what was happening and cried horribly. Then, to everyone's amazement, he fell silent. A few shovel loads later, the farmer finally looked down the well and was astonished at what he saw. With every shovel load of dirt that hit his back, Dizzy was doing something amazing. He would shake it off and take one step up.*

*As the farmer's neighbours continued to shovel dirt on top of the donkey, he would shake it off and take a further step up. Pretty soon, everyone was amazed as the donkey stepped up over the edge of the well and trotted off to the green pastures!"*

\* \* \*

Gilly's thoughtfulness in considering his teammates and stepping out of the comfort zone, was a sign of considerable authority. Like many acts of leadership, he didn't have to do it, but he did. Apart from the act alone, the point of Gilly's story was that regardless of the outside influences going on around the team, we had to be strong enough to keep stepping up and out of any perceived hole that the team was supposed to be in. On the back of missing out

on the final of the one-day series in Australia, and increasing speculation about the future of some of our more senior players, there
was shovel loads of dirt flying the way of some of our teammates.
This hurt initially, and while the guys involved could have hung
their heads and let it consume their worlds, the leaders within the
group pulled together to get them thinking about what was important. We had to win the Test series to retain the No.1 ranking in
Test match cricket, so we needed every member of the squad going
in the same direction. Thanks to strong leadership and support
from within the team, our mission was ultimately achieved and we
left the shores of South Africa as the top Test team in the world.

## THE COACH WITH VISION

Leadership encompasses many things. One of those is vision.
Throughout this book I talk about the importance of personal
vision in the form of dreams, goals and the positive picture that
you paint within your mind. Vision is as important for a team as it
is for an individual. After only three games as coach of the
Australian team, John Buchanan addressed us the day before the
Third Test against Pakistan at the WACA in Perth. His address
that day was far removed from the normal pre-Test preparation
meeting. Coming straight out with his thoughts, he asked everyone collectively what we as a team wanted to be remembered as
when we retired. He talked of the Don Bradman "Invincibles", the
"mighty West Indies" of the 80s, the "awesome Chicago Bulls", the
"magnificent Manchester United football club" and the "incomparable Hockeyroos", the Australian women's hockey team.

He asked the question so that we could come up with a theme to keep us focussed on what we wanted to achieve. "Do you want to be remembered as the "Dominators" or even the "Unbeatables"? As far as he was concerned, he knew there was enough talent in the room to consistently win games of cricket but he wanted to challenge us to take this consistency to a new level. Steve Waugh has always publicly declared that we want to win every Test match that we play. He never settles for anything less than a series whitewash when talking to the media before each Test series. I believe John was asking us to commit to this attitude by putting our thoughts down on paper.

After a long discussion we decided that our theme was to take the road less travelled in our pursuit of achieving something special. We would let the media make up names for our successes, but we would use the name of the book *The Road Less Travelled* as the theme for constant improvement in everything we do. By following *The Road Less Travelled* we were committing to having the courage to do things differently than any other team in the world. Whenever we started to drop our guard or get slack or complacent, we would remind each other of our team commitment in the changing room in Perth. This commitment was important because it allowed us to keep our minds focussed on the vision we had for what we wanted to accomplish together as a group.

It would be crazy to suggest that John's thought-provoking address that day was the sole reason we went on to win 16 straight Test matches in that period. Having said that, I am convinced that the seed or vision that he planted in our minds did make a big difference. How good can we be? How many Test matches can we win?

Why shouldn't we win every game? Why can't we continually improve? Why can't we be the best side ever? All these questions stimulated my mind, and without knowing for sure, the minds of every one of my teammates.

John Buchanan's vision and man-management skills are further examples of leadership within our highly successful organisation. In the Australian team there are plenty of people who I would stand in the trenches with, hence the camaraderie and leadership within the ranks.

## A PROVEN GAME PLAN

Apart from talent and leadership, the current Australian team has a proven game plan that we rely upon in our preparations and in the heat of the battle. Obviously there are times when we have to be flexible, but as a rule we know that we have something to fall back on when the pressure rises. Our game plan is like the foundation or platform that we revise in every pre-Test match meeting. Cricket, like most business, is a team game. But at the end of the day the team's performance also relies on the collective successes of each individual.

The Australian cricket team knows what works and therefore we stick with the recipe to ensure consistent results. We rely on a philosophy or game plan of the three Ps.

## PRESSURE

One of the main attributes of this team is that we have been able to apply pressure to every opposition that we have played against. Constant pressure means that an opportunity will eventually open up for us to bury our opponent. Steve Waugh often uses the catch cry of "seizing the moment" when he talks about finishing off the opposition. We know that if we stick to our basics and apply relentless, ruthless pressure then any side in the world will eventually crack. This pressure applies to every aspect of our game.

When we are batting we look to be aggressive and positive in order to get on top of the opposition bowlers. While we don't have a set run target each day, we do have an attitude of dominating the opposition. Regardless of who they may be, we know that no team likes having a rapid rate of scoring going against them. By scoring runs quickly we know that we are always in the game, as we will always leave ourselves enough time to bowl out the opposition. This attitude doesn't mean that we are reckless, because there are times when we have to pull back and be patient due to disciplined bowling and fielding, but it does mean that we are looking to be positive and looking for run-scoring opportunities all the time. We believe that this style of play is the best method of applying pressure to any adversary.

When we bowl, we know that pressure is built up by hammering patient lines and lengths. As a batsman, the toughest and best bowlers in the world are not necessarily the fastest or most aggressive, but rather those who eliminate your scoring opportunities. We are fortunate enough to have guys like Glenn McGrath, Jason Gillespie and Shane Warne, who deny the opposition any opportunity to score easy runs. At the end of the day, batting is about scoring runs so the aim of the best bowling attacks in the world is to disallow this opportunity. When a batsman is unable to score runs quickly, the pressure has a suffocating effect. Not only does it feel like the fieldsmen are surrounding you like a fishing net surrounds its prey, but also a slow-moving scoreboard in Test cricket usually ignites negative crowd participation. The expectation to score freely these days means that it is easy for a batsman to lose his concentration when the pressure is applied in this way.

Where we also have the advantage and opportunity to apply pressure is in the variety of our bowling attack. A guy like Brett Lee or Brad Williams may not be as tight as the other bowlers but they do have the weapon of raw pace from which they can apply pressure on the opposing batsmen. Physical fear is a definite factor because no one really likes facing very fast bowling. Some people may publicly declare they enjoy facing fast bowlers, but you can take it from me they are not telling you the whole truth. At the end of the day no one really enjoys facing fast bowlers because there is always a certain fear factor when a cricket ball is travelling towards you at 150km/h.

There is nothing better than standing at short leg when Brett Lee is roaring in to bowl. At times you can see this fear in the eyes of grown men, because they know what could happen if the ball misses their bat. You can tell so much from a man's eyes, and fear and pressure are two of those things.

The value of having extremely fast bowlers, or great bowlers like McGrath and Warne, in your team is that the pressure extends beyond the playing hours. As a batsman, a lot of the pressure comes while you are in bed the night before the contest. Your mind tends to play every possible scenario over and over, robbing you of the ability to relax and trust your instincts. We as a team understand the value of this type of pressure that comes from continued success and outstanding performances. Our body language and attitude can also help us in applying this form of pressure to some opposition teams. An intimidated opponent is an opponent ready to be beaten, regardless of the contest. When we are in the field we consciously look to cut the angles and exude energy and enthusiasm. Not only does this allow us to cut off the runs and take the catches, but it also generates a pack mentality, where 11 players are working against the two batsmen.

We also consciously apply extra pressure to opposition captains, as we know that the strongest link in the team needs to be taken out of the chain if we are to see our opponents fold.

Basketballer Luc Longley told me recently he was convinced that many of the Chicago Bulls' games were won before the match had even started. The reputations of his teammates were so intimidating that certain teams had difficulty handling the pressure.

It is all about pressure and the Australian cricket team knows it. As Jack Nicklaus says, "Pressure creates tension and when you're tense you want to get your task over and done with as fast as possible." This is why we look to apply ruthless pressure on every opposition that we play against, because we know that the team who panics last will win most contests. We can accelerate the panic stage by employing tactics that we know will put the opposition under intense pressure.

## PATIENCE

Patience, like discipline, can sometimes be an unattractive commodity, but as the old proverb says, "Patience is a bitter plant which has very sweet fruit." The second of our three Ps is patience, and it is through patience that we chip away at our opposition before taking the sweet rewards of victory. We know that if we can stick to our game plan and do all of the simple things well then eventually we will come up triumphant. Every single ball in the game of cricket is basically a contest in itself. Like taking one step at a time to complete a marathon, we understand that we have to win more single ball contests than our opponents. By doing this we will win most games of cricket against any opponent.

By patiently going about our business and sticking to our game plan, we know that we will be triumphant. Patience ensures that we don't get too far ahead of ourselves in any contest and it also gives us the courage not to alter our plans after one failure. The times that we have become complacent, or watched the outcome rather than the process, are the times when we have invariably lost our patience and therefore our control. This happens rarely, but the few times it has we have paid the penalty.

## PARTNERSHIPS

Teamwork, partnerships and comradeship in a team are like the glue that keeps everything together, especially when the pressure is on. One of the defining factors behind the success of Australian cricket is the unbreakable team spirit that radiates through the walls of the changing room and onto any cricket field around the world. It is hard to describe in words the significance or feeling of this team spirit that runs so hot within the team. It is an awesome atmosphere that can be felt the moment you walk inside the confines of our changing room. I believe this feeling is a result of the incredible respect every player has for each other. You don't make the Australian team unless you deserve it, and unless you have earned it, and therefore the respect factor is all conquering among the players. It is always difficult to describe or define a feeling, but I know it is one of the most crucial components of our success.

We enjoy each other's success because we know that if one of our teammates does well, then we are one step closer to singing the team song at the end of the game. We also understand that no one enjoys success without having paid the price one way or another. Success is a sign of strength of character. Strength of character is a trait that is easily admired and applauded.

I have gained enormously from forming a special bond with my opening partner Matthew Hayden. Australian cricket history is littered with successful partnerships: Lillee and Marsh, Lillee and Thompson, Warne and Healy, Marsh and Boon, Taylor and Slater, McGrath and Warne. The list goes on, but it goes to show how some of the most successful partnerships have formed the basis for the ongoing success of Australian cricket. We pride ourselves on sticking by our mates and the value of loyalty and friendship and that is why partnerships are one of the integral parts of our proven game plan.

## A VERY POWERFUL CULTURE

*"I would pick character over cover drives any day."*

\* \* \*

There is more to the current Australian cricket team than just skill and talent. This team has an enormous amount of character, both individually and collectively. This character oozes out in the form of leadership and performance on and off the field, and I believe this is why we have been so successful. Strong characters ensure the culture within the team remains cherished by anyone wearing the baggy green cap.

First and foremost this very powerful culture has been handed down through the ages from team to team, player to player. To the man, everyone in the Australian team cherishes and respects the baggy green cap and the history of Australian cricket. The great Sir Donald Bradman said that we are all "temporary trustees of this great game" and I believe that is how everyone who wears the baggy green cap behaves, as servants of Australian cricket. The baggy green cap is what it is all about.

Admittedly, there is more money in the game now than ever before, but regardless of the financial rewards, it is the baggy green cap that encapsulates why we play the game. Singing the team song *Underneath the Southern Cross* at the end of a triumphant Test match, wearing the baggy green cap, arm in arm with your mates, is symbolic of the great Australian spirit that has developed through our relatively short history as a nation. Everyone involved simply loves being part of the Australian cricket team and being ambassadors for our great country. There is an extraordinary atmosphere within the camp. Our running joke is that "there is a lot of love in this team", and there really is a great deal of respect and admiration within the ranks.

Our culture is not just about the players: everyone plays a part in the overall success of the business. Our support staff is as good as any in the world.

Physiotherapist Errol Alcott, who has been around for as long as anyone can remember, is quite simply a brilliant physiotherapist. His physical skills and worldly expertise and experience are invaluable assets to the organisation. The few times in the last two decades that he has been unavailable, Patty Farhart has filled in with enthusiasm, energy and passion. Just like players walking into the team to make a difference, these two guys control the changing room like seasoned maestros.

Our coach John Buchanan is without question the most innovative and visionary coach in the world. His predecessors Geoff Marsh and Bob Simpson also played crucial roles in the overall success of Australian cricket. Our fitness adviser Jock Campbell, the most unpopular member of the squad – purely a result of his job – is also a very important cog in the wheel, having taken over from champion people like Steve Smith and Dave Misson. These guys, plus our managers Steve Bernard and Mike Walsh, ensure that we have everything available so that we can concentrate on doing what we do best – playing cricket. With the support of the Australian Cricket Board and the Australian Cricketers Association, there is a very positive flow of energy in the same direction.

Our culture means that we play the game very hard on the field. We want to win and we expect to win every contest. This may sound arrogant or over-confident but, to the contrary, it is simply how we are brought up to play the game. Winning isn't everything, but there is no denying that we go out to give it our best shot every time we don the baggy green cap. We prepare hard, we play hard and we also celebrate hard. There is no doubt in my mind that we celebrate as well as any team in the world. I could quite easily write an entire book on some of the places we have sung the team song and tell stories about post-Test match celebrations. While it may sound strange as a professional athlete to describe the fun and festivity of a post-Test match celebration, I believe celebrating is extremely important. If you can't celebrate the good times, what is the point of going through all the hard toil, the pressure and the stresses of the contest? I have to say that my fondest memories of my cricket career for Australia revolve around singing the team song and celebrating a Test match victory with my mates in the baggy green cap. These treasures outweigh most of my on-field experiences by 20 to one. If *Khe Sahn* or *True Blue* is heard roaring from the Australian team changing room, then you can be sure everyone is in for a very long sitting at the ground.

## OUR VALUES WITHIN THE TEAM

We also have very strong values and ethos within the team. The senior members of the team take responsibility in handing down the traditions and values to the younger guys making their way into the culture. While everyone who earns the baggy green cap is respected, the greatest respect is earned over time by continually performing and upholding the strong name and symbol of the baggy green cap.

Before the last Ashes tour our team values were reminded to us by the captain. We take these values seriously and work to constantly sustain and endorse them at every opportunity.

**Here is the Australian team's list of values:**

— *Discipline*
— *Communication*
— *Togetherness, honesty and openness*
— *Awareness of teammates*
— *Enjoying each other's company*
— *Respect and recognising each other*
— *Respect the game – in particular the umpire's decision*
— *Aim to be the best team – on and off the field*
— *Be innovative — always one step ahead of the opposition*
— *Enjoy the experience*
— *Challenge yourself and the team out of the comfort zone*
— *Vision and goals – don't alter after one failure*
— *Ethics and integrity – recognise the difference between right and wrong*
— *Hunger and desire – no complacency*
— *Support and respect the big picture*
— *Respect image of the team*
— *Respect everyone's families on tour*

# CHAPTER 4

# Courage, Discipline and Matty Hayden

SHOT OF INSPIRATION # 4:
*The pain of discipline is nothing like the pain of disappointment. The little things today could be the catalysts for the monumental things tomorrow.*

I BELIEVE PHYSICAL AND MENTAL discipline is the key ingredient to reaching our goals and going forward in our lives. God-given ability aside, I would go as far to say that discipline has been the major reason why I have been able to make the most of what I was given through the genes of my parents.

Discipline has helped me attain my goals by ensuring that I keep my eyes firmly fixed upon my visions without distractions. It has also been the catalyst behind the best teams that I have enjoyed success with over the years.

Ever since my martial arts training I have been fascinated by the wisdom of a few of the masters. Well-known martial artist Bruce Lee explained this mind/body state to one of his students saying, "You must concentrate all the energy of the body and mind on one specific target or goal at a time. The secret of kime (tightening the mind) is to exclude all extraneous thoughts, thoughts that are not concerned with achieving your immediate goal. A good martial artist puts his mind on one thing at a time. He takes each thing as it comes, finishes with it, and then passes on to the next. Like a Zen master, he is not concerned with the past or the future, only with what he is doing at the moment. Because his mind is tight, he is calm and able to maintain strength in reserve. Then there will be room for only one thought, which will fill his entire being as water fills a pitcher. Always remember that in life, as well as on the mat, an unfocussed or 'loose' mind wastes energy."

## THE MAGICAL SUMMER OF 2001-2002

Cricket, like martial arts, is no different. During the 2001-2002 Australian summer I was out in the middle playing against a few of the best bowlers in the world, concentrating on nothing else but the cricket ball. Focussing solely on the ball took away any distraction of the past or present. By trusting my game plan I knew

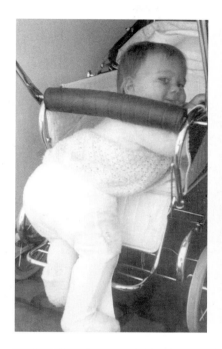

*Above left:* It all started
from here!
*Langer family collection*

*Above right:* Long distance
phone calls from home
started early on.
*Langer family collection*

*Left:* Eating has always
been high on my list of
life passions.
*Langer family collection*

First trip across the world as a three year old – Mum, Dad, Adam, a green mini and a tent.
*Langer family collection*

*Left:* A cowboy or a cricketer? The cowboy cap and pistol were always going to make way for the baggy green cap and cricket bat.
*Langer family collection*

*Left:* Warwick Junior Cricket Club with my first cricket bat, a Kim Hughes black Slazenger. *Langer family collection*

*Below:* First batting trophy and the dream was starting to evolve. *Langer family collection*

First Test match with Allan Border in January 1993. *Langer family collection*

First Test match. 'There are no heroes in Test cricket' – just ask David Boon,
Desmond Haynes and Keith Arthurton. *Langer family collection.*

*Left:* First game of club
cricket for the Scarborough
Cricket Club. My new
team-mate D.K Lillee.
*Photo: Sunday Times, 1987*

Champions… Barry Richards, Graeme Pollock, Dennis Lillee and me.
*Photo: © Tom Mucciarone*

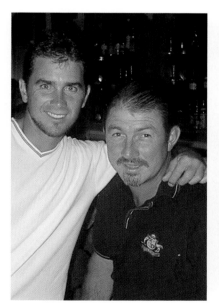

Beard growing competition with former
Australian player, coach and friend
Geoff Marsh. *Langer family collection*

Childhood hero Viv Richards in Antigua.
*Langer family collection*

Steve Smith - a heart of gold, a will of iron. *Langer family collection*

*Left:* Martial arts taught me all about discipline, respect, concentration and mental toughness. Working out with Todd Vladich.
*Langer family collection*

Golf with Sergio Garcia, Adam Scott and Hockeyroo Jenny Morris in December 2001.
*Langer family collection*

*Right:* Mentor and
close friend Nigel Wray
with wife Linda.
*Langer family collection*

*Left:* 'Perspective' – with Brett Bermingham a fortnight before he lost his battle with cancer. *Langer family collection*

Writing this book on my trusty laptop at the 'Centre of the Universe' in Manjimup, Western Australia. *Langer family collection*

the runs would look after themselves. Any concerns about the future were instantly eliminated. The past was irrelevant, as I knew nothing else mattered except the next ball bowled to me. What had happened the ball before was past and worth forgetting about, because from the moment it was gone there was nothing I could do about it anyway.

It was like Zen in the art of batting. Everything I did was centered on readiness for the next ball bowled to me. Nothing else mattered but the next ball. Every time I have enjoyed this sort of form, I have heeded the advice of all the master batsmen who have told me the same thing. Over time, Steve Waugh, Greg and Ian Chappell, Allan Border, Viv Richards, Barry Richards, Brian Lara and Sachin Tendulkar have all hinted about the importance of this process of batting. Every one of them has told me, at one stage or another, that the only thing that matters is the ball. Seeing it clearly, and then reacting to it without any preconceived notions or extraneous thoughts, is all that matters. The ball is the only important object if you want to play at your best.

There is no doubt in my mind that for six months during 2001-2002 I played at my best. While there is always room for improvement, everything felt controlled, with the rhythm and momentum running in my favour. Apart from my match game plan of seeing the ball with a clear mind, three other factors contributed to my on-field success.

One of those was my sheer determination to succeed after being dropped. This firmness of mind helped me achieve the clarity and focus required to stay on the edge of peak performance.

The second factor was my ability to concentrate on the things within my control. I have always found that the best way to achieve my goals is to work hard and concentrate on the things that I have control over rather than falling for the trap of worrying about uncontrollable factors.

In my profession as an international sportsman, I classify these controllable areas in four categories.

*Physical:* Keeping my body fit and strong, by maintaining a healthy lifestyle in terms of diet and exercise, means I will be able to cope physically with any challenges that come my way. I believe a fit body means a fit mind and I also know that the fitter I am physically the more energy I have day in day out. In this day and age, physical fitness has become one of the means of gaining the edge in professional sport.

*Technical:* Working on your skills is imperative in any field of excellence. It doesn't really matter how mentally strong you are if you haven't got a strong foundation of skill and technique to start with. Like building a house, the foundation is paramount in the final success of the project. My foundation is built around my skills, experience and technique so they need to be constantly monitored and polished up. At times my batting technique may be looser than I expect of myself, so I have to put more time and effort into this area. The rewards of this extra work will be a tighter and more effective method of countering anything the opposition bowlers have to throw at me.

*Mental:* Concentration, goal setting, positive self-talk, focus and hunger for success. Knowing that the mental approach is crucial,

I spend time working on keeping my mind clear and focussed. My dad has been telling me since I was a young boy that, "It is all in your head son, it is all in your head." He has stressed this advice to me so many times that I can hear him saying it as clearly as if he was sitting with me right now. Mastering concentration is arguably the greatest challenge in elite sport.

*Spiritual:* There is no doubt in my mind that if I am in a happy frame of mind then the positive results will follow. The more relaxed you can be in anything, the greater your chances of success. The more I smell the roses in my life and see the bright side of everything that comes my way, the happier I know I will be. Ultimately, contentment and happiness is a success in itself. Whatever it is that keeps you happy, I believe it is important to live it and do it. Some people love the ocean, some the bush; others find happiness dancing, singing and socialising. Some people like being by themselves, while others feel more comfortable in a crowd. Some people like to work hard, while others prefer to sit back and relax. Some get strength from God and their religion while others don't. Everyone is different and I think we must respect this. The important thing is that you feel happy in yourself. This is what I classify as spirituality and this is why I keep a check on it all the time.

The third undeniable factor in my recent success has been my partnership with Matthew Hayden. My own form has obviously been pleasing, but more satisfying has been the four 200-run and three 100-run opening partnerships with one of my closest mates going into the 2002/03 season. Even while typing this, I find myself shaking my head in disbelief, as life could not be more different now than it was 11 months previously in England. I could never have imagined that I would open the batting for Australia, let alone have one of the most successful statistical partnerships of the modern era. Like I say, the memories of the six months following our first jaunt to the wicket together seem totally staggering.

If I look closely at the reasons for my personal success and the success of my partnership with Haydos, I would have to say that discipline and courage have been the cornerstones of our accomplishments. When I returned to the team I vowed to enjoy the moment regardless of the circumstances. This attitude takes discipline and courage. My strategy was to smile in the face of pressure and let my instincts take over from my analytical mind. This also takes discipline and courage. I have described how being in a happy frame of mind, watching the ball like a hawk, preparing well, working hard, playing positively without hesitation, and backing myself, all formulate the recipe that I know will bring me success. The difference in 2001-2002 was that I had the discipline and courage to stick with the recipe and never waver from the things that I know work for me.

During the last Test match of the 2001-2002 Australian summer at the magnificent Sydney Cricket Ground, I was batting very aggressively just after lunch on the first day against South Africa. Jacques Kallis was bowling to me and I had hit a couple of fours from the first two balls of his over. For a few moments my mind started telling me to calm down, pull back and take it easy. With these thoughts came a positive proactive reply to "keep trusting the recipe". "Watch the ball out of his hand and trust your instincts." In the past, I may have listened to the negative thoughts and worried about the consequences of my aggression. The more I worried the more thoughts that would enter the equation and the tighter and tenser I would become.

The difference this time was that I made a conscious decision to trust my instincts and let my body react to whatever the bowler bowled to me. Having promised myself to play positively and without hesitation, I had the courage to finally back this judgement. At one stage during that first innings in Sydney I became outwardly grumpy with myself. A few doubts were creeping into my very clear mindset and I could feel the thoughts choking my flow. Recognising the signs I walked away from the crease and told myself out loud to "pull my head in and get back to trusting my recipe". Whoever the South African fieldsman was standing close by when I was talking to myself must have thought I was a little strange, but I refused to allow the negative thoughts take over my thinking. I was sick of succumbing to the doubts and fears, so this time I took a grip of the situation by telling myself to get back to the thinking that distinguishes the champions from the rest.

## THE STODGY TOP ORDER BATSMAN

The same situation presented itself in the second Test match of the 2001-2002 summer against New Zealand. On a couple of occasions since, I have heard Haydos describe the first hour of that Test match in Hobart as "the most incredible first hour of play that I have ever seen". At drinks on that first morning I was 63 runs and he was on five or six. I have great pleasure in announcing that the photo of the Bellerive scoreboard showing **Langer 63 Hayden 3** sits proudly behind my bar at home. Rarely have I outscored my big aggressive mate, so the photo acts as a reminder every time I am tagged as a stodgy, defensive top-order batsman.

For the first time in my career, I remember walking down to my partner after 20 minutes of play and saying, "Mate, I am going with my instincts here. I am seeing the ball well, I feel good and I want to go with the moment. I don't know what is going to happen but I want to trust my instincts today." As I said this, a massive smile made its way across my partner's face. He could sense that I was in control and ready to back myself to achieve something special. Usually my reaction would have been to slow down, hold back and take the safer option of a more defensive mode. In contrast, during the 2001-2002 summer I stuck with my strategy and it paid dividends.

On that particular day in Hobart, I felt that all the years of hard work on my technique were starting to pay off. Trusting my body to take over, rather that letting any thoughts inhibit my play gave me a very liberating feeling, especially during a Test match for my country. As the day crystallised, my instincts were worth trusting because we scored our second 200 partnership together while I went on to score my third consecutive century. The reason for telling you this is not to blow my own trumpet, but rather to prove that anything can be achieved if you have the courage and discipline to trust your game plan in whatever you do.

As a batsman I know that if I see the ball out of the bowler's hand then I will have an answer to anything he has to dish up. Ever since I was a young boy I have practised and practised every conceivable shot in the book of cricket technique. Physically and technically I have the ability to play every shot, because of the hours of muscle memory that have gone into my game through persistent practice of the basics. The trick is to let your body take over and put the years of practice into action on the field. This takes courage and discipline because there are fears and thoughts that inhibit the message being sent from the eyes to the brain and then to the body. Although the process of playing a cricket stroke takes about one hundredth of a second, the whole procedure relies upon a clear pathway between the three systems. Physical and mental fears hinder my ability to react and perform to the best of my ability, so the more I can eliminate these through clear positive thinking strategies, the more chance I have of success.

## WITH THE HELP OF A FRIEND

During the 2001-2002 summer I was able to achieve this process better than ever before, but all processes aside, batting with Matty Hayden was an indefinable contributor to my success. Walking into battle with a partner next to me gave me immediate strength. Usually you have to walk onto a cricket field by yourself. Sure your partner is waiting for you in the middle, but as an opening batsman you actually walk into the cauldron of the fight with a mate by your side. The fact that Haydos looks, feels and acts a bit like a Gladiator when he walks to the crease never does any harm to my confidence. He is a huge man who has supreme confidence in his ability and preparation. Every time he goes into battle I know that he is ready to answer anything our opponents have to throw at him. There are few players in the world who know their game as well as Matt does and this just adds to the aura and certainty of his presence at the crease. Batting with one of your best mates during a Test match is an inspiring feeling. Although they rarely show their emotions, I can only imagine the enormity of the bond between Stephen and Mark Waugh when they walk out onto a cricket field together.

During most of the innings that Matt and I have batted together, we have been able to feed off each other's confidence, while using our desire to wear down our opposition as a constant incentive to get the team off to a great start. We regularly set short-term targets, reminding each other between overs, and even between balls at times, of what we are attempting to achieve. I have found that this team focus has taken enormous pressure off me personally. At times I have become more nervous leading up to a 100 or 200 partnership with Haydos than I have in achieving any personal milestones. We gain enormous pleasure and pride from our work together as we set about making our own little piece of cricket history in the Australian colours. We know each other's games very well so we can sense when to talk or when to remain quiet. There have been a couple of times when we have had to tell one another to "sharpen up" or concentrate a bit better, but generally we talk very positively and proactively to keep each other going.

Another underlying factor in the success of our partnership is our commitment to enjoy every moment. We have promised each other to go about the game with a smile on our faces, and with a passionate edge that we believe should be exuded when representing your country. When I made my comeback I vowed to enjoy every opportunity in the baggy green cap. Being dropped in England during the Ashes tour the previous northern season hurt, and it made me realise how easily you can lose your most prided possession, which for me is the chance to wear the baggy green cap. Losing your dream is a nightmare and I knew that whenever another opportunity came around I was going to cherish it and enjoy it like never before.

Having travelled down very similar career paths, Matt and I have made a commitment that we will never take our positions for granted again. Playing cricket for Australia is an incredibly privileged position. We are doing what we love and we figure we should derive every joy that is possible from the experience. Playing professional sport is not going to last forever so it would be extremely foolish not to have fun and enjoy the experience along the way. Both of us tended to lose sight of this important factor earlier in our careers, so we intend making up for lost ground every time we walk out to bat together. Early in our international careers we both fell into the trap of placing ourselves under undue pressure. This thinking resulted in poor, inconsistent performances, little enjoyment and rare job satisfaction. Our remedy for this has been to play each innings like it is our last for Australia.

At times there have been a lot of hugging, high-fives and back slapping going on between the two of us, but I think this is simply a testimony to the satisfaction we get by being together out in the middle. Admittedly, there have been a few questions asked about our sexual preferences over the course of a summer. It is quite uncommon seeing two grown men showing so much emotion towards each other in a public arena. Regardless of the rumours, I can cheerfully report that neither of us is homosexual. I am happily married with three beautiful daughters, while Matt's wife Kellie delivered her first baby, a healthy baby girl, as I was writing this book. Fortunately, the two loves of our lives are also very good friends so they have no worries about our public displays of affection getting out of hand.

Despite the whispers, I make no apology for our show of energy and enthusiasm. Sport is about emotion and how an athlete reacts to any given situation. We genuinely delight in each other's successes and we get pumped up about playing for our country in a game that means a lot to us.

## THE REAL MATT HAYDEN

Channel 9's Anne-Maree Sparkman interviewed the two of us recently. One of the questions she asked was how I would sum up Matthew Hayden as a person. After careful consideration I came up with four ways to describe my mate. Firstly, he is a bit like a big friendly bear. Standing well over six-foot, he looks like a giant of a bloke.

Although he denies the story, the first time I ever laid eyes on him was more than 11 years ago at the Gabba Cricket Ground in Brisbane. I was in Queensland with the Western Australian team for a Sheffield

Shield match. Walking over the field towards the practice nets, I was nearly run over by this huge blond bloke wearing a pair of rugby shorts and a baggy singlet with World Gym printed on the front of it. He looked like he was carrying a couple of bricks in each hand as he puffed his chest out to show off the workout he had just been doing. Having no idea who this guy was, I figured he must have been one of the groundsmen. As we walked past one another, he nodded and beamed his characteristically friendly smile. My reaction was that the groundsmen at the Gabba must be a good bunch of blokes.

The following morning I was staggered when the same smiling bear walked out to open the batting for Queensland. He wasn't one of the groundsmen, but rather this Matthew Hayden bloke who we had heard about. Almost from that day forward we became mates. Sharing many of the same interests and philosophies, the big man from Queensland is a bit smarter and friendlier than your average bear, but at times he could be mistaken for one.

The second way I would sum up my batting partner is that I have an image of him as a bit of a priest. Anyone who follows the cricket would have noticed that Matt makes the sign of the cross every time he makes a century. Michael Slater kisses his helmet; Ricky Ponting jumps up in the air like he is about to fly; Steve Waugh raises both arms to the sky; Mark Waugh nonchalantly waves his bat to the crowd, while Matty makes the sign of the cross. Being quite a spiritual person, this gesture every time he reaches the magical three-figure mark suggests to me that there would be a lot of people out there praying for his success every time he is batting for Australia. This thought gives me strength because if Haydos is saying his prayers before a match and there is a collective body of supporters praying for him, I am hopeful some of the spiritual power will rub off on me. As far as I am concerned, something must be going right and if prayers are one of the things going our way then I have no complaints.

## OUR ATTITUDE IS CONTAGIOUS

Thirdly, Haydos is a self-confessed nature boy. Anything to do with nature and he is in his element. He loves fishing, surfing, skiing, the beach, the trees and the stars. The way he goes about his business, you can see the energy and enthusiasm coming through in his work. We have a saying in the Australian team that says, **"Attitude is Contagious, is Yours Worth Catching?"** I used this as our Shot Of Inspiration at the start of Chapter 3. Well, Matt's positive attitude is definitely contagious and that is why he is such an integral and respected member of the team.

Finally, I made mention earlier that walking out to bat with Haydos is like walking out to bat with a Gladiator. Although he would never admit it, I am sure my buddy sees himself as a Russell Crowe-style Gladiator when he has a cricket bat in his hands. It is not unusual to see Matt crouched down, touching the ground and settling himself down. Russell Crowe picks up a handful of dirt and rubs it into his hands before a battle; Matthew Hayden touches the turf on the cricket pitch to ground himself in readiness for his battle between bat and ball. The way I figure it is that if I have the smiling bear, the priest, the nature boy and the Gladiator looking after me in the middle, then all I have to do is watch the ball.

In a lot of ways, the successful summer of 2001-2002 was no coincidence. Sticking with the basic principles that I know work allowed me to enjoy an incredible run of success that only a short time before seemed so far away. This disciplined approach to my thinking and doing, where I relied on a couple of simple but sturdy strategies, gave me the wings to fly toward my wildest dreams. In the past, when I have lost the courage to fly and succumbed to my fears, it has been less disciplined thinking and doing that has led to my downfall.

I find these words about discipline a great inspiration in my life. Maybe you will too.

## DISCIPLINE AND COURAGE

*It takes discipline to look a man in the eyes rather than at his feet, his chest or the space above his shoulders.*

*It takes discipline to train when it is wet and cold, when all the others are at home behind the glass.*

*It takes discipline to tell the truth; remember it is just as easy to tell the truth as it is to tell a lie.*

*It takes discipline to keep your eye on the ball, the ball symbolising your vision and dreams.*

*It takes discipline to constantly work on the basics even when the basics get a little boring.*

*It takes discipline to practice under pressure so that nothing surprises you during the game.*

*It takes discipline to get out of bed early; there is nothing like a warm bed in the morning.*

*It takes discipline to keep running when your legs and lungs feel like they could burst.*

*It takes discipline to do the little things even if they don't seem important at the time.*

*It takes discipline to watch your manners, hold your tongue and respect your elders.*

*It takes discipline to do an extra lap when everyone else is in the shower or bar.*

*It takes discipline to stick with the recipe that you know works for YOU.*

*It takes discipline to guard against complacency, arrogance and laziness.*

*It takes discipline to look for the real reasons without making excuses.*

*It takes discipline to be the first on the training track and the last off it.*

*It takes discipline to make the right choice rather than the wrong one.*

*It takes discipline to be punctual, rather than just a few minutes late.*

*It takes discipline to fight back rather than quit.*

*It takes discipline to trust your game plan.*

*It takes discipline to switch off and relax.*

*It takes discipline to lead by example.*

*It takes discipline to listen and learn.*

*It takes discipline to say NO.*

*IT IS DISCIPLINE THAT WILL TAKE YOU TO THE TOP.*

# CHAPTER 5

# The Battler

SHOT OF INSPIRATION # 5:
*Focus on the positive. Don't try to be someone
or something that you are not.*

A N OLD FRIEND SENT me a note before the 2001 Australian cricket tour of England.

John wrote:

*"Well mate, you're off on another adventure!*

*This is just a quick note to wish you all the best in England. I know you will have a great time and I am sure you will score a stack of runs, so get to it! I doubt whether the boys and I will miss a ball! Do you remember the first Ashes series you watched on TV? There was something magical about it and I can't wait to share that with my sons Jacob, Mason and Dusty this year!*

*If you need any further motivation (and I know you DON'T) before you leave, how about this:*

*This Australian side you are a part of is absolutely the best side we have ever sent to England. There are about a dozen guys in the squad who will retire as "GREATS". That's nice to know . . . the man in the street loves to watch those guys go around because they know they are seeing something special.*

*But MOST men in the street cannot really relate to them - they just know they are greats!*

*What most men in the street can relate to is the guy who just works and works and works at his job - the guy who has to use e very ounce of his skills and abilities to compete. When the gritty fighter with the big heart and the positive attitude succeeds, the man in the street gets a special buzz out of it. They know they will never play for Australia, but they also know that if they stay positive and work their butts off, they can get that promotion at work, or get the bills paid, or provide for their family when they retire.*

*The man in the street NEEDS battlers in his national sporting teams and, in today's world of professional sport, the battler is less and less obvious on our sporting fields.*

*You know that a large proportion of the Australian cricketing public sees you as the battler - that guy with grit and determination who works hard at his game. That puts you in a position not many of the guys on this tour could POSSIBLY find themselves in. When you bat, all the battlers at home are willing you on, and every run you score makes them feel that much more optimistic about taking on their own struggles and coming out on top. They love to see someone like Junior get a ton, but a ton from you is more VALUABLE to them because it lifts their sprits and gives them hope. Please JL, continue providing this inspiration to those battlers out there.*

*So good luck - keep working hard and keep giving all us battlers at home a few more hundred reasons to aim up!*

*All the best, Hurls.*

\* \* \*

Once upon a time this "battler" tag haunted me. I used to despise hearing how I had less talent than a lot of other players. My skin would crawl every time I heard the statement about being a worker, who had made it to the top through toil and discipline rather than natural talent. For years I tried so hard to prove that I had the same natural ability as some of my teammates. I wanted to give the impression that it was as easy for me to perform as it was for a few of the other guys in the team.

The truth is, it wasn't. I did have to work harder than many others. I did have to spend more time working on all aspects of my game. I was never a schoolboy superstar like many of the young guys I played with and against. I was just a young person who wanted the baggy green cap more than anything else in the world. Because of this, I was willing to make sacrifices and commit myself to my dream. As far as I was concerned I would do whatever it took and I didn't care how much work it was going to take. Hard work is in my blood, keeping my eye on the vision was all that really mattered.

At times I allowed my dream to become hazy because I never wanted to accept the perception that I was less talented than the others were. It was a struggle coming to terms with just being myself and accepting who and what I was. The harder I tried and the more I listened to the critics the more I surrendered my power to everyone else. Thankfully, the passing of time and the experience and wisdom gained from life has tempered this thinking. If people see me as a battler, so be it. The truth is, whatever people think of me is none of my business. There is no point fighting someone else's perceptions of you, because you have absolutely no control over their thoughts.

In fact, the term battler now makes me smile. It invokes pride because I know how hard I have had to work and fight to make it to the top. The older and wiser I become, the more I realise that precious few make it to the top without working their fingers or minds to the bone. Like famous painter Michelangelo once said: "If people knew how hard I have had to work to gain my mastery, it wouldn't seem wonderful at all." I now know that my hard work is no different to anyone else's, and that I'm no different to those who are battling away, working hard and trying to find their way in their own personal journey.

Everyone is a battler in his or her own right. Whether they are homeless and living on the streets, rich or poor, healthy or sick, famous or not, we all have everyday battles to contend with. Ultimately, when these battles in life come our way, we have two choices. The first of these choices is how we react to the situation. The second is how we deal with the problem. These choices are crucial to our overall happiness and freedom.

The game of cricket has offered me the chance to make many choices. When Curtly Ambrose or Wasim Akram run in and bowl a cricket ball at me at 150km/hr, I have to choose in a split second how to react to the delivery. A poor choice means I am either out or in hospital.

Facing a cricket ball is a good analogy for many situations in life. For example, when the selectors have decided to drop me from a team, I have a choice to make. While the choice may not require the instinctive reaction of facing a cricket ball from a fast bowler, the decision is equally as significant. Do I cry, feel sorry for myself and quit? Or do I stand up, look myself in the mirror, confront the situation and fight my way back? The decision and choice is always ours.

## CHARACTER BEFORE COVER DRIVES

A few years ago I made up the following saying: "I would take character over cover drives any day." By this I mean that in choosing a cricket team I would look at the character traits of a person before I looked at their pure ability. In my opinion, it is a person's character that governs how far they get in this life.

If I were the sole selector in a cricket team or the boss of my own company, I would choose my staff with strong character being the major criteria in the selection process. Character outweighs skill and ability, especially when pressure is being applied. In the perfect world it is a bonus when a person has mountains of ability to back up his character. The true champions are those people who have a mix of strong character and natural God-given talent and ability.

## MAKING YOUR OWN LUCK

Over my career, I have gained opportunities when they were least expected. Some may call this luck, and while there was luck involved, I was the next cab off the rank

Not surprisingly, hard work, preparation and freak accidents have all played a part in my "lucky breaks" over the years. My Sheffield Shield debut for Western Australia against Victoria and Merv Hughes at the WACA came about when Geoff Marsh ran into Dean Jones during a one-day international. A phone call came the night before the game from coach Darryl Foster that I would be opening the batting the next day against big, bad Merv Hughes. I was lucky that the opportunities came along, but remember the selectors could have picked any of the other players around at the time. I had been training hard, playing well and striving to achieve my goal. Do we call this lucky?

A freak accident saw magical batsman Mark Lavender miss the victorious Sheffield Shield final of 1991/92. His misfortune was my good fortune and the final turned out to be a positive stepping stone in my cricket career. Whether it was luck or fate I am not sure, but I do know that whatever you call it I am glad it shined on me!

That Shield final of 1991/92 was a sensational experience. This was my first season of Shield cricket and I was playing in a team that boasted players of the highest calibre. In fact a few of my WA teammates were players I had watched and aspired to be like as a youngster. Geoff Marsh, Terry Alderman, Mike Veletta, Wayne Andrews, Bruce Reid, Tom Moody and Tim Zoehrer were the base of a very strong team with youngsters Brendon Julian,

Damien Martyn, Jo Angel and myself making up the XI. Just playing in a team like this was a great buzz for me, but to have the opportunity to play in a Shield final was a dream come true.

I learnt many valuable lessons from my debut season and from the Shield final. Throughout the season I learnt how important it is to have a strong team spirit. In this team we had a great blend of youth and experience, talent and people prepared to do the hard work. Most importantly, everyone in the team helped each other and looked after each other on and off the field. When it came to the crunch, during the real pressure times of a game, we all seemed to pull together and I honestly believe that was because we were a close unit who stayed together regardless of the situation.

## THE BATTLER AND THE INEVITABLE SETBACKS

I had an interesting experience recently when a mother of one of the kids who had attended my Sports Camp rang me out of the blue and told me that her son had just missed out on the school first XI in cricket and was very upset. She asked me if I would talk to him to cheer him up and give him some encouragement. Of course I would speak to him, but I wondered what the best approach would be to help him out. I thought about it and realised that it would be very hard to cheer him up, but I figured I could at least offer him some advice about how I thought he could best handle the disappointment.

Firstly, I told him to remember that even though it feels like the end of the world at the time, it really isn't the end of the world. Easy to say, of course, but no matter how bad something seems the world won't stop spinning because we are disappointed. It is also important to remember that we have all felt disappointment before. It is the way you handle it that makes the difference.

He found it hard to believe that I had actually felt disappointment before. In his eyes I was playing cricket for Australia and Western Australia and had made it. What do you mean you have been disappointed before? I assured him that I, like every person, had had many disappointments in my time.

I have missed out on a number of different teams in my life. I can laugh about it now, but at the time I know how hard it is to accept, and understand what it feels like when things don't go perfectly to plan.

I will never forget missing out on selection in the State under-19 team. The lead-up had been positive, I was playing A Grade cricket and had just been added to the WA Sheffield Shield squad. Before the under-19 team was selected we were invited down to the WACA for a training session. I was obviously a little nervous but quietly confident that I would be selected in the team. During the training session the coach, Les Varis, walked up to me and offered me some advice about my batting which I accepted and finished the session. Considering that this advice from the coach was the first time I had ever spoken to him, I found it hard to believe a few days later that I wasn't selected in the team because the coach thought I had an attitude problem and wasn't prepared to listen.

At the time I was devastated. I was disappointed, angry, upset and confused. Looking back, the people who decided to leave me out of different teams in my life should be the people who I am thanking today, because it was from those disappointments that I learnt a great deal about myself and about how to use disappointments to your advantage.

As it worked out I made the under-19 team the following year and we travelled to Melbourne for the carnival. I had set myself the goal of playing well in Melbourne so that I would be selected in the Australian under-19 team to play the England under-19 touring team in a Youth Test series around Australia.

Unfortunately, I had a disappointing carnival, fracturing my thumb and not scoring many runs. I wasn't selected in the Young Australian XI. While I was disappointed again, I accepted that I'd had an average carnival. but in the back of my mind I knew that the England team would be in Perth later in the summer and I thought that if I worked hard on my game then an opportunity would come up in the future.

Again, I really set about doing the extra work, believing that if I did work hard a break would surely come. To this moment I can't explain why it happens but I do know for sure that if you do give something your best shot, really give it 100 per cent, then the results ALWAYS come.

Sure enough the touring England team arrived in Perth and sure enough I was lucky enough to play a very good innings for the WA under-19s in the lead-up game to the Test at the WACA between the two Young Ashes teams. Young Australian captain, Jason Gallian, injured his foot in a freak accident the day before the Test and I was lucky to have been added to the team. It was an amazing couple of days. After the game at the WACA, I was invited to nominate for a scholarship to Australian Institute Commonwealth Bank Cricket Academy and all of a sudden what had looked like a disaster only months before turned out to be another dream come true.

Life is a struggle at times. There is no denying that it is often hard work. But when you achieve your goals, and your dreams have been realised, every modicum of blood, sweat and tears is worth the effort a thousand times over.

As I've said, I have had more than my share of disappointments in my cricket career, so you can be sure I am making the most of things since breaking back into the Australian team and becoming established at the top of the order. I'll talk a little more about the pain of disappointment in the next chapter.

In the meantime, here's cheers to the battler in us of all.

Good luck with your battle.

CHAPTER 6

# The Pain of
# Disappointment

DISAPPOINTMENT AND PAIN HURT, there is no denying that.
But always remember that the sun DOES come up tomorrow and you DO have a choice how you react to every situation in your life.

Famous Australian singer John Williamson sings in his song *Galleries of Pink Galahs*: "It takes a harsh and cruel drought, to sort the weaker saplings out, maybe that's what life's about, we must go on." This wonderful message, as tough as it may be, describes the survival of the fittest and the strength that can be gained in times of adversity.

Throughout my cricket career I have had my fair share of droughts when I have felt like I was living in the wilderness of Australian cricket. After every one of these droughts has come an oasis in the form of a triumph, and I have become a stronger person. As easy as that is to say now, each disappointment has felt like the end of the world. At the time I have felt like one of those weaker saplings, withering away and perishing in the desert sun.

On Monday, June 2, 2001, I was forced to stare one of these potentially disastrous droughts straight in the eyes.

There was a knock on the door of my hotel room at about 9:30am. With the First Test of the 2001 Ashes series getting underway the following day I was in an upbeat frame of mind. Bouncing to the door, my world turned blue in an instant, as the expression on my skipper Steve Waugh's face said it all. Without saying a word I knew I hadn't been selected. I had been dropped from the Australian cricket side for the First Test of the Ashes tour.

The moment was over quite quickly, and yet it was utterly unbearable.

My rise in Australian cricket can be attributed in some ways to the faith the captain has had in me as a player and as a person. Guys like Matthew Hayden and myself have benefited from the confidence the captain has had in us since he took over the reigns. He has a way of getting the best out of his men, like a respected general gets his men to fight to the death if necessary. Steve Waugh is the type of bloke you would stand in the trenches of war with, and to me this is the highest compliment I can pay a person.

Stephen has supported me, when others may have doubted me, and lifted me up with his words and actions in times when I may have doubted myself.

With this in mind, you may understand why the moment of my sacking was so unbearable.

Standing in front of me, with a steely look in his eyes, the captain, who was a tour selector, and a very good mate, told me: "The selectors have decided to go another way for the First Test. Sorry mate, but Marto (Damien Martyn) is in and you are out. He is in such great form and our gut feeling is that this is the way to go. This may seem like the end of the world, but there is no reason why you can't fight your way back. You have before and you can again if you work hard and keep backing yourself."

There was nothing much more for him to say.

I wanted to scream and shout and abuse him for taking away my position. I wanted to tell him that I always came up with the goods when the team most needed it. I wanted to shout out that I would put my life on the line for the baggy green cap and my teammates. I wanted to read out all of my statistics from the previous three years while batting at No.3 for Australia. I wanted to cry out for more of his support and ask him why he had turned his back on me on this occasion. I wanted to tell him that the decision wasn't fair, that I always seemed to be the easy option to be dropped. I wanted to abuse the other selectors and tell them exactly what I thought of them at that moment. I wanted to ask Steve how I was going to tell my family and friends on the other side of the globe. I wanted to plead with him to change his mind, even though I knew he couldn't and wouldn't. I wanted to ask Steve how I was going to look my teammates in the eye at training later that morning. I wanted to fight the decision, fight the moment, fight the world, fight the journalists, and fight the selectors.

But then, what would that have achieved? We were standing arm's distance from each other and for a second I can't remember if I saw Tugga as a punching bag or a big brother who I wanted to hug and use as a shoulder to cry on.

There is no doubt it was hard for Stephen to come and tell me of the decision, and to his credit he took it upon his shoulders to tell me eyeball to eyeball. I can't imagine how he was feeling as he knocked on my door that morning, but as he has confessed since, "That part of the captaincy job is the worst part."

I am not sure what would have worried him more? Would it be me going berserk and using him as that punching bag that was forming as an image in my mind, or me grabbing hold of him and crying like a baby on his shoulder?

You might have to ask him that question some time.

Either way, both scenarios would have been pretty uncomfortable, but I imagine the first script would have had the worst repercussions for both of us. But then, two blokes standing in the middle of a hotel room, one crying like a two-year-old, would have been pretty messy stuff. Luckily, I didn't have the energy to play out either scene.

At a moment like this the silence and numbness are unbearable. I imagine it is like having your stomach ripped out in front of your own eyes. Without meaning to sound too dramatic, that is what it felt like. Having played in the previous 33 Test matches for my country, and dreaming of taking on England on their home turf, my goal was taken away in a split second, in a single glance from the captain.

The emotions were incredible. So many thoughts, so many questions, so many demons started invading the space between my ears and behind my eyes. It felt like there was a little mouse inside my head scratching away trying to get out. While my heart felt heavy, my entire body felt empty as I struggled to find any perspective in the matter.

Before he left the room, Tugga simply dropped his eyes to the ground and then tapped me on the shoulder as if to again say, "Sorry, hang in there mate, keep going forward."

After he had left the room, I slumped into a leather chair at the desk in my room. The immediate emotion was like something inside me had died, and while I hadn't lost a loved one, I felt like I was entering something of a mourning period. Rather than someone dying, it was my dream, my ambition, my passion which had been momentarily destroyed, and in a way, killed. It was like the fire that had kept me pushing forward and working and striving had been extinguished, or at least dimmed for a while. I also felt like I had been let down or betrayed by my big brother. As hard a job as it is for the selectors, I felt like the man who had been one of my strongest supporters had turned his back on me. The passing of time heals these wounds and I know this wasn't the case, but at the time a tough decision had gone against me and I was having trouble coming to terms with it.

It was difficult to see past the present in the few hours that followed the captain's knock on the door. In fact, it was even hard to see past the end of my nose, let alone finding any positives in the short-term future, a future that looked gloomily bleak. In all honesty, the prospect of getting up and fighting back again seemed too hard to fathom.

## FACING UP TO MY TEAMMATES
## AFTER GETTING THE AXE

Not only did I have to ring my family back in Australia, so that they heard from me before they heard it through the media, but I had to attend a training session an hour or so later. These two things were extremely difficult. The phone calls to my parents and my wife were distressing because they know how much playing for Australia means to me. I could feel their hurt through the phone. They wanted to hug and hold me and assure me that everything would be okay, but from the other side of the world this could not happen.

After the phone calls, I sat in that leather chair until the moment I had to drag my chin off the ground and get down to the team bus for training. This was one of the hardest training sessions of my life because I had to try and stay up for the team, while all I really wanted to do was crawl up into a little ball and sleep until the nightmare went away.

I kept a diary on the Ashes tour, which I submitted to the BBC Online website in England. My diary that night read:

"*Obviously the disappointment is immense but the reality is that I have no real choice other than to get on with it. It would be nice to run away and hide, but in the real world all I can do is stand up tall and get on with it. It is no disgrace being dropped from this great team, but at the moment I feel let down and just downright shattered and sad.*

*With an Ashes series on the doorstep my enthusiasm to see the Ashes retained has not been dampened, but it is going to be tough getting myself up for the next few months. I have been here before. I will get plenty of sympathy and I will be told a thousand times to keep training hard and preparing myself for another opportunity. All the clichés will come out and while people mean well, I know I am the only one who can turn this around.*

*From as objective a point of view as I can muster, our team on paper looks awesome. The prospect of Glenn McGrath, Jason Gillespie and Brett Lee bowling in tandem is a sight any cricket lover must be counting their sleeps for. Throw in our charismatic leggie, one of the five Wisden cricketers of the century, Shane Warne, to balance out the attack, and the England batsmen will surely have as much on their minds as a novice playing a round of Mastermind.*

*On the batting front, my replacement Damien Martyn is in tremendous form, while Ricky Ponting is hitting the cricket ball like Tiger Woods hits the golf ball at St Andrews. Throw in the Waugh twins and Adam Gilchrist coming in at No.7 and you can see a depth in our line-up that leaves any team green with envy.*

*One thing I have learned in my life is that no matter what happens, the sun always comes up tomorrow, and while the jab in my stomach is sure to leave another permanent bruise, I am never one to shy away from a fight. I have fought my way back into this Test side before - there is no reason why I can't do it again. As hard as it seems right now, this could be an irresistible challenge or a suffocating nightmare. I guess I have a choice here like you do in every situation in life."*

## NOT EVEN MAKING THE ASHES TEAM

Every day that I have a shower at home, I read in big, bold letters, **THE PAIN OF DISCIPLINE IS NOTHING LIKE THE PAIN OF DISAPPOINTMENT.** This quote has been stuck in a plastic cover since 1993 when I was dropped from the Australian team to tour England.

After my first game, the Fourth Test against the West Indies in 1993, I then played in the Fifth Test of that series and went on to tour New Zealand in the lead-up to the Ashes series.

In NZ, I scored 69 in the First Test, 24 in the Second Test, but finished the series with a pair of ducks. I was then sent home while the one-day series was on, which has become common practice, and I had the agonising wait to see if I was going to be selected to tour England.

I was pretty confident that I would tour so when the selectors decided to pick a young Michael Slater and Matthew Hayden – and left me out – I was devastated. It was a massive disappointment.

A week after my omission, a letter arrived from my English mentor Nigel Wray. In it, Nigel gently reminded me about the significance of discipline in my life and the importance of dealing with disappointment. After telling me the quote that sits in my shower today, Nigel finished off by saying, "Life is challenging but also fun.

Without losing all confidence, one has to remember that around the next corner could be someone waiting to punch you in the nose, and you can't see around a corner!" In other words, always keep your hands up and your eyes open if you want to save yourself from a broken nose, or heart. I was dropped because I forgot to do these things.

Looking back through my old diaries I was amazed at how my reaction way back then was so similar to the emotional response to my axing on the Ashes tour of 2001. This in itself goes to show me that the hurt of disappointment never gets any easier regardless of how wiser or bolder you become over the years.

Here's my old diary entry from 1993.

### Friday April 2, 1993

*"I will never forget talking to Mum in the laundry, when Dad walked in with a grim expression on his face. Dennis Lillee had rung Dad to tell him about the selection. When he broke the devastating news that I had been left out of the touring team, I felt like I was about to faint. My head became light and my legs wobbly. It felt like somebody had put a hand down my throat, grabbed my heart out of my chest and threw it on the ground beside my feet. I can't believe I haven't been picked. The more I think about it the less I can understand their (the selectors) theory. The worst feeling is that I might get left behind for good. But then, I know opportunities will come up again in the future. If I am completely honest with myself I didn't really grab the opportunity with both hands. I know now that the next time the opportunity comes I will have to be more prepared. I was a bit slack all round in New Zealand. No one else is to blame. It is time to accept the fact that I am not going to England*

*and get on with the job at hand, which is to be a success by working very hard both mentally and physically. It is not the end of the world, even though it feels like it. I won't give up. This first bitter taste of disappointment in the cutthroat business of professional sport is one I want to guard myself against for the rest of my career."*

Having achieved my dream of playing cricket for Australia at a relatively young age, it was certainly a rude awakening when only a few months later my dream had been taken away from me. Or at least, I had surrendered the opportunity. Perhaps the privilege of playing cricket for my country was gone because of a lack of mental and physical discipline. I had the world at my feet one minute; the next I felt like I was free falling without a parachute attached to my back. Rather than going on an Ashes tour in 1993, I was dropped and staying at home. The disappointment was soul destroying and, like in England in 2001, I felt like I had hit rock bottom. Even though I was putting on a brave face, my world had ground to a halt. The sour experience of disappointment was arguably the worst I have tasted. Although I had time on my side back then, experience and wisdom was less of an ally.

With plenty of time up my sleeve after my omission in 1993, I had a long hard look at myself. The greatest basketball player of our time, Michael Jordan, wrote in his book *I Can't Accept Not Trying* that when he was cut from his high school team he learned that he "never wanted to feel that bad again". "I never wanted to have that taste in my mouth, that hole in my stomach." I knew what he was talking about.

Looking back, I can now see that I fell into the trap of neglecting both the physical and mental disciplines crucial to successful performance. Firstly, I got caught up in all the periphery bonuses of playing international cricket. I allowed the attention, the handouts, the money and the lifestyle to cloud my single-minded vision of what I wanted to do. Rather than preparing like a man who was hungry and broke, I was living the lifestyle of the rich and famous. Parties and late nights became a more attractive alternative to early nights and harder training sessions. What new sponsorships I could secure became more important than watching the ball and scoring runs.

In New Zealand I became scared and lost the battle to the fear of failure. Now that I was in the Australian cricket team, I didn't want to lose my spot. I wanted to be there forever. Rather than concentrating on the all-important process of exactly what I had to do to perform, I became sidetracked with other issues. These issues centered on the past and the future, taking me away from the all-important present.

I knew that the touring team to England would be selected at the end of the New Zealand tour. Throughout the entire Test series, I worried about whether I would be selected to tour England or not. Rather than immersing myself in the current series and scoring match-winning runs against the Kiwis, I was thinking about getting enough runs to stay in the team. Basically I reverted to playing "scaredy-cat" cricket. By this I mean I was batting to survive, rather than batting to score so many runs that the selectors would have to continue selecting me. I had lowered the bar of expectation, particularly in my preparation and thinking.

As hard I tried in New Zealand, I wasn't able to get the England tour out of my mind. Even though it was three months away, I couldn't regulate this thought within my mind. I kept telling myself not to worry about what might happen in the future, but for one reason or another I just couldn't shake my preoccupation. Rather than going about my business of scoring runs in a positive, energetic fashion, my mind wandered towards the doom and gloom of the road below, rather than the beautiful sunrise ahead.

Runs are the only currency of value in my game and yet I was harmfully thinking, "but what if I don't score runs?" "Will they still pick me if I don't have a good tour?" Analysing the selectors' decision to drop me in England in 2001, the honest answer is that just like in New Zealand in 1993, I conceded my position in the team because of undisciplined and negative thinking over a period of about six months.

## ACCEPTING THE SELECTORS' DECISION

As much as I tried to fight the selectors' decisions in my mind – both in 1993 and 2001 - it wasn't until I admitted to myself that I had surrendered the opportunity that I was able to get back on my feet and start again. Brutal honesty is one of the most important components of mental toughness, and a discipline in itself. It takes courage and discipline to look yourself in the mirror and admit a mistake. Even though sympathy was coming from everywhere, as it usually does when the breaks don't go your way, the reality was that I had no one too blame but myself. It was my own fault, no one else's. Not the selectors, not the coaches, not the reporters, not my teammates. It was the man in the glass:

## The Man In The Glass

*When you get what you want in your struggle for self*
*And the world makes you king for a day,*
*Just go to the mirror and look at yourself*
*And see what that man has to say.*

*For it isn't your father or mother or wife*
*Whose judgement upon you must pass?*
*The fellow whose verdict counts most in your life*
*Is the one staring back from the glass?*

*You may be like Jack Horner and chisel a plum*
*And think you're a wonderful guy.*
*But the man in the glass says you're only a bum*
*If you can't look him straight in the eye.*

*He's the fellow to please - never mind all the rest,*
*For he's with you clear to the end.*
*And you've passed your most dangerous, difficult test*
*If the man in the glass is your friend.*
*You may fool the whole world down the pathway of years*
*And get pats on the back as you pass.*
*But the final reward will be heartache and tears*
*If you've cheated the man in the glass.*

(Author unknown)

CHAPTER 7

# Tackling Inner Demons

**SHOT OF INSPIRATION # 7:**
*If at first you don't succeed, you're running about average.*

*We learn wisdom from failure*
*Much more than from success;*
*We often discover what will do,*
*by finding out what will not do,*
*and probably he who never made a mistake*
*never made a discovery.*

**SAMUEL SMILES**

L EADING UP TO THE FOURTH TEST match of the 2001 Ashes series, Steve Waugh sustained a much-publicised injury to the calf muscle in his leg that threatened to sideline him for the remainder of the tour. As a result of his misfortune a small ray of hope entered my world. Someone would have to replace him to play in the Fourth Test of the series.

Time for another life lesson.

Experience was screaming at me that team selections were out of my control and that all I could do was go out and score as many runs as possible to encourage the selectors that I was the best man for the job. Although I wanted to believe this, I went into a lead-up game trying so hard, too hard, to make the runs necessary to give me the position ahead of my close mate Simon Katich. The harder I tried, the tighter I became and the worse I batted.

The result was another failure, another nightmare and another rejection.

I will never forget walking off the Sussex cricket ground after a ball from a young county bowler had trapped me LBW for three runs. It was just before stumps on the first day, and as I trudged off the field with my head stooped, I wanted in that instant to have the ground open up and swallow me whole. I wanted to disappear from the world until I woke up from this ongoing nightmare.

To this day I can never remember feeling so low in my life, or at least in my professional life.

Sitting on the team bus that night, I was silent. While I wanted to scream and kick and throw punches at the cruelty of the world, I just sat there in silence – thinking, thinking, thinking, and staring into thin air. I was feeling lousy and very sorry for myself, as every negative thought imaginable going through my mind.

Stepping off the bus, a hand grabbed me by the shoulder and directed me to the hotel bar. Coach John Buchanan and vice-captain Adam Gilchrist guided me to a corner table and sympathetically listened to my woes.

At first it was hard to put into words precisely how I was feeling, but as the time ticked by, the feelings and emotions that had built up for the six weeks since I had been dropped, began pouring out.

In the next four hours we just sat, talked and drank a few beers. Then we talked some more and drank some more, solving some of the problems of the world along the way. For the first time in six weeks I had allowed myself to drop the cool, calm, male exterior and basically let it all hang out. John listened until I could talk no more. I told him of the questions and points I had wanted to scream at Tugga when he had first dropped me from the team. Over six weeks these issues simply got worse as they festered away in my brain.

Rather than just thinking these thoughts I let them out into the world through the ears of the coach. Rather than just *wanting* to scream and shout and abuse everyone for taking away my position, I actually did, except it wasn't really screaming and shouting. I told the coach I always came up with the goods when the team most needed it, that I would put my life on the line for the baggy green cap and my teammates. I read out all of my statistics from the previous three years while batting at No.3 for Australia and

I told him I didn't think the decision was fair. I told the coach I always seemed to be the easy option to be dropped and I let him know how hard it had been to tell my family and friends on the other side of the globe. I told John how tough it had been to look my teammates in the eye at training that day and how hard it had been keeping a happy face when everything was going along as if nothing had even happened. Finally, I told him that unless I found a way of getting over the decision, the moment, the world, the journalists, and the selectors, then I was going to self-destruct and basically lose the plot.

As he listened, John chipped in with helpful pieces of advice and a kind word every now and then. He told me that he understood my predicament and he reassured me that the decision had been a tough one and that Tugga had felt it as much as anyone. He also encouraged me to hang in there and to stay positive. Most importantly, the coach listened and I poured out my heart.

At last I felt free from the fiend that was playing havoc in my heart and soul.

By the time we left the bar, the coach and I were both a little wobbly on our feet, but I was in a far easier state of mind than when we had arrived earlier in the evening.

Then an extraordinary thing happened.

Picture this situation: as we walked up the staircase in the foyer of The Grand Hotel in Brighton we reached the point where he had to go one way to his room, while I had to go the other. At this point, while standing on the landing of the stairwell, John looked at me and dropped his bag by his feet. At that moment there was something of a tense instant as he glanced at me with a suspicious glint in his eye. Before I knew what was going on, he had grabbed me and given me the biggest bear hug of all time. Like a father giving his teenage son, or daughter, a cuddle, the coach grabbed me and hugged me with all the sympathy, love, care and understanding that he could muster.

After hugging me he said: *"I know everyone has been telling you for weeks to keep your chin up, keep working hard, keep hanging in there, but at the end of the day I realise now that you also need a hug at a time like this. I have been trying to get around to it but the timing has never been right. The timing just felt right now."*

I will never forget John's gesture. At last I felt like I had an ally on my side. He had listened and he had cared. From that moment on, I felt like a huge burden had been lifted off my shoulders.

On my wedding day, my Dad's main message to Sue and I was that the most important thing about marriage was being able to TALK, TALK, TALK. If you have a problem talk about it, don't let it fester and grow. Equally, if you are happy about something, or sad about something, or curious about something, then talk about it.

In my disappointment about being dropped I forgot this valuable advice. It had taken me six weeks to get everything off my chest and when I finally did, it was like clearing the slate and cleaning out the poison that had started to build up inside my mind. By doing this I was able to start fresh and go forward without the negative energy that had been holding me back like a ball and chain strapped to my leg.

Add to this the realisation that putting on a false bravado had been detrimental to me getting out of the hole I was in. I realised how important it is to be yourself and not try to be something you are not. Expressing your feelings in a way that is considered, and not just a knee-jerk or over-reaction, is a significant part of life. Don't hold back because speaking out isn't the thing to do. If you store your feelings without expressing them, you will risk having your heart and soul torn apart like a crumbling jigsaw.

John Buchanan's hug taught me another lesson that night. As a man in our society you are not meant to be soft or affectionate, but after realising how important this gesture was from the coach, I now say to hell with that theory. From now on, I will be a hugger because there is nothing like a bit of love and affection at the appropriate time. Take it from me, the simple hug is truly a great human gift.

# CHAPTER 8

# Fighting Back

**SHOT OF INSPIRATION # 8:**
*Sometimes you have to reach rock bottom before you*
*can start climbing back up the mountain. We learn*
*many of life's most valuable lessons at times of*
*adversity and disappointment.*

*Never give in. Never, never, never!*
*Never yield in any way great or small,*
*except to the convictions of honour and good sense.*
*Never yield to force and the apparently*
*overwhelming might of the enemy.*

WINSTON CHURCHILL

S IX WEEKS BEFORE John Buchanan's hug, Steve Waugh may have wanted to give me a hug and tell me everything would be all right, but of course that is not really the done thing. We aren't supposed to hug and show emotions, we are expected to give each other a slap on the back and say "she'll be right mate" and get on with it. If you decide not to get up and get on with it, you will be left behind like a lame animal in the jungle. It is pretty much as simple as that.

As coincidence would have it, I was dropped from the Australian team at around the same time rugby league star, and my namesake, Allan "Alfie" Langer, had made an unimaginable comeback. In an extraordinary State-of-Origin triumph over New South Wales, Alfie led his beloved Queensland teammates to an unexpected victory.

Although he had retired from Australian rugby league some time earlier, he had answered an SOS from his former coach and friend Wayne Bennett. In a controversial gut-instinct move, Bennett selected Langer to play in the final Origin encounter against the Blues. With the scoreline reading one rubber apiece after two games, Queensland were looking down and out going into the deciding rubber. In what turned out to be an amazing match, Queensland got over the line, with Allan Langer playing a major role in the victory. An Australian newspaper headline describing the event read: **"Langer makes greatest comeback ever."**

The article accompanying this headline made its way under my hotel room not long after this stunning man-of-the-match performance from the tough little Queenslander. A friend had faxed this to me, with a note suggesting that this could be a good omen for me as it was going to take a monumental effort to make a come-back to the Australian team. Every time the team checked into another hotel around England, this article, and in particular the headline, was taped to the mirror in my bathroom.

While Alfie's one-off State-of-Origin performance was out-standing in itself, it was more significant to me personally because of something I had heard about Alfie Langer 12 months before. Inspirational and highly respected Brisbane Broncos coach Wayne Bennett was the guest speaker at a pre-season Australian squad training camp in Queensland. In his position as a rugby league coach, I was surprised when he described the most courageous thing that he had ever seen from one of his players.

Because of the physical nature of rugby league as a sport, I was expecting him to describe a passage of play, or a particular tackle or rough encounter. Instead, Wayne confessed that the most cour-ageous thing he had ever seen was the retirement of Allan Langer from the Brisbane Broncos. He went on to describe how Alfie had retired at a stage when many others would have expected him to keep playing. From all accounts, the tough little halfback knew in his heart that the time was right, as he had lost his passion and hunger to train and play at the level of performance that was expected from him. He forfeited the opportunity to capitalise on his experience and skill and make the money that he was worth in the current professional game.

Wayne Bennett described how Alfie didn't want to let anyone down by playing and training below his best, and therefore he walked away from the game. For the coach to say that this decision was the most courageous thing he had witnessed is a testament to the character of one of Australia's favourite sportsmen. This courage earned Alfie even more respect from his peers, taking him to a new level of achievement and accomplishment as a player and, more importantly, as a person. Hearing this, and then seeing the way Alfie played in his comeback match, simply provided more motivational fuel to the fire inside my body.

During the period between being dropped and eventually returning to play the final Test match of the Ashes series in England, the motivation of a great comeback was at times as strong and burning as a wild bushfire. At other stages though, the thought of a comeback seemed as distant as the moon. My heart wanted a spectacular comeback but my head often told me that my chances of returning to the Australian Test team were not great.

This ongoing struggle between what I wanted in my heart and the negative thoughts I battled from time to time in my mind took me on an emotional rollercoaster. In those quieter moments when I thought about my cricket and my life, it was obvious to me that if I was going to make it back to the international arena, I'd not only have to become a better cricket player, but a conqueror of the mind games.

The thought of a comeback seemed an improbability as the Ashes tour progressed. Disappointment after disappointment, failure after failure, mind demon after mind demon took their toll on my desire to even play the game. After the first day of the Test lead-up game against Sussex, my driving ambition to play for Australia again seemed light years away.

For the last five years I have written a regular Internet article on life as a professional cricket player. Every night on tour I get back to my hotel room and spend about an hour writing a report about the day. As much as I enjoy writing, this practice takes a lot of discipline and it is basically hard work.

Surprisingly, the article that has gained the greatest reaction over the years was the one I wrote after my memorable night in the bar with John Buchanan. On returning to my room in a state of inebriation, it took me about five minutes to write and file the following 95 words.

## Rock Bottom!
## Wednesday August 8, 2001

*The purpose of this daily postcard is to give you an insight into what it is like being a professional cricket player in the Australian cricket team.*

*Today, basically, if you have heard of Brighton Rock (a name for rock candy in this part of the world), I have found some rock of my own.*

*It is called Rock Bottom!*

*Sorry if this is too sentimental or soft.*

*But it is reality, and as I type these lines, I cannot be more honest than that.*

*From Sussex.*

*After a tough day at the office!*

– JL

As I have described, this day was as low as I have ever experienced. That night I rang my Mum and Dad, my wife and my best friend in Australia. I was struggling. It is as simple as that. I knew I would miss out on the Fourth Test opportunity and the realisation had finally hit me that I may never play cricket for Australia again. At this stage I was basically at the depths of despair. I had literally hit rock bottom in my career.

How could everything have changed so dramatically in just six weeks?

Arriving in England, for the start of an Australian cricket player's ultimate tour, I was feeling on top of the world. I was the No.3 batsman for Australia, my body and mind were well rested after a few weeks' break, and I was clear on which direction I was heading.

Admittedly, there was speculation in the media about my position in the team because of the exciting form of Damien Marytn in the one-day series before the Test series, but I was used to getting through this barrier. Despite the media speculation, I was feeling as good as I had felt for a long time. I was fresh after a break away from the game, and I was as determined as ever to play my part in retaining the Ashes for my country. Besides not having my family with me, life could not have been better.

Hence my question about how could things have turned around so dramatically?

Six weeks later and here I was sitting in my hotel room in Brighton after experiencing one of the longest and hardest days of my life. There was no doubt that I was on the canvas and, at that point, looking at where I could lie down for the 10 count and just give up. It is embarrassing to admit this, but the reality is that I was ready to quit and give up the life that I had wanted since I was a young boy. Finishing like this wouldn't have been easy, but believe me it had entered my mind constantly. On this particular day in Brighton, the concept of quitting was stronger than ever.

I remember falling asleep that night with thoughts buzzing through my mind. It was like my head was a disturbed bees nest. Although my night with the coach had calmed me down to a certain point, I was still unsure of my future. While I felt more at ease with where I was going, I still had to get out of bed the next morning and play another day's cricket. This was going to be harder than usual. Not only would I be hung over for the first time in my professional career, but I would also have to watch as the rest of my teammates went through their final preparations for the Fourth Test – a Test match that I would be missing again.

My head was thumping and my mouth was as dry as sandpaper when I was woken early the next morning by the screaming telephone next to the bed. Whatever I had said to my wife the night before must have touched a nerve because she was on the other end of the telephone receiver telling me that she was flying over to England the next day.

This was great news, as the thought of her and my four-month-old baby, Sophie, coming to England for a visit was enough to bring a massive smile to my face. To her undying credit, Sue dropped everything and flew to the other side of the globe to lend me her love and support, at a time when I really needed it.

Just after Sue had hung up the phone, I was surprised by another early morning message. This second call came from my mum and dad, ringing to check that I was okay, and to reinforce their love, support and faith in my ability. Thanks to an over consumption of beer, I am not sure exactly what I said the night before to them, but by the tones in their voice I must have sounded suicidal. It is amazing what a mix of alcohol and an abundance of emotion can produce, isn't it?

These two telephone calls, plus the memory of John Buchanan's conversation and, of course, the hug the night before, were reminders that I had allies supporting me and willing me to keep fighting. This undeniable support and my own self-belief and determination, encouraged me to *really* start the long journey back. For the first time since I had been dropped, I knew clearly that I really did want to get back to where I felt I belonged. Now it was more than just words and hopes. I could feel the desire to fight my way back into the Australian cricket team. This firmness of mind was not only for myself, but also for all of those people who have so much faith in me.

As it turned out, the following night I went out to dinner with Steve Waugh and opened up to him like I had to John Buchanan the night before. This time I stayed away from the booze, and while Tugga didn't give me hug at the end of the night, I finally told him exactly how I had been feeling since the day he came to my hotel room before the First Test.

There is no doubt that this dinner conversation was another turning point in my desire to get back into the team. For six weeks I had been trying to tough it out and get through my predicament by myself. A barrier had formed between Stephen and I because I was struggling with the fact that he had been one of the selectors who had dropped me in the first place. For so long he had been one of my strongest supporters and yet I had felt like I had been let down on this occasion. It was wrong of me to think like this, but it is usually human nature to blame someone, or something else, before looking at the real cause of the problem, which you can find when you stare into a mirror.

Throughout the course of our chat, the captain urged me to continue to work hard and believe in myself. He told me to use this setback as a lesson in never giving anyone a single reason for dropping me again. He could give me no guarantees on my future but he told me that he still had faith in me and hoped I would keep challenging the rest of the guys through consistent performances. Above all else, he reminded me that anything could happen, and that I had to be ready if another opportunity came up.

When we left the restaurant and walked back to the hotel, I felt like the world had been lifted from my shoulders. I knew how hard it had been for Tugga to drop me in the first place, and I also realised that I had been foolish not to go to Stephen earlier and discuss my situation. A simple chat five weeks earlier may have saved me a lot of the uncertainty about my role in the team and the direction that I was heading. It may also have saved me from the frustration and fear of not knowing where I stood with one of the people who I most respect. This in itself is a good lesson in that you should confront a problem front on, rather than ignore it and hope it goes away by itself. Obviously I still wasn't in the team, but at least I knew where I stood and where I was going. This clearness was comforting and refreshing.

*"The darkest hour is before the dawn and that it is when the great avenger is born."* – **PAUL KELLY**

These words from the great Australian songwriter stuck in my head around this time. The day before John Buchanan, my wife, my family and the captain had reinforced their confidence in me, I felt like I had lived though my darkest hour. Now, only 24 hours later, I was clear, confident and ready to become the great avenger. Nothing had changed in regards to my current circumstance, but what had changed was how I was viewing where I was at, right at that moment. I wasn't any closer to being back in the team, but I was closer to giving myself the best chance of turning around my situation with a clearer agenda.

# CHAPTER 9

# The Joys of Touring

SHOT OF INSPIRATION # 9:
*Whatever you can do, or dream you can, begin it.*
*Boldness has genius, power and magic in it."*

HOW I WAS ACTUALLY GOING to achieve my ambition of re-selection in the Australian team on that Ashes tour of 2001 still seemed blurry, but something inside my heart and head had been released by my dinner with the captain.

At last my head had been cleared and I was ready to marry the physical and technical work I had been doing with the magic of a clear, focussed mind. This renewed focus and determination to get back to the crest of my mountain took six weeks of hard toil and self-assessment to attain but I just knew that I was back on the

path and ready to do whatever it took to climb back up the mountain. Life has a funny way of giving you a wake-up call to help you
out of your slump.

I decided to train as hard as I could, to push myself to the limit
and get myself as fit and as strong as possible. My partners in crime
on the Ashes tour were back-up wicketkeeper, Wade Seccombe,
and our team fitness adviser, Jock Campbell. We trained in the
gyms and on the roads of England like men possessed.

I knew deep down that my improved fitness level would pay off
in the future, even if I had to wait for our return to Australia for
the domestic summer. Even though the prospects of playing a Test
match for the remainder of the tour seemed as remote as a lap pool
in a desert, I was telling myself that somewhere down the track my
efforts would pay off.

In the practice nets I hit thousands of balls in an attempt to
make my game as tight as anyone in the world. My rationale was
that the next time an opportunity came I would be like a run-mak-
ing machine, which would be ruthless in my quest to fulfill my
greatest ambitions. This may sound a little over the top, but trust
me, when you are feeling like I had been, anything that can help
you maintain your focus is worth holding on to.

The only downside of my practice was that coach John
Buchanan lost his right arm and we had to strap it up with sticky
tape every time the session was completed. He will never admit
it, but I could see that look of anguish in his eyes every time
I asked him to throw a few balls at me. His look was one of, "How
is my poor arm going to get through another session, especially to

this little lunatic who won't stop hitting balls, even if he is hitting every one in the middle of his bat?"

This particular look isn't foreign, because for years I have seen the same expression on the faces of Noddy Holder and most of the members of the Meuleman family in Perth, who have thrown cricket balls at me to help improve my batting technique. The torture to their shoulders and that dreaded look in their eyes is the same every time I hand them a bucket of cricket balls and ask them for "a couple in the middle of the bat".

I was now a driven man as I tried to convince myself that if I put in the hard work eventually my fortunes would change. Lee Trevino's adage that "the harder I worked, the luckier I got" kept running through my mind.

## ONGOING PERSONAL SETBACKS

The hardest thing during my own fightback period was that although I was preparing as well as ever, my motivation was being continually undermined by what I could see as constant setbacks. Failing with the bat and negative thoughts about my future - especially the very scary thought that I may never get the opportunity to play for Australia again - plagued me day after day. Each setback was like a fire hose pointing at the inferno of desire that had been building up inside me since the day I was dropped.

Physically I was doing everything right, but my thinking was still very muddled and confused. It wasn't until I cleared the decks and got my thinking right that I was able to go forward, without banging my head against a brick wall. All that I was doing, before I had improved my thinking, was striding up the side of the mountain, getting tired and dejected, and sliding back down to the bottom.

Throughout my life, and perhaps most dramatically since the 2001 Ashes series, when ever I was able to marry my physical application with a positive mindset and unshakeable desire to reach my targets, the results were, and have been, remarkable. How many times have you heard the saying, "It is amazing what can be achieved if you put your mind to it?"

My deepest belief is that you can achieve whatever you want in this life, if you put your mind to it and follow your dreams without any distractions, and as long as you can push through the barriers that we put in front of ourselves. I really believe that miracles can be achieved if you set yourself free and let yourself fly.

I like this inspirational comment from author J. Sidlow-Baxter: "The difference between an obstacle and an opportunity is our attitude toward it. Every opportunity has difficulty and every difficulty has an opportunity."

## TEAM HIGHLIGHTS KEEP ROLLING ON

While there were tough personal times on the first half of the 2001 tour of England, it certainly wasn't all gloom and doom. Sure, I wasn't playing in the Test team, but I knew that I was still going to be part of a triumphant Australian squad that retained another Ashes urn from our closest rivals England.

There were some lonely, frustrating times but there were also some phenomenal experiences, which will remain in my memory for a long time. Looking back over my diary I realise just how enjoyable touring life is, especially when you are with a group of guys who I have been playing and travelling with for a long time. In a funny way, my team-mates are like my brothers for the majority of the year because I spend more time with them than I often do with family in Perth.

Thanks to a tough tour personally, I was able to forge and strengthen some friendships that may never have developed if the circumstances weren't as they were. The support of John Buchanan and the other dirt trackers (a name given to the boys on the bench), Damien Fleming, Colin Miller, Jock Campbell, Errol Alcott and Wade Seccombe was heartening, and I am glad that I had the chance to get to know these guys better, even if it was through our shared frustrations.

Not playing the Test matches is hard to handle, but the upside is that you get the best seats in the house, with all the same perks and less pressure. Obviously I would take the option of playing any time, but when it comes down to it, touring life is an extraordinary experience.

## THE ASHES TOUR HIGHS

Digressing a little, let me take you through a few of the tour highs.

In the First Test of the series at Edgbaston, the world finally got to see one of the most exciting bowling attacks ever unleashed on England. Glenn McGrath, Jason Gillespie, Brett Lee and Shane Warne bowling in tandem were enthralling to watch. Some outstanding batting by the Waugh brothers and my Western Australian buddies Adam Gilchrist and Damien Martyn backed up this foursome in the bowling department, allowing us to go one nil up in the series.

On Gilly's performance and winning the First Test match, I wrote in my diary:

*"The way he (Gilly) strikes the cricket ball is comparable to any of the great players, while his method seems so simple and uncomplicated. The greatest of batsmen, Sir Donald Bradman, once said that when he batted he always looked to hit the next ball for four. If it wasn't there to be hit for four, he would settle for a three, a two, a single, or as a last resort he would just survive. There is no doubt this is the same mentality adopted by our vice-captain. He is so positive in every move that he leaves the helpless bowler with very little margin for error. After Gilly's better-than-a-run-a-ball century in Mumbai five months ago, it was hard to believe that a more destructive innings could ever be witnessed. Today, my West Australian teammate played with equal contempt for the opposition bowlers, leaving everyone who was lucky enough to observe such brutality in awe of the man's talent.*

*His partner in crime happened to be my good mate from Perth and my replacement for the Test match, Damien Martyn. When he squeezed a ball through gully for his maiden Test century, my heart was pumping as though the triumph was for my own brother. Having played cricket together since we were young boys, I couldn't have been more delighted for a person as I was for Marto today. He has worked so hard over the last few years to earn the right to excel like he did today. A few years ago he was down and out and on the verge of fading away into obscurity. By disciplining his mind and body, he is now securely entrenched in the Australian cricket set-up. Through hard work and belief, he is writing his own pages in history, as he goes from strength to strength as a batsman and as a person."*

– JL

And there was more:

## Celebrations and a Wimbeldon final!
## Tuesday, July 10, 2001

*How good a time do you think the Australian cricket team has had over the last two days? After a sensational First Test result, the visitors' changing room at Edgbaston has probably never seen such carry on. Apart from being a good cricket team, it must be said, in terms of celebrators, this team is peerless.*

*Ashley Giles edged a Shane Warne leg-spinner at about 2pm. Following a few high-fives and back slaps, we walked a lap of the ground to show our appreciation to the crowd. Talk about a buzz! As a group we realise the importance of spending time acknowledging the local supporters and those who travel across the world to follow the deeds of their national cricketers. Even the local crowd seemed to appreciate this simple act, which means more to us than people may realise.*

*There is a motto within the team that says, "It is not everyday that you win a Test match." This in mind, the celebrations always fit this achievement. As the afternoon rolled into the night, the music boomed louder and the rusty but passionate singing befitted the emotions of a very happy unit of people. Rarely would the plaster-board walls of the visitors' changing room at the Edgbaston cricket ground have witnessed such euphoria and festivity. The team song, Underneath the Southern Cross, was led by Ricky Ponting at about 10pm. It would be fair to say that a few of my very professional team-mates were a little worse for wear. We know what goes into winning a*

*Test match, so it is also accepted as part of the culture of the team that celebrations at the end of the game should help everyone wind down before the next one.*

— JL

## HOW WE CELEBRATE

The question often comes up about what you can possibly do within the walls of a cricket changing room for such long periods of time. All I can say is that some of my fondest cricket memories surround the time spent listening to music, singing songs, talking rubbish and just being with your mates after a Test match victory. It is not unusual, in fact it is very common, for a session in a victorious Australian changing room to last as long as a day's play on the field. This is one of the reasons why we play the game, so that we can truly enjoy the whole package of winning Test match cricket. If only you could be a fly on the wall. Let's leave it at that!

Winning that First Test in four days allowed the guys to enjoy an incredible opportunity of sitting on Centre Court for the men's singles final at Wimbledon. With an Aussie hero vying for the cherished award, most of the squad couldn't get their hands up quickly enough when the opportunity was offered. Pat Rafter is simply an incredible person who is greatly respected not only as a tennis player but, more importantly, as a fellow Australian and outstanding character.

The Wimbledon final for most Australians is about a television set, a hot cup of coffee in the late hours of a winter's night. The mere fact that we were actually going to see the event live sent the adrenaline pumping through the veins of 15 baggy green wearing, patriotic Aussie cricketers.

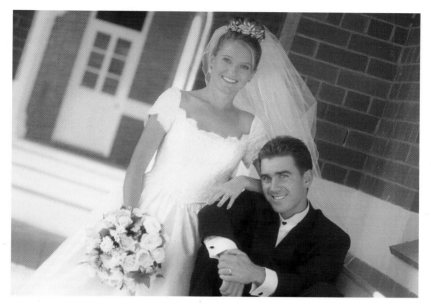

Getting married to my best friend Sue in 1996. *Langer family collection*

Arriving home after the Hobart Test match in 1999. *Photo: © Ian Cugley*

*Left:* Boxing Day Test match 1998. *Langer family collection*

*Below:* 'Always See the Sunrise' – Pop Langer. *Langer family collection*

My angels, Ali-Rose, Sophie & Jessica. *Langer family collection*

Mum and Dad - my best friends and mentors who taught me the difference between right and wrong. The best gift parents can give their children. *Langer family collection*

Me and my five girls, Jessica, Sue, Sophie, Amber (the dog) and Ali-Rose.
*Photo: © Ian Cugley*

Only hours after being dropped by captain Steve Waugh in England 2001.
*Photo:* © *Jack Atley*

*Left:* Support from team-mate and champion Shane Warne.
*Photo:* © *Jack Atley*

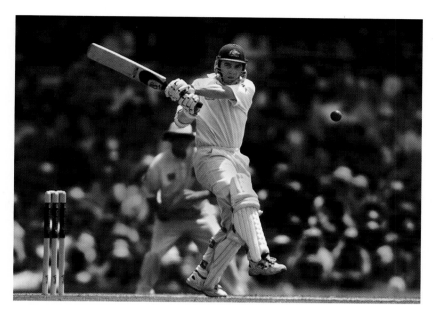

Back in action in Australia 2001/02. *Photo: © Jack Atley*

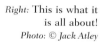

*Right:* This is what it
is all about!
*Photo: © Jack Atley*

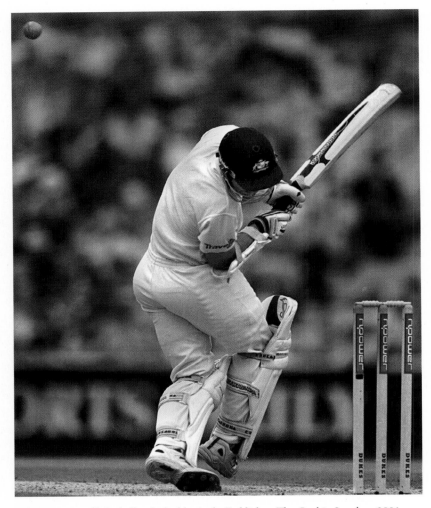

Taking my eye off the ball – decked by Andy Caddick at The Oval in London, 2001.
*Photo: © Jack Atley*

Ouch! *Photo: © Jack Atley*

*Below:* Friends for life – "well played son!" with Matty Hayden, 2001.
*Photo: © Jack Atley*

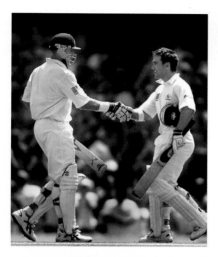

*Above:* The stodgy opener - this photo takes pride of place in my games room at home, Hobart 2001.
*Photo: Hamish Blair © Getty Images*

Runs are the only currency of value in this game. *Photo: © Jack Atley*

*Left:* Champion Glenn McGrath and the Frank Worrell Trophy, 1998. *Langer family collection*

*Below Left:* Team mascot 'Schkimpy', England 2001. *Langer family collection*

*Below Right:* Two legends of Australian cricket, Ian Healy and Steve Waugh. *Langer family collection*

Brett Lee's Test debut.
*Langer family collection*

Character… Colin 'Funky' Miller.
*Langer family collection*

On arriving at our seats on Centre Court, a thunderous roar echoed through the stadium. My initial reaction was that the players must have just entered the court to start their hit-up. Within seconds, it dawned on my colleagues and I that the band of thousands of Australian supporters there to cheer on Patty Rafter had recognised our entrance. This moment in time was nearly as proud as I have ever felt. A standing ovation at the Centre Court of Wimbledon! Wow, it is hard to put into words the emotions that flood through your body on an occasion like this. Then, to top it all off, my Hollywood hero, Mr Jack Nicholson, entered the arena to an identical reaction from the crowd. All this before a single ball had been played in the main event. Incredible!

As for the game, well what a contest. Sadly for Pat Rafter, he missed out on the title after an inspirational fight. Goran Ivanisevic enjoyed a Cinderella story for the week and was a worthy Wimbledon champion. While we all cheered our hearts out for our fellow Aussie, the Goran story was very motivating. Fighting back after years of despair to win a Wimbledon title . . . great effort mate, great effort!

After Wimbledon, and during a rain delay during our practice match against Somerset, we cheered on the Australian Wallabies to an inspiring rugby Test match.

I wrote:

*The only bonus of this morning's torrential Somerset rain was the opportunity to watch the deciding rugby Test match between Australia's Wallabies and the British Lions. After sending the Wallabies a message of luck, via Channel 7 in Australia, we were all pumped by the prospect of another Test victory for Australia. There has been so much interest in this country that the tension was intense before the first kick-off.*

*Clad in Aussie gold Australian rugby union scarves, the atmosphere in the Somerset CCC committee room reached boiling point with 15 minutes remaining in a brutal contest. When Australia scored the deciding try there was the same level of excitement as if we had just dismissed Mike Atherton for a first ball duck. To say we were pumped is something of an understatement. Not only were we excited for our fellow countrymen, but we also knew that there is no longer any chance of the tiring banter coming from the drunken mouths of sectors of the crowds we are playing in front of. For weeks we have been taunted with cries of, "You might win the cricket, but at least we will win the rugby." And "Just watch our Lions whip your convict Wallabies." It has become like a broken record, so now we just have to smile at any clown in the crowd who wants to hear his own voice. For this we will be forever indebted to the mighty Wallabies.*

The silence of the English crowd continued into the next two Test matches where I again enjoyed watching breathtaking performances from my teammates who were on fire on the field. The Lord's Test match has been a dream of mine for years and missing that was perhaps the biggest disappointment of the tour. I still have ambitions of wearing my baggy green cap onto Lord's, so I guess I will just have to wait for the next tour to achieve this ambition.

After enjoying Lord's as my home ground with Middlesex for three years of county cricket, I can say without hesitation that Lord's is my favourite ground to play at in the world.

## The Magic Of Lord's
## Tuesday July 17, 2001

*When I walked through the Long Room at Lord's today, it was like being bear-hugged by an invisible spirit, welcoming me back to the Home of Cricket. Lord's is more than a cricket ground, more than a place for which I have very fond memories both on and off the field.*

*Words don't seem to fully grasp the uplifting feeling of standing in a cricket aficionado's version of heaven. The magic of Lord's is invisible in the sense that the accompanying emotions are indefinable. In the physical sense, the magic manifests itself in many ways. The hallowed turf, the portraits, the wonderful cricket paintings, the luxuriously extravagant silver showerheads in the changing room bathroom and the long wooden tables and heavy, painted wooden doors in the Long Room. And it doesn't stop there as the players get to enjoy the greatest players dining room in the world, accompanied by the best cooks in Linda and Catherine, who prepare daily feasts fit only for kings. To top it all off, Lord's wouldn't be Lord's without George and Magic who are just two of the suited, affable ground stewards who make everything run smoothly day in day out.*

*– JL*

The statement has often been directed my way about the shame of playing County cricket at Lord's in front of mediocre crowd numbers. If truth were known, my greatest memories of Lord's are on these occasions, because during County contests it feels like you have the whole place to yourself. On these days you don't have to share the ground, and everything about it, with anyone else. There is real magic in this!

Lord's really comes to life during a Test match. As you walk through the Long Room and through the cigar smoke and delicious aroma of coffee and bacon sandwiches, the hearts of the players and umpires find a new level of activity. The expectation is immense, and if anyone forgets this, the MCC members, who are there to see a battle for which they can talk about for the remainder of their days, will soon remind you.

The portraits of Bradman, Miller, Hutton and Co. stare down from the walls, almost daring Australians to enter the arena and not come back triumphant. The incredible sense of history surrounding a Lord's Test match, and more significantly an Ashes Test match at Lord's, marks this period of any Ashes tour as an awesome experience for everyone involved.

This diary entry leading into the Second Test is a snapshot into how special it was for us on the 2001 Ashes tour.

*Training this morning was very upbeat, hardly surprising as our boys were like the proverbial kids in a chocolate factory - running, jumping, diving, catching and hitting cricket balls in front of the watchful eye of the magnificent Lord's pavilion and equally impressive high-tech media centre. We are excited about the prospect of this Test match and while the last seven days have been relatively relaxed, our preparation is now at fever pitch as we strive to win this Test and go two-nil up in the series.*

The Lord's Test also gave us the opportunity to meet the Queen of England. I have been fortunate to meet Her Majesty twice in my life and I can say that on both occasions the experience has been amazing. Both times the hair has stood upright on the back of my neck as Her Majesty came into sight. Her presence in a room is awe-inspiring, as one of the most recognisable faces in the world is actually standing, smiling only a few feet away. Our meeting with the Queen was just another incredible opportunity as a result of being a part of the Australian cricket team.

From Lord's, where the guys took the team to a decisive two-nil lead in the series, we travelled to Nottinghamshire for a chance to retain the Ashes in the Third Test. Apart from Stephen's injured calf muscle and a few tense moments, this ultimate goal was accomplished and the celebrations that followed were as memorable as ever.

Following the triumphant Third Test, the team travelled to the beautiful country of Ireland where we were treated to hospitality like only the Irish can offer. After retaining the Ashes we were able to relax by playing golf, fly-fishing and drinking a few pints of Ireland's favourite brew before returning to Headingley for the Fourth Test match of the series.

It was around this time that my wife Sue had flown over to lend her support. Among all the festivities and hard work off the field, there were times when I was struggling and feeling lonely for my family and friends. Sue's arrival seemed to mark the major turning point for me in my tour and probably my career. As I have said, she dropped everything at home and travelled across the world to give me a hug and just be there to help put things into perspective. Sue and my baby daughter Sophie helped take my mind off the disappointment of missing the Fourth Test match.

For the week of the Test I had the comfort of knowing that every night I returned to my hotel room I had my family to come home to. Rather that sitting alone staring at the TV or the walls of my hotel room, I had a baby to cuddle and a wife to talk to. Their presence made the world of difference because in the end of the day, regardless of my performance on the cricket field, they will smile and love me no matter what. This security is crucial to any success and I will cherish Sue's love and commitment during that difficult period of my life for as long as I live.

## RICKY PONTING CEMENTS THE NO.3 SPOT

As happy as I was to have the girls in Birmingham, their time coincided with the only Test match loss of the series. England's opening batsman Mark Butcher played the innings of his life to win the Test for his country. With Steve Waugh absent through injury, we obviously left our best cricket on the golf courses of Ireland, as England stole a Test match, in turn taking our pride with them. This Fourth Test marked Simon Katich's Test debut and Ricky Ponting cemented his position at No.3 with two brilliant Test innings.

We had been determined to win the series five nil and confirm our dominance over England. Losing the Fourth Test made this impossible, but it did fire the team up for the final Test match of the series, a Test match that had enormous impact on my career.

CHAPTER 10

# He Who
# Endures Wins
# in the End

**SHOT OF INSPIRATION # 10:**
*Have Fun. Make a promise to yourself that you are going*
*to have fun no matter what. It is hard to have negative*
*thoughts when you have a smile on your face.*
*Smile, smile, smile and see the difference it makes.*

HAVING MADE THE CHOICE to fight back rather than quit
after being dropped in England, I reflected on something
one of my old coaches in WA had told me years before.

Graham House had told me that **LUCK** is the point where
**OPPORTUNITY** meets **PREPARATION**. This principle has
stuck with me ever since the day he shared it with me. I have

always found that the more I prepare for something, the greater the chances are that an opportunity will present itself to me.

Preparation, in my opinion, is the single most important aspect of achievement because you have control of your preparation. In fact, your preparation is often the only thing that you do have control over. I can't remember a single time in my life when I have been thoroughly prepared for something and failed. I know that the times I have worked really hard, taken no shortcuts, and been totally committed to my training, have been my most successful times. I also know that when I have taken the shortcuts, sat in a comfort zone and made excuses about my preparation, then I have failed or at least been disappointed with a performance.

An example of Luck = **Preparation + Opportunity** happened to me toward the end of the Ashes series. This fortuitous event came in the form of an opportunity granted to me by the tour selectors. After being dropped from the Test side, I had been waiting, praying and hoping for another chance to play Test cricket for my country.

On Tuesday, August 21, 2001, exactly 51 days after I had been omitted from the First Test team, the captain told me that I had been given a lifeline. With only two days to go before the final Test match at The Oval in London, I was in euphoric shock when told I had been given my chance to wear the baggy green cap for Australia one more time.

When I had been dropped previously, it was years before I received another chance. This time it had only been 51 days — although perhaps 51 of the longest days of my life.

Here's how my recall unfolded.

Sitting in my hotel room, the telephone rang about an hour before we were due to leave for training. This training session was to be the final compulsory practice session of the tour. As I have experienced during many Australian cricket tours in the past, training sessions when you are not in the playing XI can be a dreary event. It feels like you are there to make up the numbers, as the guys in the team prepare themselves for the upcoming Test match. Like preparing for any dreary event, I was hardly full of energy as I waited in my room for the scheduled leaving time.

The ringing telephone and subsequent conversation quickly changed that.

My diary entry that night sums it all up:

### A Kid At Christmas!
### Tuesday, August 21, 2001

*The conversation went a bit like this:*

*"Lang, Tug here mate."*

*"Yeah Tug?"*

*"Just thought I would let you know that we have just had a selection meeting and you will be opening the batting with Haydos on Thursday in the Fifth Test. Slats has been left out and you are in. Good luck, you deserve the opportunity after all of the hard work you have put in since you were dropped."*

*With my heart pumping like a hydro cylinder and my mouth becoming as dry as desert air, all I could manage in the way of a reply was a meek, "Thanks mate, thanks for the chance!"*

*In shock, I had to pinch myself and clean out my ears to ensure this news wasn't something from the Sunday Sport tabloid newspaper. After what has been a disappointing tour in terms of personal achievement, this news is sweeter than the sweetest honey in the world. I feel the same way that I felt when I was first told I had been selected to make my debut back in 1993. I am pumped, absolutely pumped.*

*Steve Waugh's voice this morning sounded far more agreeable than when he came to my room six weeks ago. On that occasion, he was telling me I had been dropped from the team. This time he was throwing a life raft into the choppy seas. For weeks I have felt like I had fallen off the boat, now I feel that I am at least re-connected. Whether I pull myself back on to dry land is now up to me. Opportunities don't come around every day.*

*Although each conversation was at the opposite end of the scale, Tugga's second effort this morning was far more pleasing to the stress meter in my heart.*

*In all honesty, I thought the chance of playing a Test in this series, after I was dropped early in the tour, was highly unlikely. With every passing day this fear was multiplying like bubble bath under a pouring tap. When Simon Katich was selected to replace the captain in the Fourth Test that finished two days ago, my fears were even deeper than not playing on this tour. Katto's deserved selection indicated new blood and younger legs.*

*At 30 years of age I was starting to worry that my older legs had been put out to pasture like an old stock horse.*

*Circumstances have suggested that a recall was unlikely, especially in the short term. I thought I was going to have to wait until I got* back home to first-class cricket in Australia. I would have to wait until then to get a chance to force my way back into the powerful first XI of the Australian Test team. If I am honest, I have been thinking that getting back into the Test team was going to be as tough as climbing Mt Everest during a blizzard. Basically, I thought I was cooked, reduced to the stockpile, finished.

As fate now has it, this twist in the tale of my life and career has me primed for what I hope will be five of the most enjoyable days of my career. I know I have done the hard work; I just have to back myself now and enjoy the moment.

Of all the lessons I have learned from being dropped, the main one is that you should never take anything for granted, particularly a place in the Australian cricket team.

When my position was taken away, I realised how special it is to represent your country on the sporting field. Now that the opportunity has re-presented itself, I have vowed to myself to have the time of my life over the span of this game. It is easy to get carried away and stressed out with the occasion of Test cricket. I have done this many times before, forgetting the importance of having fun and enjoying the moment.

I am going to smile my head off and buzz around like an energiser battery for the next six days. I feel like a young kid with two sleeps left before Christmas. I am so excited; I can imagine a restless night in my bed tonight.

As for opening the batting, I have done this job on many occasions in the first-class arena. With the experience of batting No.3 for much of my career, the prospect of facing the new ball will not be a foreign *scenario. Walking out to bat with my good friend Matty Hayden will undoubtedly be one of the highlights of my career. He and I have been mates for a long time and I couldn't think of a better bloke to show me the ins and outs of opening the batting in a Test match.*

*In the past, players like David Boon have made a successful fist of changing from No.3 to opening the batting, so I am looking positively to my changing role within the team. The fact is I would be happy batting anywhere in the order, so I see this as a wonderful opportunity.*

*Whatever happens, I intend having the time of my life.*

*From London,*

**JL.**

*PS: I wonder how Slats is going. Poor bastard, I know how he must be feeling. I hope he is okay.*

I remember the emotion of writing my diary that night. I also remember the excitement in my room earlier in the day after Steve Waugh's phone call. A mundane training session had taken on a whole new meaning. As it turned out, I wasn't going to training to make up the numbers that day, I was there preparing to open the batting for Australia in a Test match.

I had gone from sitting on the bed contemplating the future, to jumping around like a kid who had eaten too much chocolate. This transformation had occurred within a 30-second phone conversation with the Australian captain. The scenes in my room were reminiscent of Popeye after he had eaten spinach or Clark Kent turning into Superman.

Until the day I die, I will never forget the very first reaction when I replaced the telephone receiver in my room. Turning to my wife with a look of humbled disbelief on my face, I told her what had just gone on. After she had screamed and jumped up in the air like an acrobat, I made her a promise. At the same time I was making a promise to myself.

I vowed that day, "Whatever happens I am going to have the best time of my life over the next six or seven days. I am going to smile and dance and run and dive and laugh and play this game like there is no tomorrow. As far as I am concerned, this might be the last time that I ever play for Australia and I am going to have fun, no matter what."

I had nothing to lose. Up until five minutes earlier I had accumulated 51 days worth of contemplating the fatalistic notion of never playing international sport again. Now I was two days away from doing what I love doing most – playing Test cricket in my baggy green cap. As unexpected as this opportunity was, I intended grabbing it with both hands, and with a smile painted all over my face.

If I scored runs then that would be a bonus. I knew I had put in a mountain of work over the previous six weeks, but regardless of this, I swore to myself that fun and enjoyment were my prime objectives. This might be my last chance. Why not have the time of my life?

# CHAPTER 11

# The Power of Positive Thoughts

**SHOT OF INSPIRATION # 11:**
*If you want more joy in your life,
do whatever you're doing now with more joy.*

O N THE FIRST MORNING OF THE Fifth Test at The Oval, this reinvigorated attitude and promise to Sue and myself, was tested to the limit. Steve Waugh, having fought back from his calf muscle injury, won the toss and decided to bat first.

Sitting down on my changing room chair, padding up, and preparing myself to bat, I remember the tension starting to crawl its way up my legs, into my heart and guts and then into my mind. As I strapped the right pad to my leg, thoughts started spearing though my mind and body like a nest of ants invading a dropped sugar cube.

These rampant thoughts started changing the feeling in my heart and the rest of my body. Where I had been loose and relaxed in the lead-up to the game, I was starting to feel tight and tense. The butterflies in my stomach were beginning to feel more like angry eagles as the nerves started to take over my existence. The clear thoughts of before were becoming cloudy as my mind started visiting the past, the future and the pit of fear that traps so many underprepared souls.

Fortunately, this drama lasted only about 60 seconds.

Once upon a time I would walk out onto the ground battling nerves and feelings of doubt.

Not this time.

Remembering my promise, I jumped up off my seat and walked over to the music box that provides so much life and entertainment to the Australian changing room. Shirtless and still only wearing one pad, I turned the music up louder than usual and danced around a little bit. This helped me loosen up my body and clear out my mind. It is difficult to feel stressed out when you are singing a song, or dancing a jig.

I then looked around the room, eventually spotting my next anti-stress, fun, fun, fun, ally. There in the corner of the changing room was swing bowler, team comedian and all-round good bloke Damien Fleming. He and I had experienced similar frustrations and disappointments throughout the tour. Consequently, we had formed a strong friendship by helping each other out along the way.

I knew he was feeling happy for me on this occasion, so I walked up to him and he had me laughing within a few seconds.

Again, this was the perfect therapy to relax my mind and body as I consciously went out of my way to stick with my vow.

Feeling calm and happy, I returned to my seat and finished off the necessary preparations. I strapped on my left pad, tucked my shirt into my thigh pad and inner thigh pad, pushed my protector into place, gave that a few jiggles, pulled up my trousers, and then threw a couple of PK "chewies" into my mouth. With a massive smile on my face, and genuinely looking forward to walking onto the ground, I then wished the team good luck, and summoned my opening partner to the changing room door. "Let's go and have some fun buddy, let's have some fun", was the advice I offered to my seasoned opening partner Hayden.

My teammates understood my excitement and joy at being picked, but I think the majority of them thought I was bananas as I walked out to bat that day. Here I was, walking out in an Ashes Test match, in front of a capacity Oval crowd, with millions of television viewers, and yet I was smiling as if it was Christmas Day. In fact, the morning of the game I confided in our team fitness adviser Jock Campbell, telling him that "today feels like Christmas Day". Such was my enthusiasm at being back in the baggy green cap, I felt like I was just about to open my first present underneath the Christmas tree.

Standing waiting for Haydos on the landing outside The Oval changing room, I remember looking down from the steps at one of the English selectors named Geoff Miller. He was wearing a very serious expression on his face. This surprised me because I knew that Geoff Miller isn't that serious a man. Having seen him earlier in the tour presenting one of the most entertaining and funny after-dinner presentations that I have ever seen, I knew that he must have been trying to act serious in his capacity as an England selector. He was a poor actor.

Staring down at him, I offered one of the biggest smiles he had ever seen. At first, he stared back at me as though he was at a funeral, but within seconds he returned the favour with a hearty smile of his own. Before he smiled though, the look on his face was one of astonishment, as if to say, "How can you be smiling like that on the first morning of a Test match against England? Aren't you supposed to be serious and somber before you walk out to bat?"

Eventually Geoff gave in and smiled back like he had just heard a good joke.

My smiling meant that not only did my teammates think I was a little balmy, but now Geoff Miller, the ex-England off-spinner and current England selector, was feeling the same way.

This impression became widespread as I offered Darren Gough and Andrew Caddick a smile and a cheery, "Good morning Goughy, morning Caddy!" This took them by surprise. Knowing they both use a fire and brimstone approach to their art of fast bowling, I think my theory of smile at all costs was working in my favour.

Before I had faced a ball I had said good morning to both umpires and had smiled at most of the England players. This behaviour may sound like madness, but I can say now that it was the best approach to a game of cricket that I have ever had.

Darren Gough was directing bouncers at me, and bowling at the pace of the wind, yet I was counter-attacking with a smile. The more I was smiling the more relaxed I felt and the better I was batting. My feet were moving like those attached to the legs of a tap dancer and my eyes felt soft, allowing me to see the ball like a hawk sees her prey.

The loose fibres in my body were giving me strength and power as I batted with the freedom of an un-caged bird.

At the other end, Matty Hayden was encouraging me to keep going. In our first partnership together we passed the 100 mark. Before he left the crease we had set the scene for future milestones. The more I smiled, the more he did. With this relaxed spirit we went about our task like two mates on a fishing trip. I can't remember a more enjoyable partnership.

Until a ball from Andy Caddick rose steeply and hit me in the helmet, I felt in full control of my innings. I went hard at my ex-Middlesex teammate Phil Tufnell, who was also making a comeback appearance, and I played debutante James Ormond with a genuine respect that he earned in gaining selection. While the battle in the middle was intense, I felt the more I was able to relax, the more I was able to control my emotions and subsequent actions.

## A CENTURY IN MY COMEBACK TEST AT THE OVAL

Although I was eventually forced to retire hurt by the Caddick blow – I must be getting soft in my old age – I vividly remember the moment when I square cut Tuffers for four to bring up my century. Even while I write this line I can feel the emotions pouring back through my body. When the ball left my bat I ran down the pitch and jumped into the air as if I was taking off to fly. I felt so happy at that moment that I am a little surprised I didn't actually grow wings and fly up onto a cloud and stay there for the rest of the day.

Because man wasn't designed to fly, I instead turned my energy to the changing room where my teammates were standing with their hands raised above their heads. Pumping my right fist at my mates, I felt so filled with emotion and lost in the moment that I must have forgotten to watch Caddick's bouncer a few overs later. The result of this was an earlier than desired departure from the ground and a trip to the local London hospital emergency ward.

I was forced to retire hurt on 104.

Again, my diary account of that day summed up my emotions:

### What A Day!
### Thursday, August 23, 2001

*Today has been like a dream.*

*Fifteen days ago I wrote an entry describing how I felt like my career was at rock bottom. Dropped from the Test team, struggling to score runs against the county attacks and basically feeling down and out, I felt like the whole world was against me.*

*When I was told of my selection for this Test match I vowed to myself that whatever happened I was going to enjoy the next five days and have a lot of fun in the baggy green cap. This attitude helped me go into the day brimming with enthusiasm and energy. Now as I write this entry (with an icepack strapped to my throbbing left ear thanks to a quick Andy Caddick bouncer), I can admit to feeling on top of the world.*

*It is said that having reached rock bottom, you can then start climbing up the mountain towards the pleasing reward of the summit. Having experienced emotions at both ends of the scale over the last six weeks, I can recommend the latter to anybody. By working hard, trusting your instincts, backing yourself and enjoying each experience, you can expect to enjoy the rewards down the track. These rewards taste so much sweeter when you have tasted the bitter tang of disappointment. The key as I found out today is to trust the process and the results will follow.*

*This entry tonight is a short one because my bed is calling. Luckily, a CT scan cleared me of any internal damage to my head, and I am happy to report that I will have my hand up to go in at the fall of the next wicket. I have had too much fun not to get out there and bat again tomorrow. A sore left ear aside, I am feeling pumped right now. It is as simple as that.*

*We have had a great day today. Batting with Matty Hayden was even more fun than I could have imagined. I think this opening the batting gig could be the change in career that I have needed. I don't think that this will be the last time I open the batting in my life. I hope this is the case in a few more Test matches for Australia. Time will tell.*

*From London,*

**JL.**

# CHAPTER 12

# The Smiling Assassin

SHOT OF INSPIRATION # 12:

*The best things in life aren't things.* – ART BUCHWALD

THROUGHOUT MY CAREER I HAVE always maintained that when I am in a happy frame of mind, the results – which in my case means scoring runs - look after themselves. The image of the smiling assassin has now made itself into my pre-match psyche. I know that a smiling face means a loose body, which in turn leads to the most powerful and effective execution of my skills.

Reflecting on my career until now, I remember that all of my best innings have been played in this relaxed free and easy manner. My comeback innings in London was almost as enjoyable as the time I batted with Adam Gilchrist in Hobart against the talented Pakistanis in 1999.

Australia came back from the jaws of defeat to beat Pakistan in this Test after Gilly and I shared a long partnership. While I remember the innings well, the image most vivid in my mind is of a picture on the front page of one of the national newspapers.

Leading up to this Second Test in Hobart, I had to undergo dental treatment on my right eyetooth. Years before, the same tooth had been knocked out of my mouth by a fierce bouncer from South Australian speedster Shane George. Unfortunately the therapy hadn't gone exactly to plan and I had to go into the game with a gaping hole protruding from my smiling face.

For four days I had hidden this horrific sight by pulling my top lip over my remaining top teeth, like a teenage girl who had just had braces fitted to her mouth. So embarrassed was I about looking like a toothless rogue that although I may have been smiling on the inside, I was saving my best smiles for my post dental surgery after the Test had concluded. How vain is that?

A smile-less game was at least my game plan, as I tried to retain the squeaky clean Ken Doll image expected of an Australian sportsman. Unfortunately, one ball from the world's fastest bowler Shoaib Akhtar exposed my dreadful smile, which ended up splashed all over the front page of the newspaper. Shoaib had let go a very, very fast bouncer that hit me flush on the left shoulder. At the moment the ball careered into my body, a massive smile beamed from my face. Don't ask me why or how this happened? Usually a ball like this would have had me grimacing and swearing and cursing back at the bully fast bowler. Not this time. Instead, I was smiling and laughing, as if to tell Shoaib that he would have to come up with something better than that to knock me over. The feeling was extremely liberating and although my toothless smile was exposed, I was so pumped up and lost in the moment, that I couldn't have cared less. My outward smile had returned and I knew that this calmness would be instrumental in me being able to play a good innings.

## A DAY TO REMEMBER AT BELLERIVE OVAL

History now records a victory to Australia on that fifth day at Bellerive Oval in Hobart. Not only did this victory act as a stepping-stone for me personally – not in my modelling career but in my batting career – it was also a monumental stepping-stone for the Australian team, which went on to win 16 successive Test matches. If we could win from this position, we felt that we could win from anywhere.

I'm sure many cricket fans will remember this incredible day and fighting effort by the Australian team. After going in at No.3, I watched as wickets fell around me. We had been chasing 368 runs in the final innings to win the Second Test.

We were in tatters at 5-126 when Gilly came to the crease at the drinks break on the last session on the fourth day. After sharing an incredible four-session partnership with Gilly, I was out trying to win the game with a big hit – caught off the bowling of the off-spinner Saqlain – for 127. We were just four runs short of our target. Gilly remained 149 not out – an amazing innings – and Australia had come back from the dead to win by four wickets.

Here's what I wrote about my partnership with Adam Gilchrist and our subsequent team triumph:

*What a day!*

*When Gilly met me at the crease on day four of the Second Test in Hobart I looked at my good mate from the west and said, "You just never know mate, you just never know." He had walked out to bat just as the drinks were being dragged onto the ground, an hour before stumps on the fourth afternoon. The Pakistanis were cock-a-hoop. They were smiling and laughing and having the time of their life. They had us on the ropes and could taste the blood of their toughest opponents. They were ready for the kill.*

*Unfortunately for them, we weren't quite ready to be killed.*

*"If we can hang in here until stumps we might be half a chance tomorrow. We might even make Test cricket history here. This would be an amazing victory from here", I said to Gilly with a nervous smile and laugh.*

*Admittedly, I was talking more out of optimism than realism, but even still, my heart told me we were some sort of chance. If the truth be known I was trying to calm Gilly's nerves, as I could half see the Test match being over tonight if we didn't do something special. With our most senior batsmen licking their wounds in the Bellerive changing rooms, I had a funny feeling that something special was still to come. The loss of our fighting skipper Steve Waugh and Bellerive's golden boy Ricky Ponting in a few balls had dampened my optimism for a Test victory. Rather than conceding defeat, I decided it was time to fight like a wounded tiger to stave off an early defeat.*

*As luck would have it, Gilly and I were able to fight through to stumps on the Sunday afternoon. Walking off the ground, I couldn't help but notice the scoreboard, which read Gilchrist 45, Langer 53. My partner had scored his runs so quickly that a strange confidence was building inside my veins. I had been batting for about three hours and yet my partner had nearly overtaken me in a mere 60 minutes. That's Adam Gilchrist for you. Only an hour into our partnership, the Pakistanis had quietened down but they knew they were still in the box seat. One early wicket the following day and they knew the Test match would likely be theirs.*

*Although we were still a long way off the target, I felt unusually calm about our prospects on day five. With heavy rain forecast for the following 24 hours, I expected grey skies and wet roads to greet me when I opened the curtains of my hotel room the following morning. As I have seen before in Hobart, another abandoned day's play would mean a one-nil lead going into the final Test match in Perth. This would be a WACA administrator's dream and a comfortable buffer for my teammates and our supporters.*

*With this scenario in mind, I fell asleep like a tired baby.*

*What transpired on the final day was miles from my wildest imag-ination. Firstly, clear blue skies smiled through my bedroom window when I woke up in the morning. This perfect Hobart morning paved the way for a great day of Test cricket. Blue skies meant a competitive draw was out of the equation. A full day's play would mean a tense and entertaining finale to a magnificent Test match. Day five was going to be a fight of wits and skills for yours truly, Gilly and the remainder of our tail.*

*When we arrived at the ground, our chances of survival, history, and the bookies' odds, were stacked heavily against us. The pitch was deteriorating and the Pakistanis boasted one of the great bowling attacks. If we wanted to win, something special would have to occur.*

*As the day progressed, something special did transpire.*

*In one of the most incredible run chases in Australian cricket history, Gilly and I were able to chip away at the target and eventually come up trumps. When our veteran teammate of just two Test matches, Adam Gilchrist, hit the winning runs with a trademark hoick over long-on, the scenes in the Bellerive viewing room were unforgettable. The atmosphere was euphoric as we began to realise the enormity of the moment.*

*Admittedly, the event was especially momentous for Gilly and I as we had shared a fantastic partnership and helped pull an unlikely victory from the jaws of defeat. But, much more importantly, the victory for the entire Australian team and our support staff was a major stepping-stone for things to come. Personal glory is always sweet, but it never matches the giddiness of sharing such triumph with your teammates. The moment was extraordinary as everyone savoured the elation of an historical Test match victory.*

*From my part, scoring a century was great fun, but I would have to say it wasn't as much fun as my partnership with Gilly, who made my job easy. Every minute of our time together in the middle made the odd bruise, the odd strain and any previous doubts and fears immaterial. Throughout the innings I remembered something my dad had told me in my first Test match against the West Indies. "If you are still there, the team is always a chance."*

*My partner was magnificent, as he played with a fluency and confidence reserved for a champion sportsman. He is in superb form as he goes from strength to strength with every outing in the Test match arena. His skill and poise simplified my role, as his ability to score runs freely reduced the pressure to a simple battle of wits.*

*The success of our partnership can be attributed mainly to our ability to stick rigidly to a game plan of playing one ball at a time with sharp concentration. Before each delivery we were speaking to each other and encouraging one another to concentrate on "this ball" and "keep watching the ball like a hawk". Our communication helped inspire each other as we kept pushing ourselves to the limits of our beliefs to record an unlikely Test match victory.*

*At lunch on the last day, our teammates were so pumped up that it wouldn't have seemed right to leave the job unfinished when we returned after the break. With a Test match and subsequent series win within sight, everyone within the walls of our changing room was tense, but extremely excited. The feeling within the team was one of unwavering belief in the final result. Initially there was silence in the room before we went back out to bat after lunch, but just before we walked out of the room it felt more like the atmosphere I would expect from a football dressing room. There was plenty of backslapping and noise. When I crossed through the gates onto the oval, I felt like I could charge through the enemy lines on a battlefield. Where the Pakistan players had tasted blood the night before, I was starting to sense something incredible.*

*Our teammates' enthusiasm was highly infectious. To say we were pumped up is something of an understatement. As each run was ticked off the ledger, the energy in the centre of Bellerive was as intense as the local power station. It was inspiring, exciting and one of the greatest experiences of my cricket career. With 20 runs to go, I turned to the changing room and pumped my arm like Lleyton Hewitt after he has won a big point. I was so absorbed in the contest that I was doing things that I would never think of doing on a cricket field. For a time there, I could understand what it must feel like for Hewitt or Pat Rafter when they have won a big tournament.*

*What started out as an optimistic hope was becoming reality as the minutes ticked by. My game plan was to count down the runs 10 at a time. On the other hand, Gilly opted for the approach of playing out time. He knew that batting time and "just being there" would eventually mean victory. He would say to me, "C'mon, let's bat well for the next seven minutes and get to 2:30" or "15 minutes until the drinks break, hang in there mate". My dialogue was more along the lines of, "Seven runs and we only need 140" or "Another five and we are down to 100". Our different approaches kept us going individually. Like all good partnerships, two sound individual game plans ultimately blossomed to form a great team effort. Our partnership was most definitely a fantastic team effort on that day.*

*As 150 runs was reduced to 100, and then 100 to 50, 50 to 40, 40 to 20, down to the moment when the victory had actually been secured, the tensions and excitement exploded in hugs, cheers and singing. Winning a Test match always means a great deal to anyone wearing a baggy green cap. Because this particular Test match was without doubt the toughest and most intensely competitive that I have ever been involved in, this triumph felt even more unique. The pressure was so high for the full five days, it was no surprise to see the sheer exhilaration that accompanied the victory.*

*Equally, the disappointment painted on the faces of our opposition was as relevant to this drama as the smiles of delight etched under 12 baggy green caps.*

*It was like living a dream. Playing in a winning Test match for your country is always a joy, but playing a big part in a winning Test match for your country is unbelievable. The pride on our captain's face was unforgettable as we entered the changing room. His pride in the team made the moment even more significant than that of a normal victory.*

*For me, I knew my dad had been sitting in the crowd for every ball of the Test match. When I walked from the ground, he was the first to grab me and give me a bear hug over the fence. This in itself was like a fairytale. A Test victory, a Test century, an unforgettable partnership with a good mate, and then a hug from my father to top it all off. This really was a Cinderella story for yours truly.*

*I have never had so much fun on a cricket field!*

*– JL*

## FACING THE WORLD'S FASTEST BOWLER AND NOT KNOWING WHETHER TO LAUGH OR CRY

Three days after winning that historic Test match in Hobart, we started the Third Test of the series at my home ground, the WACA in Perth. With Pakistan trying to restore some pride after the Second Test, Shoaib Akhtar was roaring into bowl with the famous Perth sea breeze howling behind his back. There is no doubt in my mind that this was the fastest over of bowling I have ever seen and will ever see in my career. Fortunately I was standing at the non-striker's end as Shoaib sprinted in to bowl his thunderbolts at Ricky Ponting.

The first ball of the over flew past Rick's nose and into the out-stretched gloves of Moin Khan. With this, Rick looked at me and offered a very nervous grin. The second ball was a little closer to my partner's nose and a little faster than the ball before. Again, Rick looked at me for support. All I could offer him was a "keep going mate" with a sheepish smirk on my face. By the time the umpire called "over" after six balls of pure aggression, both Ricky and I had been reduced to good-hearted belly laughter. This was easy for me because I didn't have to face one ball in the over, but our instinctive reaction to this vicious onslaught was to smile and attempt to enjoy the contest.

This reaction took some courage from my younger teammate. In his previous four innings, Rick had been dismissed for a duck. On the back of a run of failures like this, all batsmen feel the pressure building up. Now he was not only fighting his form, but he was standing at the crease of one of the quickest, bounciest pitches in the world facing up to the fastest bowler in the world. Most players would go to water under this sort of pressure. Instead, Rick decided to smile and enjoy the challenge. He backed himself regardless of the circumstances. He smiled in the face of pressure.

Pressure is a big man, and so is Ricky Ponting because in that innings he scored 198 of the most entertaining runs I have ever seen. Under enormous strain he backed his instincts, smiled and came out triumphant. He once again showed why he is one of the mentally toughest players currently playing the game.

CHAPTER 13

# Laughter is Inner Jogging

**SHOT OF INSPIRATION # 13:**
*When we are at peace and in a happy frame of mind,*
*we create success with effortless ease.* – SHAKTI GAWAIN

I HAVE READ ABOUT SO MANY athletes who have backed up the theory of using a loose, relaxed body and happy frame of mind to help them attain their peak performance.

Andre Agassi said: "Sometimes I find myself getting a little too serious. When I am having fun it breaks the tension and I play much better." Andre's equally successful wife, Steffi Graf, backed this up by admitting: "As long as I can focus on enjoying what I am doing, having fun, I know I'll play well."

I once heard Michael Jordan say: "I first realised how much I loved the game of basketball when I began to look forward to practices as much as the games. Money is nothing to me. The bottom line is that I'm playing. I have a "love-of-the-game" clause in my contract, which allows me to play basketball any time I want during the off-season. Basketball makes me smile, I love playing the game."

## WHY PEACE OF MIND CREATES RESULTS

Being a curious sort of person I asked a doctor and a psychologist if there was any physiological or psychological evidence proving that a smiling face makes a difference to how the body functions. There is no doubt in my mind that there is a very strong link between the mind and the body. Both medical experts confirmed this by saying that there is a definite link between a relaxed body and a higher level of performance.

The evidence shows that the effects of pressure and over-excitement lead to both physical and mental effects on performance.

### Physical Effects Under Pressure

— *We hyperventilate, not exhaling enough air.*
— *Blood flow is adversely affected by our tightness.*
— *General muscular constriction results.*
— *We have a reduced range of motion.*
— *Movements become less smooth or fluid, often becoming tight.*
— *Our ability to see clearly may also become impaired.*

## Mental Effects Of A Tight Body

*– Messages from our eyes and ears become unclear and distorted.*
*– Our judgments are not as accurate.*
*– Indecisiveness sets in.*
*– Our minds jump from one place to another – we are literally out of control.*

The effects of fear, anxiety and tension cause muscular tightness and poor breathing patterns. These affect concentration levels because the eyes may react to irrelevant cues. Under pressure a person may tend to force performance rather than just letting his or her body flow and react instinctively. Negative self-talk will tighten muscles and interfere with the messages being delivered from the eyes. When the individual tries to handle more than one function at a time, he/she will divide their attention. The message from the eyes will not be clear, as the eyes need a clear channel to do their job.

Whatever the pressure – whether it is to do better, try harder, accomplish more, be perfect, not fail, whatever – the individual should be aware that their best will come when their performance is effortless, not forced.

Ever since I was a young boy, Kenny Meuleman, my long-time batting advisor and friend, has described to me the importance of having loose, soft forearms when holding the cricket bat. His theory is that loose arms are a sign of a relaxed body. In this state, you give your feet the best chance of moving like a dancer and your body the freedom to move with the fluency and rhythm required to extract your optimum performances.

This is no different in any sport or function that your body is required to perform. The looser and more relaxed you can train your body to be, especially under pressure, the better you will move, and ultimately perform.

In martial arts, I learned that the calmer and more relaxed that I could keep my body, the quicker I could move away from an opponent and the more powerful I could punch or kick. When fighting, this can be difficult because an aggressor is always confronting you, but the reality is that the best way to confront an aggressor is with a calm and focused mind and body.

## ENJOYMENT AND POSITIVITY –
## THE SERGIO GARCIA AND CURTLY AMBROSE WAY

One of the most enjoyable afternoons of my life was when I was invited to play a round of golf with the brilliant Spaniard Sergio Garcia. During this pro-am event – I am definitely an amateur on the golf course – I quizzed the little superstar on the finer details of his success. Without flinching, he looked at me and said, "The most important thing for me to play good golf, is that I am smiling." Pointing at his caddy, he then said, "That is why I employ him to be my caddie. He has good golf expertise, but much more importantly he makes me laugh and smile in all situations. He is invaluable because he always makes me laugh and smile and when I do this I know I will play good golf. Even when the pressure is on we have a laugh together and that helps me stay focused without worrying too much."

I was expecting one of the game's best players to describe concentration, technique or visualisation, but rather, he simply confirmed what I believe is one of the keys to success. Obviously physical, technical and mental preparation are crucial, but when you have done these things, the ability to smile, relax and enjoy the pressure of the event is paramount to your success.

Every time I faced West Indian fast bowler Curtly Ambrose I was intimidated by the fact that he always smiled at me. It didn't matter whether he hit me on the body, I played and missed or I hit him for four, Curtly would just smile at me. Obviously this smile was bigger than the Grand Canyon when he had taken my wicket, but even when I was having a good day surviving the great Antiguan, he still smiled like he was at a comedy show.

He was the best technical bowler and one of the most feared exponents of fast bowling that has ever played the game, and yet he always (or at least nearly always) played with a smile on his face. It is well known that he was something of a joker in the West Indian changing room and while he conjured images of fear in any batsman, he was more like a friendly giant in real life. Curtly was able to break the fast bowler's stereotype of being like a fire-breathing dragon, simply by smiling and laughing at his opponent, or the situation of a game. Although he ignored the archetypal style of most fast bowlers, Curtly was one of the most breathtaking and fiercest bowlers to have played the game.

## WHY WE CAN LEARN SO MUCH FROM OUR CHILDREN

Do you ever watch children at play? They can create enormous fun, enthusiasm and joy from any situation. Since I have become a father, I have learnt some incredible lessons from my kids.

Although they are still only very young, their thoughts and actions provide a wonderful insight into a beautiful world. While we as parents are supposed to be the teachers, my kids, and kids in general, have helped me see life from a much more innocent, stress-free and imaginative perspective.

My young daughter Jessica is a night owl who hates going to sleep at night. Recently I quizzed her about her lack of motivation for early nights, as I was worried that perhaps she was scared of the dark, or scared of being alone, or just scared of something. Looking at me through her sparkling blue eyes, she told me in no uncertain terms that the reason she didn't like going to bed is that she hadn't had enough time to play during the day.

When I returned the idea that she had played all day and needed the sleep to gain energy for the next day, she came out with another magnificent theory on life. "Yeah, but Dad, wouldn't it be just great, in fact wouldn't it be perfect, if we could play all day, and then all night, and never have to go to sleep. It is too much fun playing and I can't have fun while I am asleep."

What a marvellous way to see life and although she will probably learn to love her sleep as she grows into a teenage girl, her sweet passion for life is a reminder to us all.

## MADNESS IN MUMBAI

If worse comes to worse and you are struggling to find a smile or laugh, you could always travel to Mumbai and venture down to the Gateway to India. Just as the sun is rising over the horizon, you can experience an event more humorous than a Billy Connolly concert.

Every morning that I was in Mumbai with the Australian team, I was inevitably woken from my sleep by raucous bouts of laughter.

The first morning of this unusual early morning wake-up call, I thought the people in the room next to mine must have been having a very late party. The laughter was very loud and very infectious. Although it woke me up, it brought an instant albeit curious smile to my face. When the laughter stopped I thought nothing more of it and went back to sleep.

The following morning the same thing happened. Rather than be woken up by a ringing telephone and an Indian receptionist wishing me "good morning", I was shaken to life by another bout of boisterous laughter.

Two mornings in a row seemed unusual, so this time I fell out of bed to investigate the cacophonous rumblings from outside my hotel room. Looking down the hotel corridor I found nothing, and it wasn't until I opened the curtains in my room that I caught the end of a group of people standing around in a circle laughing their brains out.

My curiosity turned to intrigue. The following morning I set my own alarm clock for 5:45am. When the buzzer jolted me from my sleep, I opened the curtains and looked out to the lawn surrounding the majestic monument at the Gateway to India. Within a few minutes I watched a small Indian man who was dressed in a white cloak, walk into the centre of a circle of 11 people. He looked around, nodded and then started howling with laughter. With this, the group followed his lead and for the next 15 or 20 minutes they laughed and laughed and laughed.

This was undoubtedly one of the most extraordinary things I have ever seen.

Later investigations showed that this event is a daily form of meditation designed to free the soul and start the day with a smile. As crazy as this story may sound, the sentiment behind the event is brilliant. While it was hilarious watching the event from afar, I can only imagine how good it must be, being part of that sunrise laughing group. It was so refreshing seeing these people replacing any negative energy they may have with pure, positive energy. It is hard to be angry or negative with a smile on your face. If the laughing meditation is anything to go by, then maybe we should all have a dose of laughter with our glass of orange juice in the morning. It is amazing the effect a good laugh in the morning had on my daily frame of mind in India.

\* \* \*

In summing up, in Joshua Kadison's moving song, *Beautiful In My Eyes*, he sings: "There are lines upon my face from a lifetime of smiles."

A smile is worth a thousand words. A simple smile is a gift to someone else, but more importantly, it is also a gift to you. Every now and then take time to smell the roses and smile. This is a great life to be enjoyed. Don't let small insignificant things get in the way of your happiness. It is not worth it. Make the choice to be happy.

# CHAPTER 14

# Backing Yourself Takes Guts

**SHOT OF INSPIRATION # 14:**

*If you don't back yourself you can be sure no one else is going to.
Believe in yourself, believe in your dream and don't let
anyone tell you anything different. This is your life and you
need to back yourself every step of the way.*

*It is not the critic who counts, not the man who points out how the strong
man stumbles or where the doer of deeds could have done them better.
The credit belongs to the man who is actually in the arena, whose face is
marred by dust and sweat and blood, who strives valiantly, who errs and comes
short again and again because there is no effort without error and shortcomings,
who knows the great devotion, who spends himself in a worthy cause,
who at the best knows in the end the high achievement of triumph and who
at worst, if he fails while daring greatly, knows his place shall never be with
those timid and cold souls who know neither victory nor defeat.*

**THEODORE ROOSEVELT**

THERE IS NO DOUBT IN MY mind that the reason I was able to fight back in England was because I had the courage to stick with the recipe that I know works for me. When you hear testimonies about, or from, the best performers in any field, the underlying message tends to be that they know their own games so well. Elite performers tend to understand their strengths and weaknesses and they trust what works for THEM. What works for someone else isn't necessarily the answer for you.

I know that if I am in a happy frame of mind and smiling, if I watch the ball like a hawk and see it released from the bowler's hand, if I am well prepared and know that I have put in the hard work, if I am positive and play without hesitation, then I will be successful.

I am putting the percentages in my favour and therefore giving myself the best chance of success. The key is to continually trust this recipe and stick with it day in day out, regardless of the circumstances.

Unfortunately it is not always that easy. If I allow outside influences to get in my way, then I tend to put ingredients into the recipe that will make my performance flop. Critics, fatigue, poor preparation or complacency can lead to failure. Consistent failure leads to self-doubt and, in my opinion, it is this self-doubt that has been my most brutal and destructive enemy.

*"Justin, you just have to believe in yourself, trust your ability and believe you are good enough to make it."*

A rich man I would be if a dollar were dropped into my piggy bank every time this old cliché has been directed my way. Mentors

like my Dad and Steve Waugh have often echoed the same sentiment, as I struggled for years to come to terms with playing international cricket.

In past years I would try and re-assure my ego, through words
and a bold front, that I did believe in my God-given talent, but if
I am completely honest this underlying message of doubt was true.
Rather than trusting the recipe that worked for me in Sheffield
Shield cricket, I battled the demons in my mind that were
constantly teasing me that I wasn't really good enough to make
it to the top. These demons acted to cloud my vision, not only
of the little red thing called a cricket ball, but also of my ultimate
life goals and ambitions.

Opportunity and confidence are major factors in embracing
this belief in yourself. It is not until you truly feel it in your heart
and your bones that you can take the power and benefit from this
self-belief and use it to go forward.

It is all a vicious circle because belief comes from confidence
and success, and yet you rarely gain these two assets unless you
have the courage to stick to your recipe and believe that you have
the foundation to succeed. It is easy to say "believe in yourself"
but in reality these words are worthless unless you honestly feel
and embrace the message behind the words. My view is that belief
in yourself comes with time, and while your self-belief is always
being chipped away at, you have the choice to trust in yourself,
what you are doing, and where you are going.

## MY FIRST TEST CENTURY –
## THE TURNING POINT IN MY CAREER

It obviously took quite some time for me to understand these words and the profound impact they can have on your life. After making my Test debut for Australia in 1993, I was only able to play three Test matches in the following five years. There were many tours in between where I made up the numbers and ran the drinks out to my teammates, but basically I was unable to secure a permanent place in the team.

As frustrating as this period was, these were times and experiences that helped strengthen my resolve to force my way into the side. The consistent feats of Steve and Mark Waugh, David Boon, Glenn McGrath, Shane Warne and Ian Healy in these years were acting as an inspiration and a benchmark for where I wanted to be. Where Kim Hughes, Allan Border, Viv Richards, Dennis Lillee and Rod Marsh were my heroes in the backyard, and on the television, I was now playing with real-life heroes who were emulating my dreams. I was so close, and yet so far, away from doing exactly what I wanted to do and that was being a regular member of the Australian cricket team.

Here I was rubbing shoulders with the best in the business and yet for years I doubted my worthiness to be in this environment. It was a fantasy being in the Australian changing room and wearing the green and gold tracksuit, but early on I was never really at ease with myself, feeling that I was yet to earn my stripes within the team.

It took some time to make the break, and when I eventually scored my maiden Test century in Peshawar, Pakistan, in 1998,

I started to feel the power and confidence of knowing that I could succeed at the highest level. This was the same game that Mark Taylor smashed his record-breaking score of 334, and although the match ended in a draw, the memories are sweet. My maiden Test hundred was undoubtedly a breakthrough innings for me. It was also a valuable lesson in the fine line between success and failure, triumph and disappointment.

## BUT FIRST... A GOLDEN DUCK IN KARACHI

Having been selected back into the Australian team after another extended period in the wilderness, I was full of confidence, hope and expectation when I walked out to bat in the First Test in Karachi. Facing up to my first comeback ball in the green and gold colours, I looked up to see Wasim Akram steaming into me like he was the 100m sprint champion. The crowd was screaming, the air was hot and humid and my heart was pounding. As usual I was telling myself to "watch the ball, watch the ball, watch the ball".

History will tell you that obviously I wasn't watching the ball and listening to my own good advice, because that same ball that I was supposed to be watching like a hawk focusing on its prey thudded into my right pad at about 150km/hr. Without hesitation the umpire had his finger pointed to the sky and I was on my way back to the pavilion for a batsman's worst nightmare, a golden duck.

"Here we go again" was the negative affirmation that kept running through my mind. Thoughts of another failure, another setback and another missed opportunity for Justin Langer in Test cricket invaded my mind, like hyenas encompassing a carcass.

These thoughts dominated my mind, even though I kept telling myself not to be so stupid and pessimistic. I knew that this was only one innings, but I also knew that my mindset was in danger of falling apart like it had done so many times before in my career.

There was an upside to my personal batting failure. Eventually, we won the First Test, giving ourselves an enormous chance to beat Pakistan in a Test series away from home. Because of this, the team celebrated with our normal gusto. Thanks to a team beer sponsorship, I am sure we drank more Foster's beer than has ever been consumed in Pakistan previously at one sitting. We had a magnificent celebration to mark an historic victory on Pakistani soil.

Amid the cloudy, Foster's-induced haze of that particular night I can clearly remember two incidents. At one stage, and this is quite embarrassing to admit, I remember standing in the toilet of the Australian Club in Karachi, staring at myself in the mirror and telling myself out loud that I was good enough to play for Australia. Had anyone walked in on my pep session, I would have died of embarrassment. Here I was talking to myself in the mirror, promising myself to think and talk positively until my next opportunity in the Second Test. Sounds crazy now, but I knew that I was on the verge of giving in to the negativity of my mind. I also knew that I didn't want to do that any more!

Later on that night, I sat down beside captain Mark Taylor at the bar. For the first time in my career I spoke to him about where he thought I was at, and how I was feeling about getting a golden duck in my comeback game. The one thing I particularly remember about this conversation was Mark telling me to, "go back to your room tonight and ring Sue (my wife) and tell her that you are going to enjoy the next two Test matches no matter what. If these are your last Test matches for Australia, tell her that you are going to have the time of your life." Mark also told me that he knew I was very self-motivated and determined to make it to the top, but added, "in my opinion, you are a little too intense, and therefore not allowing your natural instincts to take over." He went on, "you are trying way too hard and not relaxing enough to give yourself a chance of success."

Basically he was advising me to relax and enjoy the challenge of Test cricket rather than fighting myself to be a success at the next level. Sometimes the harder you try the worse it gets.

With a week to go before the Second Test I decided to take the skipper's advice. My preparation was as perfect as I could have it leading into a Test. In the practice nets I was hitting the ball in the middle of the bat. My feet were dancing and my face was smiling. For some reason I could see the number 125 next to my name on the scoreboard. I was feeling as confident as I had ever felt going into a Test match. On the eve of the Second Test I was ready to go. I had not only had the ideal physical preparation, but my mind felt clear, as if I had slain the fire-breathing dragons that had kept me out of my dream castle for so long. I wanted to be the king of this castle in the Second Test. Surely it was time for me to step up?

Before I go on, I must begin the remainder of this story by disclosing two facts.

The first one is that the umpire officiating the Second Test in Peshawar in 1998 was a six-foot something Jamaican named Steve

Bucknor, who is one of my favourite umpires on the international panel. One of Steve's idiosyncrasies is that he traditionally takes a long time to make his decisions. After a bowler has appealed he will look once, look twice, and then look one more time for good luck, before making his decision. It is not uncommon for him to take about five to 10 excruciating seconds to make up his mind on the fate of the batsman at the other end.

The second fact is that the first ball I was facing in the Second Test of that 1998 tour of Pakistan was from a man by the name of Shoaib Akhtar. Now at the best of times there is little fun in facing Shoaib because he regularly bowls a hard little red cricket ball at more than 150km/hr. He also comes in off the longest run-up in the game, which gives you far too much time to think about how fast that same hard little red cricket ball is about to come at you. Add to this fear factor, the fact that I was walking in to bat with a golden duck in my last outing and my career up for grabs, and you might understand that regardless of how well prepared I was feeling, I was under the pump.

Now, back to the story.

Unfortunately for then Australian opening batsman Michael Slater, I was required to bat 45 minutes before lunch on the first day of the Second Test. The dismissal of "Slats" meant the moment of reckoning for yours truly.

Like in Karachi during the First Test, I stood ready and determined, telling myself over and over to watch the ball like a hawk. The crowd was roaring and it felt like I was a Christian facing the lions in a Roman Colosseum. If it was hot and humid in Karachi, it was hotter and much more humid in Peshawar. As loud as it was in Karachi, it seemed far louder on this particular occasion in the Second Test. If my heart was racing in the First Test, then it was literally out of control now, as Akhtar charged at me like a raging, insane bull.

In he comes, my heart feels like it is about to burst out of my chest as I strive to focus on the shiny red ball in Shoaib's sweating hand, while his long hair fringe bounces around on top of his head.

"Watch the ball, watch the ball, watch the ball." It's my mantra at the crease. In times of pressure it sounds like I am screaming this at myself, but in reality it is nothing more than a silent thought occupying my mind.

## ON A GOLDEN PAIR AGAINST SHOAIB AKHTAR

As Shoaib reaches the crease, he jumps into the air and lets go of a thunderbolt. He has the crowd behind him. His adrenaline is pumping like a stainless steel piston as his insatiable desire to send me packing is at fever pitch. As he lets go of the pill, I am sure that I have seen it leave his hand.

Obviously I didn't.

In almost identical circumstances to Karachi, Shoaib Akhtar's thunderbolt hits my right pad as quick as a bolt of lightning lights up the southern sky. Whack! Not only did the ball buckle my right knee, but also, for the next 10 seconds, I felt like my heart was making its way up my chest, through my mouth and on to the dusty Peshawar cricket pitch. I can never remember being more anxious.

If you can remember that feeling when you were young, and the school bully held your head under the water in a swimming pool, you may understand how I was feeling right at this moment in my life. It literally felt like I was underwater, on the verge of oxygen-deprived panic. I was struggling for that breath of beautiful oxygen while Steve Bucknor stood, stared and decided which way to go.

From the moment that ball from Shoaib hit my pad, I could feel the school bully's hand pushing me under the water. In an instant, my career passed in front of my eyes. It could have gone one of two ways. Steve Bucknor could have looked once, looked twice and eventually given me out, and basically drowned me on the spot. Two golden ducks in a row would have been pretty hard to fight back from.

Slowly I looked up and stared into the eyes of the Jamaican. Staring back at me, he tilted his head to the right, and then to the left. He then took one last glare at my pads before looking me in the eyes and saying, "NOT OUT".

Lightning never strikes twice!

The beautiful taste of fresh oxygen came in the form of this Steve Bucknor reprieve. I was still alive and kicking.

The next ball from Shoaib was even quicker than his first. He was angry and fired up. He felt that the umpire had made a mistake. But then, to be fair, fast bowlers always think that.

As the second ball screamed past my nose, I looked back down the pitch to see a furious Shoaib standing and cursing about three inches from my nose. I can't remember facing a faster delivery in my life. He was probably sledging me, but fortunately I can't talk Pakistani, so I had no idea what he was firing at me. My instincts told me that whatever he was saying, he wasn't a happy young man.

It was at this point that I clearly remember a real moment of truth. With Shoaib swearing and cursing, and my career in the balance, I found a renewed energy that I will never forget. It was like something inside of me had decided in that split second that I didn't want to die like this. I didn't want to play Sheffield Shield cricket and County cricket for the remainder of my career. I wanted to play for Australia and this was the time to seize the moment.

Banging my bat a little harder on the turf, and staring at the ball like it was my worst enemy, I went after the Pakistani bowlers like never before. I backed myself and hit the ball without hesitation. I felt resolute in my actions and I let my instincts take over. When I was finally dismissed, I had 118 runs on the board. I had been given a chance and I had taken it with both hands. This was a defining moment. Whatever happened from here on, no one could ever take away from me the fact that I had scored a Test century. At last, after five years in the wilderness, I felt like I belonged in the Test arena.

Had Steve Bucknor raised his finger that morning in Pakistan, who knows what would have happened to my career? As I have said, there is a very fine line between success and failure, but at the end of the day, the world has a funny way of smiling on you if you are doing everything right. Leading into the game, I felt as if my preparation was perfect. Some would say I was lucky to have survived that first ball from Shoaib.

Maybe I was, but as far as I am concerned I deserved a little bit of luck for all of the work I had put into that first Test century. Lucky or not, I was happy with the result.

## THE DAY I EARNED THE NICKNAME ARTHUR MORRIS

A nickname given to me by my teammates after that Peshawar Test match summed up how I had felt about being an Australian Test cricket player during that wilderness period of my career. The guys started calling me Arthur Morris, not because of my ability with the bat, but because of a story that Arthur had shared with the team years before.

Arthur is always asked about the great and late Sir Donald Bradman. Having played with the game's greatest ever player, the public wants to know little else about Arthur's era in Australian cricket, other than The Don. He knows only too well that the mention of Sir Donald Bradman secures total attention to his every word, especially when he is speaking to an audience.

A question often asked of Arthur, who himself was one of the best players to have ever represented Australia, was whether he played in Sir Donald's famous last game at The Oval in London, where he was bowled for a duck, denying him of a Test average of 100? With a wry smile, Arthur's reply is always "Yes", he did play in that game, and in fact he scored 196 runs himself, "not that anyone would ever remember that minor detail."

Hence my new nickname, Arthur Morris. Did I play in the famous game in which Mark Taylor scored an incredible 334 in Pakistan?

My reply is, "Yes, in fact I batted with him and scored my maiden Test century. Not that anyone would ever remember that minor detail of course."

The feeling of being an invisible member of the Australian cricket team plagued me for years. This was brought about by a lack of belief in myself, and it was this lack of self-belief when I was playing at the higher level which ultimately led to a lack of opportunity after my early Test debut.

I believe it is impossible to succeed in anything unless you truly believe that you can do it. As hard as it is to admit, it was no coincidence that I felt, and basically was, invisible in the Australian cricket set-up for so many years. There is no doubt that my lack of self-belief was brought upon by myself. There is also no doubt that this lack of self-confidence was the major factor holding me back.

## TRYING TOO HARD TO REACH MY GOALS

It is difficult to answer the question, why did I lack this self-confidence? When I was young I always had constant love and support from my parents. I was never under any pressure to perform and they never pushed me in any particular direction. Mum and Dad encouraged me unconditionally to enjoy what I was doing and I always played a number of different sports. At school I worked pretty hard and was always looking to learn what I could through my education. My base of friends is very loyal and strong and they have been constant supporters regardless of the direction I have chosen to take.

Having thought about it closely, maybe I was so desperate to reach my goals that I tried too hard to reach them. It became something of an obsession. My uncle Robbie, who played World Series Cricket for Australia, once rang me and warned me about making my goal an obsession. I will never forget him ringing me out of the blue and saying, "For what it's worth, I watched you batting on the television today and I could see it in your eyes that you are trying too hard. It looks to me like it has become an obsession to play for Australia. I think this is dangerous. If you don't let go and enjoy what you are doing then you will do yourself more harm than good."

For many years it was like I was aiming for perfection rather than settling for my best. With this, I was putting myself under enormous pressure. Every failure felt like the end of the world. Until I was able to find some perspective, I wasn't really giving myself the best chance of success. Because of this, I would perform under my peak and this would have an effect on my confidence. When anyone's confidence diminishes there is a danger of negative self-talk and a downward spiral is likely to eventuate.

## POSITIVE SELF-TALK

Over many coffees, psychologist and friend Victor N. Smith has listened to me talk about the ups and downs of my career. During the times I have fallen into the trap of negative thinking I have obviously forgotten Vic's great little story about the importance of changing negative self-talk into positive self-talk. His story is an excellent reflection on mental discipline.

JL, I would like you to imagine that you're at the British Open at St Andrews having a coffee with friends. You are waiting in anticipation for the first round, which will start shortly.

You look up from your drink to see a tall, slim, blonde gentleman walking towards you. He's healthily tanned and is wearing a large hat with the emblem of a shark on the front. He beckons your attention and says, in what seems to be a cross between an Australian and an American accent, "Hi, I'm Greg Norman and I've got a favour to ask of you. You see, my caddy's just pulled a hamstring muscle and I need another caddy in a hurry, as I'm just about to tee off. Do you think you can help me out?"

You readily agree, pick up his bag, and head to the first tee.

Not being shy about giving a little advice when it's needed, you advise Greg that, "This is a really important hole . . . if you mess up your tee shot you'll be in lots of trouble. How embarrassing would it be if you played a poor shot first up?"

He seems to ignore your advice and promptly hooks the tee shot into the rough.

Seeing this, you try again. "What a terrible shot . . . this round is looking pretty bad already. It is going to be a long, hard day if you keep playing like that!"

Fortunately Greg recovers and puts the second shot on the fairway. Impressed, you pass on a little positive reinforcement. "Phew . . . you were lucky to get out of that mess, you don't want to stuff up the next shot or you're back in bogey country."

Like a champion, Greg plays a great shot onto the sloping green, below and within three metres of the pin, so you voice a bit of *encouragement. "The first putt will tell us if your putting is on today, so you'd better sink this one!"*

*Your advice falls on deaf ears and Greg leaves his difficult up-hill put about half a metre short of the hole. Out of frustration you yell: "You wimp! Why didn't you have a go. If you continue putting like this, you won't have a chance of making the cut."*

*JL, I often tell this story to young golfers I am working with, and watch as they grimace, like you have, with each negative comment I attribute to them. After running through a series of negative affirmations, I then ask: "If you were really caddying for Greg Norman, would you talk to him in this fashion?"*

Shaking my head I tell Victor that of course I wouldn't talk to Greg Norman like that.

*That is what everyone says: they always emphatically answer NO.*

*I then ask them how they talk to themselves during an important round, and watch in amusement as they exhibit a sheepish grin. If you wouldn't talk to Greg Norman like that, then why do we talk to yourself like that?*

*To finish off the story I then ask them, as I am asking you now, what they would really say to Greg Norman after he had played a poor shot. The answer is always that they would reply with a series of very positive statements such as:*

*"You're bound to play a couple of average shots per round . . .that's one of them out of the way! The next shot will be fabulous."*
*"You've been in this position plenty of times and always play a great recovery shot . . . you can do it!"*

*"Keep sticking to the basics and everything will turn around for the better."*

*"You have everything required to play this next shot . . . back yourself and hit the pin."*

Victor finished by telling me that the moral of the story is that if you want to give yourself a chance of playing terrific golf, talk to yourself as a great caddy or coach would talk to you. This is no different to anything we do in life. Always talk to yourself as if you are the best coach in the world.

Practice giving yourself the type of advice that the world's best coach would give to you. The best coach is you. Trust your own advice and listen to the positive reinforcement and ignore the negative rubbish. Self-talk is invaluable if you use it to your benefit. There is no doubt in my mind that the way we talk to ourselves is reflected in our feelings and therefore our actions.

## DAMIEN MARTYN – A RARE TALENT

If a lack of self-belief wasn't due to trying too hard or negative self-talk, then maybe I simply was not born with the same level of ability as some of my peers.

In the early days I could never understand why some players could do things that I found more difficult to do. Damien Martyn and I have been mates since we were young boys. In a sense, we were also rivals because we were the new kids on the block in Western Australian cricket. This led to comparisons between the two of us and a certain pressure resulted. He was so naturally talented, with every shot in the book, and I found this frustrating.

Why was it so easy for him and yet I had to work so hard to gain similar, but far less attractive results? Maybe I resented not being seen as good as the other kids. Again, maybe I tried too hard to be as good as everyone else rather than just being the best I could be.

## WHEN MEDIA COMMENTS HURT

In the past, I think I have made a massive mistake in listening to everything the media has had to say about me. Rather than putting the media into perspective and realising that the guys in the press are doing a certain job, I have tended to take personally every comment that I perceived to be negative. After my second or third Shield game against Queensland, I read a very critical article by News Limited journalist Robert Craddock about my innings and his opinion of my ability, or lack of it. Even though I had scored a century, it had been a tough innings and I had taken a long time reaching the magical milestone of my maiden first-class century.

Having never experienced the media before, I was shattered reading this man's opinion of me. I had just scored a century and yet I was basically reading that I had little future in the game.

People suggest that we shouldn't read what is in the paper, but take it from me this is a lot harder to do than it sounds. The problem is that everyone else reads the paper, and invariably any negative comment will be brought to your attention at one stage or another. Like many things, information sounds far worse second hand. I would rather read the opinion myself and then make a critical judgment of what is being said.

The criticism that hurts the most is when it comes from former Australian players who have found a place for themselves in the media. I once read that Kerry O'Keeffe "would rather watch ripe bananas go brown than watch Justin Langer bat". This sort of comment may sound funny, but I can tell you that this touched a nerve. I was disappointed that a person who knows how hard it is to play for Australia could be so critical. The other thing that hurt was that earlier in my career, O'Keeffe had helped and advised me while I was at the Commonwealth Bank Cricket Academy. Now he was writing me off in the public domain. I had trouble coming to terms with this.

Who really knows, maybe the more I read negative press reports the less I believed in my own ability. The more bad press I read the more I let myself surrender my power to outside influences. It really is difficult to answer why to the question of a lack of self-belief, but all I know is that if you allow yourself to succumb to this trap you will pay the price. I certainly have in the past.

## ADVICE FROM BIG MAL MENINGA

Advice has come from many corners of the globe over the years. Australian rugby league star Mal Meninga once sat with me in a hotel in England encouraging me to believe in my dreams and take the necessary steps to achieve them. His words of wisdom were that it didn't matter how many other people believed in my ability, if I didn't have faith in myself then I would ultimately come unstuck.

I will never forget that night in the bar with one of the giants of Australian rugby league. Within the Australian team there is always massive admiration and respect for any other sports men or women who represent our country. The team often sends faxes and messages of good luck or congratulations to Australian teams or individuals in other sporting codes. Whenever the opportunity presents, there always seems to be a bond between high-achieving sports men and women.

On this particular night during the 1997 Ashes tour of England, Mal and a few of the Australian rugby league players were staying at the same hotel as us in Leeds, in the north of England. Once again the Test team had been announced, and once again I was feeling like an invisible member of the squad, because my name wasn't called out in the final team selection meeting. This dejection must have been showing on my face. Within a few minutes of entering the hotel bar, this enormous looking bloke with jet black, curly hair, and hands the size of two baseball gloves, came over and introduced himself. Of course, I knew exactly who he was, but I was taken aback by his warm and sudden welcome.

"G'day Justin, I'm Mal Meninga, it is really nice to meet you as I am a great admirer of you cricket players," said Big Mal.

But then this: "It looks like someone's just stolen your favourite mate, what's up?"

Mal couldn't have been more direct, but in the same instance he sounded like he was genuinely interested in why I was looking so blue.

For the next three hours he sat with me at the bar and we talked about everything from rugby league, to cricket, to life's lessons.

At one stage of the night he stormed over to the in-house telephone and demanded that Steve Waugh come down and join our conversation. I couldn't believe that he had the nerve to ring Tugga up in his room. But, as Mal said, "It is blokes like Steve Waugh who can help you make it to the top and I know he is the sort of person who will be interested in helping you out. He should be down here having a beer and talking it through with us."

To be honest, I didn't think Steve would come down to the bar at 10 o'clock at night. But, in hindsight, and knowing Tugga like I do, I shouldn't have been surprised when he arrived within a few minutes of Mal's invitation. Shaking Mal's hand and giving me a curious nod, Steve was soon engrossed in what had turned into a very deep and meaningful conversation.

Although I had heard the advice of believing in myself many times before, the strength of this particular company added extra impetus to the message that was coming my way. Mal's message was the same as Tugga has always given to me. "You must believe in yourself and back yourself. When you play, play without hesitation or doubt. Have the guts and determination to back yourself in every situation."

Before we left the bar that night, Mal squeezed my hand, looked me straight in the eyes and told me to, "get off your backside, poke your chest out and start believing in yourself." He told me that I was, "a very, very good player and that I was the only one who couldn't seem to see this fact. I was crazy not to believe in my ability and that I would go nowhere unless I did something about it."

I haven't seen Mal Meninga since that night in the bar, but his message sure had an impact. I started feeling the power of self-belief, his passion that night stayed with me for some time. I hope big Mal gets a little smile on his face whenever he sees me raise my bat to the crowd, because I am grinning as I recall that night he took me under his wing in Leeds.

## THE MIRACLE OF ADAM GILCHRIST

Lacking belief in yourself is like running to the finishing line with a rubber bungy belt wrapped around your waist. You may be running as hard as you can, working like a Trojan warrior and giving it your best shot, but eventually the belt will hold you back from the finishing line. It will pull you back and deny you the chance of living your dream. Every now and then you may experience a brief taste of success, but like hitting the water in a bungy jump, your moment of victory will be fleeting.

On the other hand, when you do embrace self-belief and trust your ability, the feeling of freedom and confidence is powerful. The possibilities are limitless when you truly believe in your capabilities and unconditionally back yourself.

In 1995, while working as a scholarship coach at Australia's famous Commonwealth Bank Cricket Academy in Adelaide, I received a phone call from a guy by the name of Adam Gilchrist.

There had been pre-season whispers that this ambitious, young man from NSW was keen to move States in a bid to further his career. As a wicketkeeper, who was also pretty handy with a cricket bat in his hands, Adam wanted to marry both skills and develop

*Right:* Pace great…
Glenn McGrath with his
faithful bat on ice.
*Langer family collection*

*Left:* Superstar…
Shane Warne.
*Langer family collection*

A great Australian team – International team of the year, 2001. *Photo:* © *Jack Atley*

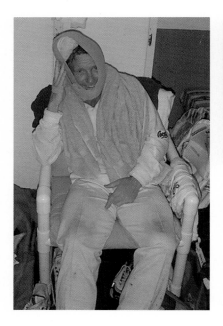

*Above Right:* Coach John Buchanan and superstar Mark Waugh.
*Langer family collection*

*Left:* Not all fun and games, Ian Healy on ice. *Langer family collection*

A breadcrumb in an ants nest, India 2001. *Langer family collection*

*Left:* Life in Trenchtown Jamaica, 1998.
*Langer family collection*

Winning the Ashes, battling cancer… Adam Gilchrist, Mark Wornum and Brett Lee. *Langer family collection*

Three nil – winning the Ashes at Trentbridge 2001, Jason Gillespie, Matt Hayden and Damien Martyn. *Langer family collection*

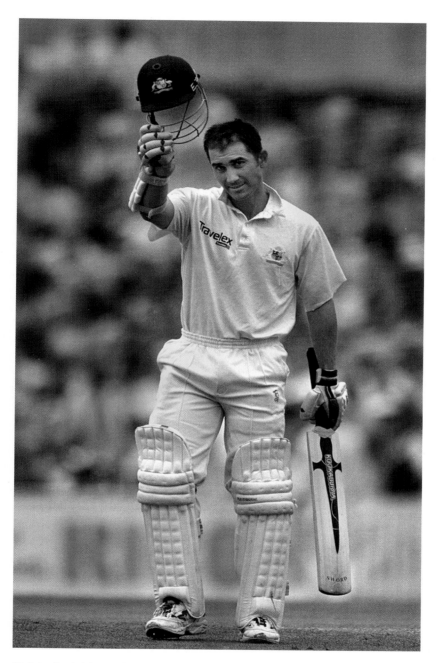

Fighting back, The Oval in London 2001. *Photo: © Jack Atley*

Down and out, rock bottom, Sussex 2001. *Photo: © Jack Atley*

*Left:* In the middle with champion player and good friend Ricky Ponting.
*Photo: © Jack Atley*

*Right:* Watching the
ball like a hawk.
*Photo: © Jack Atley*

*Left:* Backing
yourself takes guts,
England 2001.
*Photo: © Jack Atley*

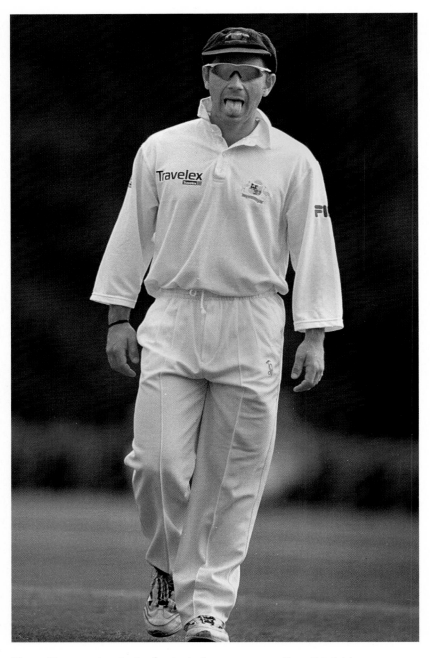

The smiling assassin – having fun in the baggy green cap. *Photo: © Jack Atley*

into an allrounder, rather than just settle for being a middle-order batsman for the Blues.

The thought of Gilly travelling across the country and setting up in Perth seemed remote, but the fact that he was on the phone quizzing me about the west, reflected more than a little curiosity about this prospect. The sheer magnitude of the decision to leave his home State for greener pastures on the west coast suggested that it was a brave man taking the plunge.

Having played a handful of games for NSW as a batsman, he had been unable to secure a position behind the stumps and was finding this situation increasingly frustrating. Gilly's ambitions stretched far beyond batting in the middle order for NSW and he knew better than anyone that, locked inside him, was a potential impatiently waiting to be expressed. He was desperately keen to unleash his natural wizardry but felt that his hands were tied while he was playing, and waiting, in NSW.

Throughout his formative years, Gilly was always a wicketkeeper who had the ability to hit the cricket ball like others hit a golf ball. Unfortunately, due to circumstances, NSW were unable to offer him the chance to blossom and combine both talents and therefore take steps forward in his quest to realise his childhood ambition of donning the baggy green cap.

Talking on the telephone on that fateful day in 1995, it became apparent that he would enjoy his cricket to the fullest if he were able to spend the majority of his time standing behind the stumps with a pair of leather gloves on his hands. As he could see it, the permanency of veteran Blues gloveman Phil Emery would restrict any hope he had of developing this side of his game. The short term looked bleak at home and he thought a change in environment, plus the whisper of a changing of the guard in WA, might be the opportunity he needed to shine

After months of soul searching, he made the difficult decision to move west. In making the decision, he had the advice of his family and peers to consider, but in the end it was he who had to go with his heart and make the move. History now suggests that his decision to migrate to Perth was the right one, but I can tell you his decision was full of courage, determination and character. Not only did he have to leave his home – a heart-wrenching decision at the best of times – and set up in a foreign environment away from his family and friends, but he also had to forge his career from little more than potential and hope.

Arriving in Perth he had to deal with speculation about the future of the ultra-gifted wicketkeeper Tim Zoehrer, who was in the twilight of his career, as well as his own doubts about whether he had made the correct decision to change colours. The self-doubts and the negative karma of the sceptics who doubted his decision to move, or arrive, depending upon which pasture you are sitting in, must have added weight to the enormity of his initial resolution to leave.

It is a credit to the man and an indication of his strong character that he was able to make the decision and then, more importantly, make his decision work. Making the decision is one thing, making it work is another. It is no surprise or coincidence to see Adam play cricket the way he does. There is no doubt he has mountains of natural talent, but it is what you do with your natural talent that really matters. There are few people I know who capitalise on their God-given ability as well as my Australian and Western Australian teammate and friend.

To his credit, Gilly plays Test cricket like a boy would play beach cricket or a backyard Test match. The freedom and majesty that he exudes every time he walks on to a cricket field are inspirational to watch. Just as inspirational is the fact that, before he was a superstar, he had the guts and the nerve to back himself against the odds to make it to the top. He had to make many tough decisions early to reach his goals, but now he is rightfully reaping the benefits of his early resolve.

## IN THE SAME VEIN AS SOBERS

In every "Team of the Century" or "Greatest Team of All Time", the name Sir Gary Sobers is penned in the middle order. His all-round ability with the bat and ball has made him arguably the best player to have ever played the game. It is said that Gary Sobers was so destructive with the bat that he would destroy a bowler's confidence when he started wielding his willow with an ease and grace reserved for few.

Over and over, Adam has given us a taste of what it must have been like to watch the great Sobers in full flight. Regularly, the Australian vice-captain has batted with the destruction of a hurricane through a coastal fishing village. His class and unadulterated power while batting will have him selected alongside the great Sobers in hypothetical cricket selections for many, many years to come. His all-round ability with the bat and wicket-keeping gloves has him in my best team of all time. There has never been a wicketkeeper in the history of our wonderful game who could brutalise opposition attacks like he so regularly does. This, plus his work ethic, natural charisma and success behind the stumps, sees him revered around the globe.

Imagine if Adam hadn't backed himself in coming to Perth, and if he didn't continue to back himself 100 per cent now. He continues to provide us all with a lesson in self-belief and determination.

## A MEMORABLE ALLAN BORDER PEP TALK

Some of the best advice about "backing yourself" came my way during a conversation with Allan Border in Harare, Zimbabwe. Standing in as the interim coach, between Geoff Marsh resigning and John Buchanan taking over the position, AB was instrumental in helping me turn my career around. Having arrived in Zimbabwe in October, 1999, from a tough tour of Sri Lanka, I was feeling pretty low in confidence, wondering where my next run was coming from.

During a centre-wicket practice session, my confidence was sent lower than ever as I batted like I was wearing two concrete boots attached to my feet and a blindfold covering my eyes. After being totally humiliated by Glenn McGrath and Shane Warne – not that I am the first player to have felt like that – I walked from the pitch with my tail between my legs and my chin scraping along the dirt.

Sensing my frustration, AB asked me if I wanted to have another session against the practice bowlers in the nets. Sheepishly, I told him how I was feeling and that I didn't know if another session would help me or make things even worse.

At this point he said something that has stuck with me to this day.

"Batting, like most things in this life, is all about your attitude. Go into those nets and I want to see you hit the ball. Don't worry if you get out a few times, just go in a whack the ball over the place. Look to score runs, back yourself to hit every ball in the middle. You have nothing to lose because you can't feel any worse than you already do. Just get in there and hit as many fours and sixes as you can. Don't worry about anything except hitting that ball. Watch the ball and hit it like there is no tomorrow. Back yourself, have a bit of fun and take them on. It is all about your attitude Justin; it is all about your attitude. Back yourself and believe in yourself. It is all an attitude."

Two minutes before this pep talk I was embarrassed and feeling like a novice with the cricket bat. Now, I was pumped and determined to change things around. Taking AB's advice I walked into the practice nets and hit every ball like there was no tomorrow. What I found by doing this was that my feet were starting to dance again, my hands were working perfectly and I was actually smiling and enjoying the exercise. Rather than getting out, I remember walking out of the nets feeling a lot better about the world. I felt powerful and confident and ready to make runs. I was smiling, and there was energy pumping through every vein in my body. The adrenaline rush had me fired up and raring to go.

The next day I walked out and hammered a century in the lead-up game to the inaugural First Test against Zimbabwe. From there I became a permanent member of the team during the next 16 victorious Test matches. By making a decision to look at my attitude, life changed within 15 minutes. It was incredible that I had gone from feeling at the depths of the ocean to the summit of a mountain simply by changing my attitude.

Instead of batting to survive, worrying about the future, and questioning my ability to cope with the skills of opposition bowlers, I was going forward and backing myself to come up trumps in any situation.

In a short space of time I had turned my attention towards my attitude, rather than my technique or my physical capabilities. By doing this I had transformed my thinking to a point where I could go forward without any barriers. The liberty that comes with a change of attitude is stimulating and energising. A positive attitude to life is the key to freedom, happiness and ultimately success in whatever you choose to do. I encourage you to change your mind and change your life.

## JASON HONEYCHURCH – A REAL LIFE INSPIRATION

Jason Honeychurch, a 16-year-old schoolboy from country Western Australia, is one of the most extraordinary young people I have met. I was invited to speak at a camp just outside of Perth. To say my thunder was stolen is something of an understatement, because Jason told a story of courage and self-belief that had the audience gasping for air and wiping the tears out of their eyes.

After years of misery, Jason told me that the best day of his life was when he woke up and was told that his right leg had been cut off. Can you imagine that?

Against all the advice from his doctors, he requested that his leg be amputated. Jason's heart told him that the removal of his leg would be the turning point in his life. While a decision like this is difficult, if not impossible to contemplate, he swears that losing his right leg was the best thing that has ever happened to him. Having made the decision, he stands proud and says that his life has moved forward in leaps and bounds since the brave judgment was made.

When Jason was only nine years old he was run over by a crane while riding his bike. "I was riding on the path and could see the crane coming towards me, but then the rest is a bit of a blur. I was in shock after sitting up and seeing my legs splattered all over the place. The wheels were huge, but I just sat there looking at what used to be my legs. There was blood and bone everywhere, I was in shock and just sitting there."

For the next six years doctors tried to save his legs with constant operations. Luckily his left leg recovered, but until he was 15 years old his right leg was basically that of a nine-year-old's leg attached to his 15-year-old body. No matter how hard the doctors tried, the leg did not grow. There was no bone strength and even the slightest of bumps could cause the leg to break.

His disability wreaked mental heartbreak. As he told me, it was this mental torture that was arguably worse than the physical suffering. He often felt lonely and ashamed to the point where suicide became an unwelcome option. According to him, his teenage years were dark years filled with fear, resentment and pain.

After winning a scholarship to Aquinas College in Perth, Jason decided that his only way forward was to have the amputation.

"The idea of having my leg cut off was always on my mind. Eventually I decided that the only way to get on with my life was to have it taken off. I thought that this would be the perfect time to make a fresh start. I didn't want to go to a new school feeling like I had been feeling for so long. While it might sound like a tough thing to do, I can honestly say it is the best thing that has ever happened to me. Now I can walk around with my new leg. I feel happy and proud of my decision. This really is the best thing that could have happened."

Meeting Jason was a great privilege. Basically he lost his leg to better his life. He backed his heart's judgment and made an incredibly tough decision by himself. He took responsibility for his actions and is now running toward the finishing line like he has a tornado behind his back. By losing something, he gained so much. The smile on his face, and the message of determination in his words, are testament to this young man's courage. It might be worth watching for the name Jason Honeychurch in the next Paralympics. He is wonderful example of self-belief and determination.

## ENJOY THE GOOD TIMES

I believe it's important to enjoy the good times – the fruits of your hard work – when you do back yourself and it pays off.

During the Australian summer of 2002, I experienced 30 of the sweetest seconds of my life that made any of the tough times seem as insignificant as single grain of sand on a wind-swept beach. History now reads that South African spin bowler Claude Henderson came in to bowl a ball to yours truly, who was 96 runs on the grand Adelaide Oval scoreboard. Letting go of the ball, I noticed that Henderson had thrown the red leather projectile a little higher in the air than usual. Throwing off any apprehensions of the nervous 90s, I danced down the Adelaide Oval pitch and swung my favourite Kookaburra cricket bat as hard as my arms and body could muster. The moment the blade of my bat met the ball I knew that I had hit it right out of the centre of the willow.

For those next 30 seconds it was like I was living in a vacuum and in my own fantasy world. From the instant the ball left my bat I watched it sail high into the air and over the mid-wicket boundary for six. It was like everything was happening in slow motion. For those few moments in my life I felt untouchable. My world was silent but euphoric. It was the most exhilarating moment of my cricket career. A six meant a century, and a century in a batsman's world is a milestone to cherish at any level, let alone a Test match against South Africa.

Raising both arms above my head and smiling like I had just won the lottery, I felt like the happiest man on the planet. It was at this instant that I realised that these magic moments in your life outweigh any bad times by a thousand to one. From the second that single ball flew over the Adelaide Oval fence, I proved to myself once again that there is only one option in life, and that is to keep fighting back no matter what.

Although this was only one of the hundreds of thousands of balls I have faced up to in my life, it was one that will remain with me forever.

Matty Hayden has since described the smile on my face as priceless. At that very moment in my life I was standing on the dais receiving the gold medal. Test matches come around far more than every four years like the Olympic Games, but I felt like I was standing with a gold medal around my neck. Having met a few Olympians in my life I know that a gold medal takes a lot of blood, sweat, tears, ups, downs, highs, lows and constant challenges. This time for me was as close to a gold medal as I could achieve. The only thing that was missing was the national anthem and a few tears.

Unfortunately, in my Olympic Games in the centre of the Adelaide Oval, I was required to face up to the next ball and get on with the job. I wish the moment could have lasted forever.

## Winners Versus Losers

— *When a winner makes a mistake, he says, "I was wrong."*

— *When a loser makes a mistake, he says, "It wasn't my fault."*

— *A winner works harder than a loser and has more time.*

— *A loser is always "too busy" to do what is necessary.*

— *A winner goes through a problem.*

— *A loser goes around it, and never gets past it.*

— *A winner makes commitments.*

— *A loser makes promises.*

— *A winner says, "I'm good, but not as good as I ought to be."*

— *A loser says, "I'm not as bad as a lot of other people."*

— *A winner listens.*

— *A loser just waits until it's his turn to talk.*

— *A winner respects those who are superior to him and tries to learn something from them.*

— *A loser resents those who are superior to him and tries to find chinks in their armour.*

— *A winner feels responsible for more than his job.*

— *A loser says, "I only work here."*

— *A winner says, "There ought to be a better way to do it."*

— *A loser says, "That's the way it's always been done here."*

**PAT WILLIAMS – NBA General Manager and Vice-President**

CHAPTER 15

# Mind Power
# and Creating
# Our Dreams

**SHOT OF INSPIRATION # 15:**
*We can use positive mental energy to reach our goals.*

GREAT AUSTRALIAN ULTRA-MARATHON runner Pat Farmer once told me that he always sees the finish line before starting a race. Before setting out on his physically and mentally punishing runs he visualises the finish line. Every time his body screams out in pain or his mind starts playing funny tricks, he imagines himself finishing the race.

With this vision of running through the finishing tape secure and clear in his mind, he takes one step at a time towards fulfilling that ambition.

Having seen Pat on *This Is Your Life*, I always wanted to meet him in person. Fortunately this opportunity came during the first Test match of the new millennium in Sydney against India in January, 2000. Pat was running a celebratory lap of the magnificent Sydney Cricket Ground during the lunch break of the first day's play to promote another of his exceptional two-month charity runs around the eastern states of Australia. This was a chance for the vocal Sydney crowd to pay tribute to an exceptional Australian.

The rain was falling in Sydney while Pat was circling the ground waving to his admirers in the SCG grandstands. This rain was frustrating from a cricket point of view, but welcomed by me because it meant a longer than usual lunch break and a chance to meet this man whom I had come to admire from a distance. Never one for missing an opportunity I sent a message around to Pat, inviting him to come in to the changing room and meet a few of the guys. Before long, Pat was sitting around talking to the team and offering a few pearls of wisdom that helped him get through his marathons on the roads, and also through some of the toughest periods that he had encountered through his life.

Sadly, Pat lost his wife, and the mother of his two kids, to an early tragic death. I had seen this on the *This Is Your Life* program and I was intrigued by what had given him the strength to get through this and also through his treacherous mind/body torture sessions of ultra-marathon running. Apart from just being a very good bloke, Pat said two things that have stuck with the Australian cricketers ever since our meeting. He told the team that as far as he was concerned, you could achieve absolutely anything in your life if you put your mind to it, and if you really want it enough to make the necessary sacrifices to achieve whatever it is you want to achieve.

He also made the point about seeing the finish line first. He suggested that it is important to see the end goal first, before setting out on your journey. This vision helps to keep you motivated, no matter how hard the journey may become along the way.

During my private conversation with Pat, I shared with him how I had at times found it hard to see the finish line every time I was playing at the SCG.

Up until that day I told him how I was averaging about 15 in Sydney and that I felt uncomfortable, for one reason or another, every time I walked out to bat at the SCG.

## VISUALISING MY WAY TO A TEST HIGH

Pat urged me to paint a positive "perfect world" picture in my mind of exactly what I would like to achieve in this Test match. With nothing to lose I started to think about a century in Sydney. I pictured how I would play each of the Indian bowlers and how I would acknowledge the crowd when I went past my first century at the SCG.

Until the time I went out to bat, and even during that particular innings, I kept this picture in my mind.

Call it a coincidence, call it luck, but to this day that innings in Sydney has been my highest Test score for Australia. Two hundred and twenty four runs later, I had destroyed the demons that had haunted me in Sydney and come away triumphant, having learned a valuable lesson, from a valuable bloke named Pat Farmer.

Statisticians pointed out to me later I was the first cricketer to score a Test century in the new millennium.

## STEVE WAUGH AND VISUALISATION

Batting guru Steve Waugh has shared with me on a number of occasions how he often sees a certain score on the scoreboard the day before a Test match. He has said that a figure enters his mind, he visualises it on the clear scoreboard, and then he uses the picture as something of an incentive in his preparation for a Test match.

I have since used this technique to good effect in my cricket and in many other areas of life. Early in my career I had a vivid experience when I obviously programmed my mind to head in the right direction. Before the first Sheffield Shield final that I was lucky enough to play in, I remember writing in my diary the number 150 all over the pages. I can't remember what possessed me to do this but I do remember writing over and over and over and over that particular number. This sounds a bit freaky now as I think about it, but that is exactly what I did. I covered my diary pages in this number and kept telling myself that I wanted to make a difference to the result of the game by making a big score in the final.

After my first innings, in which I was dismissed cheaply for three, this self-prediction of scoring 150 looked about as likely as me falling pregnant and having a baby. I had been so nervous in that first innings that I didn't even look like scoring 15, let alone 150. It is funny how the mind works though because in the second innings I again fell short of the 150 mark, but this time it was only by one run. In my best innings to that point in my career, I had managed to get over my nerves and inexperience to post 149 runs, which helped Western Australia win the 1992 Sheffield Shield final.

In 1998/99, when England were last out in Australia for an Ashes series, the same thing happened before the Adelaide Test match. For about the thousandth time in my career, the critics were suggesting I wasn't the right person to be batting No.3 for Australia. In the lead-up to that Third Test I remember spending more time than usual running and working harder on my fitness. Every time I was out on the road, or on the beach running, I was thinking about scoring a big century in the Adelaide Test match.

I went as far as thinking about every bowler and how I was going to score runs off them. I visualised the ground, the conditions and what I thought the England bowlers would say to me. With every step I was programming myself to focus on exactly what I wanted to achieve.

Around the same time I was telling myself, and anyone else who wanted to listen, that I was the master of my own destiny. If I scored runs I would stay in the team, if I didn't I would be out of the team. It didn't matter what anyone was writing or saying in the press, I was in control of my own destiny. This motto ran through my mind as I trained hard and focussed on what had to be done.

The day before leaving for Adelaide, a psychologist friend of mine, Vic Smith, dropped around to see me. I explained how I had been preparing for the Test match. Nodding his approval he asked me if I wanted to take my preparation one step further. Of course, I was very keen to have a successful Test match so I agreed with anything he thought would help. Lying me down on the ground, Vic told me to take a few deep breaths and relax. After a few minutes he prompted me to see the beautiful Adelaide Oval scoreboard. Picture the crowd, the grass, the umpires, the fieldsmen and the bowlers. He then told me to see the number 200 on the scoreboard next to my name. See it clearly he urged me. Now feel the elation and the joy of achieving this milestone. See yourself raising your bat to the crowd. Feel the bat in your hands and picture yourself playing your best shots.

After about 30 minutes I was shaking his hand and waving him goodbye from my driveway. I knew I had already prepared well for the Test match, but now I felt I would arrive in Adelaide with an extra polish added to my inner game. The end result was out of my control but the fact was I had a very clear picture in my mind of exactly what I wanted to achieve.

Once again that picture became reality five days later when I scored 179 not out in 40-degree heat. My physical hard work had complimented by mental practice and I had accomplished what I had set out to achieve in very trying conditions. Again I was blown away by the power of the mind.

## CAPTAIN WAUGH –
## THE MENTALLY TOUGHEST ATHLETE I'VE SEEN

Watching Stephen Waugh over the years, it seems to me that this mental imagery goes much deeper. The mentally toughest cricket player I have ever come across, Steve's record in the second half of his career has been nothing short of phenomenal.

Talking to former Australian cricket captain and Australian of the Year, Mark Taylor, who played most of his career alongside Tugga, he believes that one of the main reasons for his mate's success comes down to discipline, particularly in his thinking. Mark told me: "After Steve was dropped from the Australian team, it was as if he decided to trade flamboyance and flashiness for runs. No matter what the situation, he refused to give his wicket away and was determined to make the bowlers bowl at him, no matter what level of cricket he was playing."

When he came back from being dropped, Stephen had decided that he wanted to do things much better than he had before. Tugga has told me that in the period between being dropped and coming back into the team, he decided that he wasn't satisfied with what he had achieved up until then. He knew he had more to offer to himself and to Australian cricket, and that he would always regret it if he didn't make much more of his obvious natural talent.

When he was reinstated to the team he began scoring runs in Test cricket like no other player in the modern game. He painted a picture in his mind of being the best in the world and after setting his mind to where he wanted to go he never wavered from the course that he had set himself.

Often Stephen has glanced at me with that curious look in his eye and said, "It is amazing what can be achieved if you put your mind to it." Because he is such a deep thinker about the game of cricket and also about life, I know that he, like me, is inspired, and at times awe-struck, by examples of how the mind conquers all.

At the end of day three of the final Test match of the 2001 Ashes series in England, I wrote a diary excerpt that concentrated on the unbelievable rehabilitation of our captain in getting himself fit for the Test match. After suffering a severe injury to his right calf muscle, most people gave him only the slightest chance of playing another game in the tour. History reads that this wasn't the case.

My diary read:

*Steve Waugh's incredibly courageous performance in scoring yet another Test century is a tribute to our captain's strength of character. Batting on one leg for most of his innings, he proved that anything can be achieved if you put your mind to it. When he scored his century, you may have noticed him pointing to the changing room. He was signalling to our fantastic physiotherapist, Errol Alcott, as an acknowledgment for the tireless amount of work that they have put in on rehabilitating his calf since he was injured during the Third Test a couple of weeks ago.*

*For five or six hours a day the two of them have worked on getting the skipper back for this final Test of the summer. While stretching tonight after the game, Stephen confided in me that during every minute he was being treated, he was thinking about scoring a century in this Test. The captain's determination has never been questioned but considering this may be his last Test match in England, I think his determination in playing was stronger than ever before. Most people wouldn't have even tried to get fit in such a short space of time. The difference is that Steve knows the power of the mind, and in this instance he has used this knowledge to his incredible advantage. The fact that he was even out there on the field sends a very strong message to England that we mean business.*

*– JL*

## USING MENTAL IMAGERY TO BECOME A RUN MACHINE

On returning from England at the end of the successful 2001 Ashes series and after making that memorable century in my comeback Test at the Oval, I vowed from that day forward to play my cricket with more enthusiasm than ever before.

At the same time another funny thing happened. To this moment I don't know what sparked this moment but I am glad it occurred. Driving down Wellington Street in Perth, on my way to training at the WACA, a thought entered my mind. It wasn't like any normal thought, but rather like a bolt of lightning running deep into my conscience.

Whether it was something I had seen, a song on the radio, or just a message from above that sparked this emotion, I really don't know. My mind flashed a picture or an image that stuck with me all season. I decided that I wanted to be a run machine, who was going to play with a smile on my face, whatever the circumstances. Beware the smiling assassin run machine, was my new motto.

In everything I did I was going to be a run machine. Like Steve Waugh, I was going to score runs, as many of them as I could, every time I walked onto a cricket field. It didn't matter whom I was playing against or where I was playing, I was going to display a ruthless determination to score the amount of runs that I had always dreamed about scoring.

The very thought of bringing this decision of mine into the public forum, through these words, scares me because it makes me sound a little egotistical. This is not my intention. The point is that I had painted a picture of exactly what I wanted to achieve from the upcoming summer. In everything I did, my focus was around being a very prolific run-scorer. I used the affirmation of being a run-machine to help me remain focussed day in day out. The affirmation and "perfect world" picture of being a run machine, was like my end goal for which I would strive and eventually conquer.

As a result, my training was sharper, my thinking clearer and my focus was definite. Every time a negative thought entered my world, I would quickly dismiss it with my vision of where I was headed. Not only did I now have a real image of where I wanted to go but I also had a strategy when negative, useless thinking interrupted this vision. For example, if I failed in the first innings of a game, I would remind myself of my target of being a run machine. If I was feeling lazy or flat at training or in a game, I would have a word to myself and encourage myself to find the extra energy and enthusiasm required to play and to act as a run machine would. If I ever let negative thoughts of losing my position in the team or the uncertainty of the future enter my mind, then I would simply smile and remind myself that if I lived up to my expectation these issues were of no concern. If I started getting too intense or started taking myself too seriously then I would shake my head, tell myself to get my thinking right and smile at my foolishness.

The results of this thinking were fantastic. Not only did I score more runs than ever before, but I also enjoyed the 2001-2002 season more than any other I had in the past.

The million-dollar question of course is which one came first? Did I enjoy myself more because of the success? Or did I enjoy myself more because I had a clear picture of exactly how I wanted to go about my life, ultimately leading to more success? Looking back, I think the latter was more crucial.

## SEEING THE SUNRISE

In my teenage years, my grandfather, who was an absolute hero in my eyes, taught me one of life's most valuable lessons.

Growing up, he was like most grandfathers in that he was someone to look up to, admire and love. Not only did he make the best boiled eggs and toast soldiers in the world, he was also a tough old man – an ex-boxer who worked in the pubs for most of his life and looked strong and uncompromising.

As a youngster, yours truly was scared of heights. In fact, it was more like petrified, manic and desperate when my feet were anywhere above ground level. In those formative teenage years my Pop recognised this fear and told me that he would help cure my fear of heights.

One Saturday morning there was a loud knock on the front door. It was 5am and like every teenage boy the very thought of waking up and getting out of my warm bed at this hour was repulsive. Having no idea what the noise was at this un-Godly hour, it was something of a surprise when the banging stopped and footsteps crept towards my bedroom.

Within a few moments, Pop was standing at the edge of my bed beckoning me to wake up and get dressed. My mind was in a state of confusion as it was very unusual to have my grandfather in my room at 5am.

After dealing with this momentary puzzlement, I focussed my tired eyes on the loving but stern look on Pop's face. When our eyes met, he finally explained that he had decided that this morning was as good a time as any to cure me of my fear of heights.

"What?" was my initial reaction.

"What are you talking about," I argued, while rubbing the sleep out of my eyes.

All he could say was that this problem of mine had been bugging him and it was time for me to trust him and come with him right away before it was too late.

"Too late for what?" was my obvious question, a question that was quickly dismissed with, "Please just trust me on this one."

By the time a shirt and shorts had been thrown over my body, Pop was sitting impatiently outside in his car.

For the next 15 minutes we drove toward the centre of town in relative silence. He sensed my discomfort, but in his way he simply stared through the front windscreen with a quiet but determined look upon his face. Driving slowly but purposefully, we finally pulled up outside a construction site with a large sign saying, "DANGER – Keep Out – Construction in Progress."

At this obscene time of the day there wasn't a soul to be seen, and when Pop said, "Come with me", as he headed towards a dusty concrete doorway, it would be fair to say my apprehension was growing with every tick of the clock. The sight of a ghostly 20-storey construction site and the brief knowledge that we were here to cure me of my fear of heights was enough to send me running as fast as my teenage legs would take me. The flight or fight mechanism in my body was beginning to take effect and if it wasn't for the sheer respect for my grandfather the lesson that I was about to be taught may never have happened.

Having eventually mustered up enough courage to pass through the doorway of doom and no return, Pop started walking up a flight of stairs. Before he had reached the first landing, I meekly suggested that he could cure me of my fear from this sandy, but very safe ground-floor level.

Shaking his head slowly, he told me that this cure was an experiential lesson and that I would have to follow his every command if I were to grow and develop from this day forward. As scared as I could ever remember being, I eventually followed my Pop to the landing at the first level. With the stairwell being open to the elements, my heart was beginning to race as we climbed toward the second, third, fourth and fifth levels of this construction site building.

For those of you who know the fear of heights, you will understand that as we got higher and higher from the ground my heart was thumping so hard it felt like it would break through my chest bones and out onto the grimy floor. The palms of my hands were as clammy as the inside of a dirty old sock and my legs were turning to jelly with every upward movement.

By the time we had reached floors 10 to 15, my head was aching like a sprained ankle and my mouth was as dry as desert sand. Sweat was pouring out of every pore in my body and the demons in my mind were going off like the fireworks on New Year's Eve in Sydney.

Between the final stages of this horrific trek I had gone from holding onto the walls with both hands, to crawling on all fours, to finally scrambling like a snake with my chest not leaving the hard concrete steps.

When we reached the top floor, which was an open landing with walls standing about one metre from the ground, Pop reached down and grabbed both of my hands and pulled me up to the standing position.

My stomach was churning and the strong feeling of nausea was overtaking my shaking body.

"Pull yourself together" was the sentimental relief offered by my Pop who told me to muster all the courage I had and walk over to the edge of the building.

"You must be kidding," I said as my world was starting to spin out of control.

Looking at me again, as only he could, he held me by the shoulders and looked straight into my eyes.

"Do you trust me son."

My reply was that "of course" I trusted him, but right now I thought he was "the meanest person in the world".

This didn't seem to deter him one bit as he ordered me to, "Take one step at a time and go over to the edge of the building and listen to every word I say."

Knowing that there was nowhere to run or hide and that I was at the point where the bungy jumper has no choice, I crept like a snail to the edge of the building. When I was there, Pop told me to hold onto the edge of the brick wall and look down at the ground below. With my knuckles as white as winter snow and my muscles as taunt and tense as a tightrope, I held onto the side and somehow looked down at the ground below.

Within two seconds, a time frame that felt more like an eternity, I had turned around and was again on all fours ready to throw up everywhere. Before long, Pop was again standing near me asking how I felt? In a nutshell, I explained that I felt just like I felt every time I was off the ground – like I was going to die or at least that I thought this must be the feeling just before I was going to die.

"Okay," he said, "now I want you to get up and walk to the edge one more time and again listen to my voice."

Almost crying, I asked him if he had listened to what I had just told him and if he could see what this crazy joke of his was doing to me. It was like being tortured, although this torture was worse because I wasn't being tortured by an enemy, but rather by one of the people I most loved and respected in this world. It was like the ultimate betrayal.

Again he pleaded for my trust, telling me that this ordeal was almost over and that this one last effort would be worth all of the pain.

Out of anger and determination for this nightmare to end, I eventually dragged my sorry backside off the dirt and headed towards the other side of the building. When I reached the eastern wall the same intense fear ran through my fingers as I held onto the edge of the brickwork as tightly as a beggar holds onto his last penny. This time though, before I looked down at the frightening fate below me, Pop's voice rang through my ears.

"Justin, this time don't look down, look up and see the sun rising over the hills, look up and enjoy the start of this new day."

In an amazing moment in my life, I stared out at the magnificent red, orange, pink and apricot colours of the rising sun. Having never seen a sun rise before, I was in awe of this incredible feat of nature that happens every day. I couldn't remember seeing something so beautiful as I looked out into the distance admiring this awe-inspiring view of a new day.

Within a few seconds a light touch awoke me from this trance-like state. My Pop was standing next to me asking me how I now felt.

Rather than crawling like a scared baby on the ground, I was standing upright, feeling relaxed, cherishing the moment and enjoying what I was watching. Instead of fearing for my life I suddenly felt secure and safe, free of the nightmare that had been haunting me only minutes before.

With his arm around me, Pop explained that he had not only cured my fear of heights but he had also taught me one of the most important lessons that I would ever learn. He went on to say, "You must always look to where you want to go, rather than where you don't want to go. By looking down at the ground all you are seeing is the long fall, the heavy landing and the consequent pain that comes with such a fall. If you can learn to always look where you want to go, in other words, look at the sun rise rather than the road below, then you will find that all of your fears, not only the fear of heights, will disappear forever."

This lesson has served me well over the years.

Not only has my fear of heights gone, I now remember this lesson every time I let my mind wander away from the path that I want to be travelling along. It is important to paint the picture in your mind of where you want to go rather that where you don't want to go. Work out exactly what you want to do and keep your mind focussed on that perfect picture. By doing this you won't have time to worry about taking the other destructive path that your mind can so easily retreat to.

Being dropped from the Australian cricket team is an example in my life of how poor thinking led to poor performances on the field, which ultimately led to me being omitted from the team. Rather than focussing on developing into one of the best batsmen in the world, in one of the best teams in the world, I allowed my mind to get distracted.

The fear of failure, the insecurity of not being good enough, or the trap of sitting in the comfort zone are examples of poor thinking and a destructive attitude.

These fears are no different to the fear I had of heights. Many of us tend to focus on the doom and gloom of the road below, rather than the beautiful sunrise that represents the dream of where we want to be, and doing exactly what we want to do.

## HAYDEN AND MARTYN – OTHER GREAT EXAMPLES

My good mate Matty Hayden relies on the constant affirmation of "world-class thinking". He wanted to be world class in the game of cricket and by using this affirmation he set out to be world class in everything he does. His preparation is world class, his technique is world class, his temperament is world class, his discipline is world class, his thinking is world class and, as a result, his performances have been absolutely world class.

Any time he feels himself slipping into a comfort zone or feels that his mind is wandering from the path of excellence he relies on his affirmation of being world class. He has a clear picture in his mind of exactly how he wants to live his life and, as a result, he is living it and feeling it and loving it.

Early in his career, Matt wasn't as confident playing against spin bowling as he was against fast bowling. This in mind, he set about improving this area of his game to the point where he is now one of the best players of spin bowling in the world. His dominance over spin bowling is incredible and I get the feeling the little red cricket ball grimaces and shakes every time it leaves the spin bowler's hand. Not only does he hit the ball as hard as a boxer hits a punching bag, but he also seems to hit the ball to whatever part of the boundary he likes. Through constant hard word and a clear game plan, he dominates spin bowlers like Tiger Woods dominates the current men's golf circuit. His efforts have been rewarded because he stopped worrying about his perceived weakness against spin bowling – instead spending his time doing something about getting it right.

This confidence and improvement didn't happen by coincidence. A few years ago Matt asked the Australian selectors to consider sending him on a short trip to India with a group of players involved in the cricket academy. He was resolute in his goal of improving this area of his game and he felt that the best way to improve was to visit the country that could best teach him the lessons he needed to learn.

If you want to learn how to make the best pasta or pizza in the world you go to Italy. If you want to learn about spin bowling you go to India. Hence, Matty's desire to visit the sub-continent. He knew what had to be done, he put a plan together and then, most importantly, he followed up his plan with actions. As a result he benefited from making the effort and getting out of his comfort zone. The rewards speak for themselves.

Even now, it is not unusual to see my big mate roughing up areas of the Brisbane practice wickets to test himself against any spinner who cares to challenge him. The rough areas give the spin bowlers a target from which they can produce extra movement. This exercise makes it more difficult for the batsman and subsequently means he has to be at his best to get through the session unscathed. This method of practice is highly effective, as it follows the Ric Charlesworth coaching philosophy of always training and practising harder than you would ever experience in the game. If you can learn your skills under a pressurised environment at practice, nothing will surprise you when you are in a competition.

There is no doubt that Matt Hayden has the most specific practice methods that I have ever seen.

Another living example of a person who painted a picture in his mind before setting out to achieve his greatest ambition in life is Damien Martyn. After years on the outer of the Australian cricket team he made a concerted and determined decision to make more of his awesome natural ability. To his undying credit he decided to take a very close look at everything he was doing in his quest to get himself back into the team.

As a young player he always possessed more natural ability than any other player I have ever seen, but for a number of reasons he had a fall from grace from which it took incredible courage to fight back. For two or three years, Damien struggled to regain his early career sparkle, but after a great deal of soul searching and decision making, he is now one of the best players in the world.

One of the areas he wanted to improve was his physical fitness. Through sacrifice and discipline he transformed himself into an outstanding athlete. He lost eight kilograms in weight and trained as hard as any player in the Australian team. He painted a very clear picture in his mind of how he wanted to look and feel and, of course, how he wanted to perform. It is no surprise that he is now one of the fittest members of the Australian cricket squad who has had one of the most inspiring comebacks in Australian cricket history. His vision and subsequent accomplishment has been a shining example to all. He has shown that you can accomplish your dreams if you clearly define in your mind what it is that you want and then take definite steps towards attaining that vision.

## DIET, PHYSICAL FITNESS AND MIND POWER

Depending upon the stage of the season, my workload will vary, but I like to maintain a healthy lifestyle all year round to keep my fitness at the level that I know makes me feel fresh and strong.

Different people maintain their fitness in varying ways. I love eating and therefore would rather work harder on the track than sacrifice one of the great things in life, food. Damien Martyn, on the other hand, works hard, but is also extremely careful about what he puts in his mouth. His dietary habits became legendary in the Australian team as he dropped a lot of weight to help him achieve the fitness level that he felt would enhance his performances on the cricket field. He was obviously spot on in his thinking as he is now one of the best-performed batsmen in the world.

Walking every morning, an incredible work ethic at training and marrying a first-class dietician is the key to Adam Gilchrist's sustained fighting weight. Shane Warne has recently lost a mountain of weight by sacrificing his beloved pizza, french fries and cheese sandwiches, and working like an Olympian in the gyms around the world. Everyone is different, but the most successful people I know recognise the significance of a fit and healthy body.

To his credit, Brett Lee, one of the fastest bowlers in the world, made a sacrifice for a year that made a difference to his performances and overall physical fitness capabilities. He decided, after a run of injuries, to stop drinking alcohol. At the tender age of 24, and living in the environment that he does, this was no mean feat. Even during Test match celebrations he would stick to a bottle of water or mineral water. It took courage and strength to say no, time after time, to the offers of a cold celebratory beer or a drink at the pub, but he did, and as a result he turned his body into a high-performance machine.

Not only did he get through the year injury free, but he also enjoyed what he saw every time he took his shirt off in front of the mirror. All of a sudden his baby fat turned to lean, hard muscles as his stomach region turned into a six, or maybe even an eight-pack, underneath his cricket shirt. This feeling of health and well-being bred more confidence and with this confidence came more consistent performance. He and the young brigade of fast bowlers are showing the way in terms of physical fitness.

Every morning, Jason Gillespie is down at the hotel swimming pool stretching his body in preparation for the day's play. He spends hours maintaining his cardiac fitness and flexibility in an effort to improve his on-field performances. His effort allows him to recover more quickly and perform at his peak day in day out.

In this day and age, physical fitness has become one of the means of gaining the edge in professional sport. A leaner, fitter figure is important, not only to professional sports people, but also to anyone who wants to live a more invigorating and energetic lifestyle.

You will not only look better in a pair of bathers, but you will also wake up with more energy every day. Physical fitness is paramount to my success and that is why it is high on my list of controllables that I check off every week.

## THE INNER GAME

I have heard people say about Steve Waugh, who has been one of the leading batsmen in the world for many years, that he doesn't have a great technique but because of his incredible mental toughness he is able to perform at the level he does. As far as I am concerned, every player has his or her own style, but there is no way that someone like Steve Waugh has anything less that a very, very good technique. In terms of the basics of the game, he is very sound as he plays most balls with a straight bat and he watches the ball as closely as any player in the game, which in itself is a learned and practised technique. I don't believe anyone makes it to the top of their field without having mastered, or is at least striving to master, their skills.

Nevertheless, you will often hear statements that cricket at the top level is a mind game, a mental battle with one's self, a game played as much between your ears as it is with the opposition.

Professional sport today features players, administrators, coaches, computers, video feedback, fitness advisers, nutritionists and sports psychologists. The current-day professionalism in cricket has led to an increasing incentive for players to use every available resource to ensure that they maximise their potential and make the most of the opportunities now available.

Strangely though, sport psychology, "the inner game", whatever you like to call it, seems to be the least studied of all cricket skills, even though it is widely accepted as being the most important ingredient of success.

This has always astounded me, but in the same breath it has made me more determined to study the mind and work out how I can use the power of the mind to get the edge over my opponents.

At present, the Australian team has a number of players who have been able to achieve this mind/body synergy and as a result they will always be remembered as great players. The list is phenomenal within this current team and it is no wonder there has been so much success over the last few years.

Names like Warne, McGrath, S. and M. Waugh, Gilchrist, Hayden, Ponting and Martyn, belong to people who have reached the very top of their game by mastering aspects of their mind and technique.

## THE ULTIMATE IN POSITIVITY – MUHAMMAD ALI

Do you think Muhammad Ali ever let negative thinking or negative self-talk get in his way? If he did, he never let anyone know about it. He may have been more vocal and public than most others were, but you can be sure the picture he was painting with his words were helping to program his mind to where he wanted to go.

"The Champ" predicted early in his career:

*This is the legend of Cassius Clay,*
*the most beautiful fighter in the world today.*
*He talks a great deal and brags indeedly*
*of a muscular punch*
*that's incredibly speedy.*

*This fistic world was dull and weary;*
*with a champ like Liston,*
*things had to be dreary.*
*Then someone with colour,*
*someone with dash,*
*brought the fight fans*
*running with cash.*
*This brash young boxer is something to see,*
*And the heavyweight championship is his destiny!*

# CHAPTER 16

# Mentors

SHOT OF INSPIRATION # 16:
*Surround yourself with good people who you know have characters
of steel. Listen to their advice and take careful notice of
the way they carry themselves in everything they do. There are
answers in watching and talking to successful people.*

W HAT IS A MENTOR? The World Book Dictionary describes
a mentor as "a wise and trusted advisor". It goes on to say,
"A faithful friend of Odysseus. When Odysseus went to fight the
Trojans, he left his own son with Mentor to be taught and advised."

Other definitions include coach, counsellor, guide, instructor
and highly respected, loyal and reliable friend.

In my development there have been a couple of people who
have taken the form of all of the above descriptions. They have
been crucial in helping me attain my goals, but more importantly
they have become "faithful friends" along the way.

In my life I have been lucky to rub shoulders with many famous people. I have met the Queen twice, shaken hands with Prime Ministers, dined with elite sports men and women, and talked with some of the great achievers of this world. Many of these people have been instrumental in teaching me some of the thoughts that I am sharing with you in this book.

I have read about, listened to, met and been touched by numerous examples of courage and character over the years. In every story there is great inspiration, and a message of motivation, to be gained. The history of the world is made up of wonderful deeds of men and women who have battled all odds to come out triumphant. Their leadership and grace have inspired many followers to draw inspiration from their leadership.

Growing up I always wanted to write Sir Donald Bradman a letter. I figured that he was the best ever cricketer so surely he would be the best person to ask for advice on cricket. For one reason or another I put off writing that letter until I was 24 years old. At 24 I had reached an intersection in my cricket career. I had been lucky enough to realise my initial dream of wearing the baggy green cap but after surrendering the opportunity I was in life's wilderness.

The naivete of my letter makes me laugh now:

*15 August 1994*

*Dear Sir Don,*
*I feel a little shy about writing this letter but I felt you might be able to offer me a little advice, which may help me achieve my goal of becoming a very successful Australian Test cricketer.*

As I have heard you describe, I am one of the "temporary trustees" of our great game who is very determined to play a part in helping this young Australian team develop into an entertaining and dominant force in international cricket. I have a burning desire to wear the baggy green cap with pride and distinction and I am determined to grab my opportunity of playing for Australia with both hands.

With the tour of Sri Lanka and Pakistan only a few weeks away, I thought, if it was not an inconvenience, you might offer me advice on a couple of aspects of my game which are playing on my mind.

I am very curious what you used to think about, how you prepared yourself mentally for a Test series, a Test Match, a Test innings? Your consistency was obviously remarkable and I am interested if you attribute that to your preparation or purely your natural ability?

Through my involvement with the Australian Cricket Academy, I believe that I have prepared myself physically for the next six months of cricket and I believe that the key to me succeeding for Australia will be my ability to prepare my mind for the action ahead.

As I am predominantly a back-foot player, I wonder if you have any ideas on playing medium pace bowlers. I tend to have more difficulty with my rhythm against these bowlers than the quicks and spinners.

If you could offer me any advice I would treasure it and value your opinion and thoughts. For me it would be an honour and privilege to be given a few words of wisdom from a person who has obviously a great knowledge of the game.

Yours sincerely,

Justin Langer

Incredibly a reply came two days later. More incredible was the second line of Sir Don's return note.

*August 17, 1994*

*Dear Justin,*

*Thank you for your letter. You flatter me by suggesting that an old octogenarian like me can help you with your cricket.*

*When I finished playing I summarised my thoughts in my book "The Art Of Cricket" which deals with all facets of the game and if you haven't got a copy I think you will find it worthwhile.*

*Also, I made a video on the art of batting and this should be available almost everywhere.*

*My success in the game was I think more a matter of natural ability than anything else. I did not do anything special – I did not take any measures to fit me physically other than live a normal and sensible non-smoking and non-drinking career, and I relied on the practice nets to work out any chinks in my batting.*

*You mention specially the medium pacers and a slight problem you have with them. Against them, I always started to move just before delivery by going slightly back and across. In fact the main basis of my batting was back play because I think this gives the batsman greater flexibility in making shots and taking the initiative than the forward player who becomes stuck in a grave.*

*I suppose the one outstanding feature of a good player is his ability to concentrate and to impose his will on the bowler.*

*I always played cricket for fun and because I loved the game. It never became a boring pastime.*

*I am sure you have the right attitude and I congratulate you on your success so far. Follow your own instincts and don't be a slave to coaching.*

*I wish you good luck in the future.*

*Kinds regards,*

*Don Bradman*

Sir Don's letter remains one of my most treasured items.

## DENNIS LILLEE'S INFLUENCE

When I was a young, wide-eyed 16-year-old, Australian cricket legend Dennis Lillee gave me wonderful support and advice. Being one of my absolute childhood heroes, anything Dennis had to offer me in those developmental years of my career was like gospel. One of the main reasons I wanted to play cricket for Australia was because Dennis Lillee cleaned bowled the great Sir Vivian Richards on the last ball of the Boxing Day Test many years ago.

As a result, playing in a Boxing Day Test match became one of my most desired life goals and to this day, remains one of my favourite events in the calendar year.

In my first season of club cricket in Perth, I was lucky to be a teammate of the great D.K. Lillee, who was making a comeback to the first-class arena. Every Saturday afternoon I would sit in the changing room and watch in awe as Dennis went about his business with the professionalism of a 20-year old.

When we were out on the ground I would stand at mid-on with a smile on my face, pinching myself to wake up from this incredible dream.

One afternoon after club training, Dennis asked me if he could join me in some extra running I was doing. Knowing that Dennis's work ethic was legendary and that he prided himself on being first on the track and last off it, I wasn't overly surprised at his request. For half an hour we ran until our legs felt like jelly and our lungs were like a smoking furnace.

I can say it now, but the old bloke was determined to do everything I was doing and he wasn't going to give in for anything. When we finally finished the session, Dennis told me that he was impressed by the extra work I was putting in but that, "when you make it to the top that is when the hard work really begins." At the time I thought he must be crazy because of the work I thought I was already putting into my game.

He went on to say, "You have to work hard to get to the next level, but when you have reached that point then you have to work harder and harder to stay there. Always look to constantly improve and be disciplined in everything you do. If you really want to make it to the very top you must be willing to make the sacrifice. You must be ready to do the little things extra. The people who don't quite make it are the ones who aren't prepared to make those sacrifices and who aren't prepared to do that little bit extra."

On a number of occasions I have watched Dennis address a group of up-and-coming fast bowlers. On each occasion, the first thing he has said to the boys is, "I want to share with you all the secrets of making it as a fast bowler."

With this, all of the boys step a little closer and you can see their eyes opening wide and their ears beginning to twitch in anticipation of the great man's advice. Lowering his voice a little he whispers, "I want to give you the recipe right now because I know one of you wants to take it away with you and do something with these secrets."

At this stage the boys are almost salivating with excitement to this secret recipe that is about to be uncovered. Dennis pauses for a few seconds before saying: "The three things you must know about making it to the top are these: one is hard work, the second is hard work and the third is more hard work. These are the three secrets to making it to the top. It is up to you how much you want to listen to these secrets of success."

With this the boys almost collapse at the let–down of this advice; even though it will probably be the best advice they ever get, in whatever they choose to do with their lives.

## A FITNESS NUT CALLED STEVE SMITH

While I have had the privilege of meeting many high achievers, there have also been a number of so-called "ordinary" people who have had an indelible effect on my development as a person.

One of the men who continue to leave their mark upon me is a short, bearded, red–headed, red-blooded, tattooed, ex-navy diver by the name of Steve Smith. Not only does he inspire and moti-vate people in his every day job as an elite fitness trainer, but he has also overcome some battles of his own to be where he is today.

Smithy is not everyone's cup of tea because he calls a spade a spade, he loves working hard and he doesn't like people making excuses. He is as tough as old navy rope, but although he would hate to admit it, everyone who comes across him knows that he has a heart of gold. He is, at the very least, respected by everyone who knows him.

In November 1985, Smithy was involved in a climbing accident in the navy and fractured a number of the discs in his lower back. After months of physiotherapy and constant misery, he decided in April, 1986, that the only way he was going to fix his back problem was to take control of his own destiny and do it by himself. Doctors and physiotherapists had had their chance; it was now time for him to take responsibility for his actions and his life.

The frustration of his injuries was driving him to despair. He knew that unless he was proactive in his thoughts and his actions, then he would continue leading a life of continued disappointment, feeling defeated and angry. Not one for sitting around feeling sorry for himself, Smithy wanted to take control of his own destiny.

One of the steps he decided was important in turning his life around was to give up drinking alcohol and smoking cigarettes. Considering he had enjoyed a drink or a hundred over the years and that he was smoking a couple of packets of fags a day, this was no mean feat.

Given that the accident had left him hardly able to walk, this initial resolution took some guts. He could have quite easily felt sorry for himself and given up hope, but as he has said to me over

MENTORS

and over again, "You have to get up and get on with your life. Whatever happens you, just never give up, no matter what."

Smithy started programming his own rehabilitation, step by step towards regaining his peak physical and mental fitness. He enrolled in university to study how the body works and learned the basic principles that laid the foundations for a very successful business that he appropriately called "ASPIRE Health and Fitness".

Every morning that I walk into his gym I am greeted with a motivational message that he has written up on the whiteboard next to the front door. Along with the message comes a smile and a handshake from the man who happily claims to jump out of bed in the morning and promise himself: "Today is going to be a GREAT day."

I met Smithy when Geoff "Swampy" Marsh, who was the captain of the Western Australian cricket team, invited me to come for a run with him one Friday morning. My only instruction from Swampy was to be at the Langley Plaza Hotel at 6am "and whatever you do, don't be late".

As you do on these occasions, I woke at all intervals throughout the night so that I wouldn't miss the 5:30am alarm that was designed to shake me from the slumber that I usually enjoy so much. When the scream of my alarm finally came, I dragged myself out of bed, jumped into the car and drove into the Langley Plaza car park, arriving at about 5:59am. Having to get up the stairs in less than a minute, I leapt out of the car and ran into the hotel.

As I arrived in the hotel foyer, I could see the back of Swampy and this little red–headed bloke, who were already leaving for their run. Meekly, I shouted out an apology for being late – even though

I thought I was on time – only to be greeted gruffly by this five-foot-nothing red–head who had the following piece of advice for me.

"Get rid of your bloody bag upstairs, you young blokes are all the bloody same. Catch up with us if you can and if you don't, I never want to see you again. Don't ever be late again, we have taken your lateness as an insult." With this, he stared a hole through my retinas, turned, and jogged down the street.

In view of the fact that I had never met this guy before in my life, my initial reaction was that this was an extraordinary response. Perplexed, somewhat taken aback, and unsure of what to expect next, I did just as he had commanded. Dropping my bag into the hotel gymnasium, I ran like Carl Lewis until I finally caught up to my so-called running partners. On arrival, this little psycho whom I had met for the first time 10 minutes before, turned around and beamed a massive smile my way. With that, he extended his right hand and shook my hand with the warmest greeting of all time. From that day forward we have never looked back.

"A fit body means a fit mind," has been Smithy's motto from the first day we ran together.

For years now, every Friday morning that I am in Perth, Smithy and I will go for our early morning run. Even though it is quite a tough run, it is the most enjoyable training session of the week. Yes, it is early, and yes we do run – rain, hail or shine – but I wouldn't miss it for anything.

Firstly, I wouldn't miss it because I know Smithy will be there no matter what, and secondly, because I know that every Friday morning run I will learn something new about myself or about life.

He often reminds me along the way that not many other people, especially cricket players, are likely to be running at 6am.

This motivation alone helps maintain my hunger and edge over my direct competition. Whether it is the bowlers I have to face or the other batsmen challenging with me for a place in the team, I believe that this extra work will give me a mental and physical edge over my contemporaries. This itself is a lesson.

Despite the fact that Smithy is short in stature, he is like a little Jack Russell terrier during these runs. It is not uncommon for him to run up alongside me, sledging and cursing me as he tries to get into my head, as if he is Curtly Ambrose or Wasim Akram. Often he says at the start of our runs, "I'm Curtly Ambrose today", and along the way he bumps me into bus stands or into puddles, while chipping away at my mind. As crazy as this scenario may sound, he wants me to concentrate and block out all of the distractions that are coming my way.

These mornings have been valuable practice for mentally toughening me up. While I can smile now at how silly some of our behaviour must look at the time, there is no doubt that Smithy has helped me steel my mind for batting.

## AN AFL LEGEND CALLED CRAIG BRADLEY

When I was about 18 years old, I was playing a colts game of cricket for Western Australia in Victoria. The game was being played at the beautiful Albert Oval. During the course of play I was standing talking with Darrin Ramshaw, when a black convertible sports car drove by and parked on the grassy bank of the ground.

After a few seconds another short, fit–looking bloke wearing a pair of running shorts stepped out of the car and walked over to the pavilion. Darrin looked at me and asked if I knew who that was. When I told him that I didn't, Darrin said, "That's a guy called Craig Bradley. Do you know what he does for a living?" Shaking my head, he finished off by saying, "He gets fit for a living. He runs and runs and runs and gets paid for it. On the weekend he plays AFL football and for the rest of the week he gets himself as fit as possible. Not a bad way to make a good living, hey?"

From that moment on, I wanted to be Craig Bradley. How good a life would that be, I thought. Getting fit for a living! An incredibly gifted all-round athlete, Craig Bradley remains an inspiration to me, as he continues writing his own legend as one of the most esteemed players to have played AFL football. Craig Bradley would have no idea that he was an inspiration early in my career and continues to be one of my most admired sportsmen to this day. I guess that is what being a hero or role model is about. With the character, skill and supreme fitness that he possesses, he would have inspired thousands of kids through his actions on and off the football field.

It is funny what can grow when a seed has been planted. One vision of Craig Bradley sparked a desire in me to be a professional athlete for a living. Just like Kim Hughes playing a cover drive down on one knee, or Dennis Lillee bowling Viv Richards on the last ball on Boxing Day many years ago, a seed was planted in my youthful, imaginative mind and I wanted to be an Australian cricket player. Thank heavens for heroes in this life.

## A TEACHER WITH VISION

It is funny how a few incidents can leave a mark that end up being as permanent as a tattoo. Looking back, one such incident in my life, involved one of my schoolteachers at high school. Thanks to his vision and care, he helped re-direct the path I was taking. In the process he taught me an invaluable lesson.

Having changed colleges for the final two years of school, I was trying to make an impression on my new peers and fit in with the crowd, while still looking to make the most of the benefits of my new school. After a month in my new uniform, my economics teacher, Rod O'Meara, asked me to stay in my seat at the end of class.

Obviously this is a pretty nervous time for any young bloke, especially when the teacher asks you to stay behind with a hint of aggravation and frustration in his voice. When the class had cleared, he sat down, looked me straight in the face and told me that in his opinion I was wasting an opportunity of a lifetime. He explained how he thought that I had fallen into the wrong crowd of mates at school and if I weren't careful I would find myself wasting what he saw as great potential. He went on to say that the school would hand consequential opportunities to me, in both my education and sport, and unless I lifted my game then it would all be wasted. He pointed out that it was totally up to me whether or not I wanted to live up to my perceived capabilities and make the most of my God-given talent. He also said that he was not the only teacher who was worried and frustrated by my attitude and performances up until then.

To this day I owe a great deal of gratitude to Rod O'Meara, who was also my school cricket coach and is now a friend. He did not have to take the time to warn me of the signs of underachievement. His message was a wake-up call and while I initially may have reacted like most teenagers, "what does he know anyway", or "why is he picking on me", my heart knew that his message was spot on the mark.

There is no doubt that his advice eventually sank in, as from that day forward school life changed dramatically. My workrate increased markedly, resulting in a dramatic improvement in my grades. I had to put up with a few smart comments from the blokes who were more interested in seeing me smoke a cigarette behind the trees, or making a smart remark to one of the teachers, but so what?

It took some courage to turn my back on the poor influences around me. Eventually the small pains of dealing with the peer-group pressure went away and ultimately those few early jibes have proven to be insignificant in the overall scheme of my life.

Apart from being honest with myself and accepting responsibility, Rod taught me about the importance of grabbing an opportunity with both hands. I have learnt from a number of personal experiences that opportunities don't come along every day and if you surrender those opportunities then disappointment will follow.

If you are completely honest with yourself, then, no matter how many excuses you make, and no matter how many other people you blame, there is rarely anyone else to point the finger at other than yourself for missing an opportunity.

## ALAN JONES AND HIS PRE-TOUR PEP TALK

A man who has been a mentor to many is Alan Jones, the highly successful media giant from Sydney. Before the Australian team left for the 2002 South African tour, Jones addressed the team. One of his pearls of wisdom centred on this very point of grabbing an opportunity. In his passionate and entertainingly enthralling way he said, "Gentlemen, there are four things that you can never take back in this life." After a pause of a few seconds, he looked towards our eager eyes and finished with, "those four things are the shot arrow, the spoken word, the passing of time and, most importantly, the missed opportunity."

Jones was specifically talking to us about the opportunity to retain the No.1 Test ranking in world cricket by beating South Africa on their home soil. He was passionate about our opportunity to silence any critics, and for the team to get behind Steve Waugh, who had just been left out of the one-day team. On a number of occasions during this successful tour, Alan Jones's words were recalled as we pushed towards realising our goal of beating the South Africans in their environment. A seed had been planted and we made it blossom through a concerted team effort.

My second daughter, Ali-Rose, looked at me on the day of her third birthday and whispered, "Daddy, I am never going to be two years old ever again." Her expression then reminded me of one of the four things that Alan Jones suggested could never be taken back. This day, that conversation, this moment, your experience yesterday, will never happen again. Like an opportunity, it will never present itself in the same way a second time around, so always keep your eyes open and recognise when it has presented itself. Be ready, so that when an opportunity comes you have both hands out in front of you, prepared to grab hold of it. Enjoy every moment because our life passes by in a blink of an eye.

One of the other things Alan Jones asked the team was whether we wanted to represent the bacon or the eggs on our upcoming tour. He went on to explain that the pig and the bacon are fully committed to the cause whereas the hen and the eggs are simply involved in the journey. There is no doubt that he got his message across very strongly. To be successful you must be fully committed. It is easy to be involved in something without committing to it. Commitment, like passion, is crucial to enjoying success and satisfaction.

## A WILY OLD ENGLISH SPINNER

In 1992 I approached ex-England spin bowler Tony Locke, who was also one of Western Australia's best cricket players and captains. I told Tony that I wanted to leave university for a year and play cricket in England for six months. English summers run adjacent to our winter so I could play cricket in England for six months then return for our season back home.

Before I could blink, Tony said, "Justin, I know the perfect place for you, let me see what I can do." Within a few days he had given me the name of an English gentleman by the name of Nigel Wray and suggested I give him a call. This I did, and after a few letters and a number of phone calls, all was set and I was off to England to play league cricket.

Now this was also a very interesting period of my life.

Firstly, leaving university was a big step in itself. For years I had studied like a trooper in the hope of getting enough marks to get into the damned place, and now I was dropping this goal for another.

Most people told me I was crazy. The general thought was that I should gain a university degree so that I had security behind me. The most popular consensus was one of, "Get your degree first then you can go off and play your cricket."

The more people I talked to the more confused I was getting. If I just packed up, followed my heart and gave this cricket caper a go, would I be putting my life and my career in jeopardy?

It sounds dramatic, but at the time it felt like a massive decision. The more people who guided me down the path of perceived security and responsibility, the more I started to panic and question what I really wanted to do with my life.

Thanks to a piece of advice from a family friend, I took my desired path without any regrets. This wise friend told me, "You have to go with your gut feeling and follow your instincts. If you do this always, you can't go wrong because you are taking total responsibility for your actions. By following your gut feeling and instincts you eliminate blame from anyone else because you are following what your heart really believes."

This advice has been invaluable wisdom for me and I now strive to live by it and pass it on to other people every day.

My decision to go to England was based on belief. If I gave cricket 100 per cent and it didn't work well I could always go back to university and study for a so-called real job. But, of course, at that stage of my life the thought of failing never really entered my mind.

While I had the perceived security blanket of university to fall back on, my heart guided me to the destination where I truly wanted to go.

I could have stayed to please people and look to be responsible, but sometimes you have to say "what the heck" and go with what you feel is best for you.

I knew in my heart that I wanted to take the plunge and go to England. I wanted to go and learn more about the game, learn how to adapt to different conditions, play against different oppositions and, above all, play a lot of cricket. England could offer me this; university couldn't at that stage.

So, before I knew it, I was off to England. My close friend James Brayshaw had talked me into stopping off in Greece before we arrived in the UK. It sounded unbelievable - a week in the Greek Islands at 18 years of age.

The day before we left, I remember vividly a phone call from Tony Locke. He wished me all the best, then said to me in his sternest English gentleman's voice: *"Now Justin, I suggest when you get to England and meet Nigel Wray that you show him the greatest of reverence and you must always call him Mr Wray."*

He explained how Mr Wray was a very wealthy English gentleman who had been kind enough to find me a place to live in England. He was known to be a very generous man and if I played my cards right I would be "looked after" for six months.

"It is up to you though Justin, this is a great opportunity that we are offering you, don't mess it up son, don't mess it up."

Now I was under pressure: six months away from home, a week

in the Greek Islands, followed by an imminent meeting with a man named Nigel. Sorry, Mr Wray.

What had I gotten myself into?

## EARLY DAYS IN ENGLAND

Suntanned and relaxed after my Greek Island holiday, I rang the Wray residence from a public phone in Athens. Due to a faulty phone line I had been cut off just after reminding them that I would be arriving at Heathrow at 9.30pm. Throughout the flight to one of the world's busiest airports I was having nightmares about arriving in this foreign land with no one there to greet me. The mind plays terrible games with you in moments of uncertainty.

Thankfully, I should never have worried, as the first sign I saw when I stepped through the arrival gates was a big card with the name JUSTIN LANGER written in bold, black print.

Standing in front of me, just as I had imagined him, and exactly how he had sounded on the phone, was Mr Wray. He was a short, bald, bespectacled man, grinning from ear to ear, and exactly how I imagined an English gentleman to look.

You know when you speak to someone on the telephone and you form a picture in your mind of what they may look like? On this occasion the image in my imagination was picture perfect.

Nervously I approached him, extended my hand and said, "Mr Wray, it is an absolute pleasure to meet you sir." I laid it on thick and was really outdoing myself in the manners stake this time. Mr Wray just smiled at me, picked up my bags and took me out to the brand new Land Rover in the Heathrow car park.

I remember it was pouring with rain - a great introduction to English weather - but for the hour-long journey I chatted away and he simply continued to smile.  Just as we pulled up to the heavy wooden electric gates of this magnificent English mansion known as *The Priory*, Mr Wray looked at me straight in the face and said, "Justin, I guess you must have realised by now that I am Mr Wray's chauffeur, Ron.  It has been a pleasure meeting you and if there is anything I can do to make you feel at home, don't be afraid to ask."

I couldn't believe it; I had been done beautifully.  No wonder Ron had been grinning from ear to ear for the last hour or so.

This meant I had to go through this nervous greeting once again.

As I opened the door to the most beautiful house I have ever seen, there, standing in the hallway, was this tall, fit man with long dark hair and a caring smile on his face.  This time it was him who came up to me, extended his hand and said, "Hello, Justin, my name is Nigel Wray, welcome to my house, please make yourself at home and if there is anything you need, just ask and we will look after it for you."

I was dumbfounded.  He definitely didn't look like I had expected and when I called him Mr Wray he just laughed and told me that Nigel would be fine and that Mr Wray made him feel old. He was only 40.

From that moment a great friendship was formed and some of my greatest lessons in life were about to be learned.

After an amazing night's sleep in a bed that I needed a step ladder to get into, I decided to have a look around *The Priory* and see if it was really as big as it had seemed the night before.  I felt like a kid in *Willy Wonker's Chocolate Factory*. I had only reached the steps leading down into the main part of the house when an attractive blonde lady and a young girl greeted me. After last night's fiasco with Ron the chauffeur, I couldn't help but wonder who these people were.

Before I could speak, Linda and Lucy Wray introduced themselves as the wife and daughter of Nigel. Again, these weren't the images I had in my mind of Mrs Wray. I was half expecting her to be round and plump and permanently wearing an apron around her neck. I must have read too many kids' books when I was younger.

What a relief and what a thrill! These people actually seemed like normal people; certainly not the posh, rich, untouchable family that Tony Locke had hinted at.

My shyness soon turned to enthusiasm as I learnt of what the Old Millhillians Cricket Club had in store for me for the next six months. The first step was to find a place for me to stay because *The Priory* was only a temporary resting place until I got myself on my feet. The plan was to stay with the other overseas Australian, who was teaching at Mill Hill College and playing for the OMs cricket club.

After a couple of days living in luxury, my first meeting with John Hurley was set. I rang the doorbell and walked into what was going to be my home for the next six months. My first reaction was, wow! This place was something else. John was sitting on his couch watching *The Blues Brothers* for the 47th time. In one corner there was a pile of pizza boxes stacked to the roof – a competition he was having with one of his mates apparently. On the inside dining table was a Bundaberg Rum umbrella, secured by a hole that had been drilled into the middle of the woodwork. There were dishes everywhere and the whole apartment was about as big as the bedroom I had been staying in for the three days before this encounter.

All sorts of thoughts screamed through my mind, not least of them being, "where's my Mum?" But after meeting Hurls, I started to relax. Maybe this would be a good start to my manhood. By living in the ultimate bachelor pad, I would surely learn a lot about life. It would toughen me up a bit and make me a much wiser and worldly person. I would go home a man; if I could survive this, I could survive anything.

By the time I had convinced myself that this was going to be a great place to stay while I was in London without my Mum, I heard the doorbell ring.

There at the front door was Linda to pick me up from the Hurls Bachelor Pad, my home for the next six months. I shook Hurls' hand and said, " I'll see you tomorrow mate, and I will bring all my things over in the morning."

That morning never came. As I opened the door, Linda nearly fainted. She had heard all about the famous Hurley residence, but until now she had never believed it. Politely she smiled, said goodbye and then spent the journey home apologising. "We can't let you live there, we will just have to find you somewhere else to live. You leave it up to me, I will talk to Nigel as soon as we get home."

I tried to convince her that living with Hurls would be a great life experience, a great growing up adventure.

She wouldn't believe me. For the next six months we kept looking for another place for me to stay, but unfortunately we just couldn't find anyone else to take me in. This meant that I had to endure six rugged months of luxury at *The Priory*.

What a six months this turned out to be, with the generosity and friendship being simply amazing. To this day I am still bewildered how they put up with me for so long; it is a time I will never forget.

Nigel Wray is a great teacher in his own quiet sort of way. He probably wouldn't admit it, but deep down I am sure he knows that he has had an amazing influence on my life. For the wealth he has accumulated through his diversified businesses, he leads a pretty simple life. He could be forgiven for leading a flamboyant lifestyle but that is not his way. He once contrasted himself with Aussie tycoon Alan Bond. "Sure I could live the very public life, drive around in limousines and be a media figure, but it just doesn't interest me. To my way of thinking that is flaunting with danger."

He did have Ron driving him around those days, but that was mainly to avoid the London traffic and to allow him to do some work during those monotonous traffic jams. He loves his sport and likes the idea of being able to jet off to his favourite sporting event around the world or take his family, which now includes his son Joseph, on holidays when they want to get away.

But he is generally a man who has worked very hard and smartly to build up one of the most successful businesses in the UK. That in itself is something I admire and respect about him.

During my time in England with the Wrays and the Old Milhillian Cricket Club, I experienced a shock to the system about three months into the season. I felt like a brick wall had been dropped on my world, thanks to a few home truths from this man for whom I was gaining enormous admiration.

This particular summer's afternoon, while driving to a game of village cricket in Sussex, I was chatting away about this and that, but specifically fishing for Nigel's thoughts about the most important traits of being a successful person. He was giving me the answers to all my questions and talking me through his ideas of why he thought he had done so well in business.

The usual things came up like perseverance, hard work, determination, dedication, sacrifice, discipline, self-belief and so on. I was getting all inspired, generally pumped up, and feeling good about myself when, from out of the blue, I was knocked out by what was equivalent to the best right hook I had ever received.

Despite the fact I have spent plenty of time in the boxing ring through martial arts or boxing training, this pseudo right hook hurt more than any I have experienced before.

The jolt wasn't an actual right hook of course, but something that felt 10 times worse. Nigel pulled over in his car, looked at me and said: "While we are on the subject, there are a few things I would like to talk to you about. As far as I am concerned I am afraid you don't really possess any of the things I have been talking about. Sure you talk a good game, you keep saying that you want to be a Test cricket star, and yes you do have some talent, but I haven't seen anything yet to indicate that you will make it to the top."

I couldn't believe what I was hearing as my jaw hit the car floor and for once in my life I was lost for words. As far as I was concerned I had been making plenty of runs for his club and was a bit of a star. Everyone at the club was telling me what a good player I was and I guess I just believed it.

Anyway, he went on, "I have been watching you. I have never seen you do any extra training, no extra running, no extra work at all. To be an elite sportsman, surely you have to have an elite and superior level of fitness to everyone else. Your preparation is poor, you are out until all hours drinking and hell knows what else. You are playing a fairly average level of cricket and while you may think you are making a lot of runs, you aren't making anywhere near the amount of runs I would expect you to be making.

"You are making silly mistakes on and off the field and to me this is just an indication of your attitude and the lifestyle you are leading. You haven't got the discipline I would expect from an aspiring cricket professional and to me it is disappointing. Remember it is not whether you have talent or not, it is what you do with the talent that makes all the difference.

"You should be looking to dominate the level you are at if you want to keep improving and I wouldn't say you are exactly dominating here, would you?"

Like I say, I was a shattered unit. It pretty much came out of the blue. Until that moment I had no idea Nigel thought that way of me. We had been getting along like a house on fire, I was living in his house and I was feeling like a part of the family.

At the time I really thought I was doing okay. It wasn't until it had been pointed out to me by someone who I really respected and admired that, for the second time in my life (remembering Rod O'Meara), I thought I had better have a good hard look at myself.

That night I went home and wrote in my diary what had happened. I concluded with the words, "Nigel reckons I won't make it, I'll show that bastard." I must have been fired up, because Nigel is the furthest thing from a bastard that I know. It is crazy the things you say and think when you have been criticised or hurt.

Nigel's wake-up call certainly worked as my attitude changed completely. It was like Rocky Balboa's boxing coach telling him that he was fat and slow and lazy and good for nothing and that Apollo Creed was going to murder him in the ring unless he got off his backside and started clicking into gear.

Nigel's verbal rocket had exactly the same effect on me. From that day I started training harder than I had ever trained before. I was running, doing weights, swimming, skipping, saying "No" more often when people asked me to go out drinking and partying, and generally focusing on what I had been talking so much about.

John Hurley was throwing and bowling hundreds of practice balls at me, helping me develop my technique and improve my concentration. In other words, things changed.

Today, I am very glad that Nigel took the time to tell me the truth, even if at the time it really hurt to hear that truth. He didn't need to take the time, but like one's greatest mentor, he cared enough to go out on a limb and give it to me straight.

His encouragement ever since then has been unbelievable. After that day in the car, Nigel always promised me that if I continued to work hard and was fortunate enough to play Test cricket then he would be there to watch my first Test, no matter where it was in the world.

The day I left England I reminded him of his promise and he just smiled and said, "A promise is a promise!"

History now reveals that I have been lucky enough to play Test cricket for Australia. History also shows that I found out about my Test selection only 24 hours before I was due to walk out onto the beautiful Adelaide Oval.

This wasn't exactly a lot of time to prepare myself for something that I had dreamed about since I was a little kid, but I wouldn't have given it up for the world.

As the match progressed through the first day, I was 0 not out overnight and facing the fiery West Indian attack on day two of the Fourth Test in the Frank Worrell Trophy series of 1993.

After a restless and nervous night's sleep I had a shower, nibbled on some breakfast (I was far too nervous to eat) and took the lift downstairs to where the team bus was waiting to take us to the ground.

As I stepped out of the lift and walked towards the reception desk I thought that I could see Ian Baker-Finch standing at the reception desk. When I looked a little closer, the man was tall, with long dark hair, but it definitely wasn't the famous British Open golf champion.

There standing at the reception of the Hindley Park Royal in Adelaide was my friend, my mentor and "that bastard", Nigel Wray.

It was one of the most amazing acts of faith I have ever experienced. Most incredible was the fact that Nigel had dropped everything in London and within such short notice had booked on to a plane and travelled to the other side of the world.

Thankfully, Nigel's right-hand lady and personal assistant Gina Wernham had a few tricks up her sleeve, allowing Nigel to get on to a plane from Heathrow to keep his end of the bargain after my late call-up.

When he arrived at the Adelaide airport, Nigel hailed a taxi and asked the Italian taxi driver to take him to a nice hotel somewhere in town. Having never been to Australia before he was relying on the advice of a cab driver who could hardly speak English to find him somewhere pleasant to stay while he was in town. He had no idea where we were staying, but simply took the advice of the driver. The driver, in his wisdom, recommended the Hindley Park Royal, to which Nigel obviously agreed.

At 9am, Nigel was checking into the first hotel he had ever stayed in Down Under. At 9am, I just happened to be walking through the foyer of that same hotel. I simply couldn't believe it. Call it luck, call it fate, call it whatever you want, but it was a great moment in my life.

Nigel had made a promise and he had kept it. He had inspired me and pulled me into line previously, and now he was there for one of the best days of my life – it was simply unbelievable.

In one of the greatest Test matches ever played at the Adelaide Oval we fell one excruciating run short of beating the West Indies in a Test series. So close yet so far.

Two nights after the game I was having dinner with Nigel before he flew back to London. At the end of the night he said to me,

"Remember that day in the car when we had a talk about a few things to do with your attitude and goal of playing for Australia?"

How could I ever forget?

"Well, can you also remember writing in your diary that I will show that bastard?" he asked.

Once again my jaw hit the ground. "How did you know about that, Nigel?"

He finished, "You left your diary open on your bed one day and Linda saw it lying there. She sneaked a look at what you had written. After she told me, I watched you change and I am proud of what you have done. For once in my life I am happy to be thought of as a bastard."

I couldn't believe it. The man is full of surprises.

Interestingly, also at my first Test was John Hurley, who had flown from Sydney to be there. He had obviously forgiven me for not moving in with him and he and I, as you read earlier in the book, have been friends ever since my early initiation to England.

I often look back and wonder how different my life would have been if I had of moved into the "Hurls flat" the next morning? I would never have experienced the things that I did, yet I would have still been experiencing life in a different way.

I wonder if I would be a different person today? I will never know. I wonder if I would be where I am today if I hadn't been offered the lessons from Nigel Wray?

There are definitive moments in your life that change or re-direct the course of your life's journey.

## Little Eyes Upon You

*There are little eyes upon you*
*And they're watching night and day.*
*There are little ears that quickly*
*Take in every word you say.*
*There are little hands all eager*
*To do anything you do,*
*And a little boy who's dreaming*
*Of the day he'll be like you.*

*You're the little fellow's idol,*
*You're the wisest of the wise.*
*In his little mind about you*
*No suspicions ever rise.*
*He believes in you devoutly,*
*Holds all that you say and do,*
*He will say and do, in your way,*
*When he's grown up like you.*

*There's a wide-eyed little fellow*
*Who believes you're always right,*
*And his eyes are always opened,*
*And he watches day and night.*
*You are setting an example*
*Every day in all you do,*
*For the little boy who's waiting*
*To grow up to be like you.*

(Author unknown)

CHAPTER 17

# Keeping Life
# in Perspective

SHOT OF INSPIRATION # 17:
*Don't worry! If you have a problem and it is fixable, then there
is no need to worry about it. If you have a problem and it is
not fixable, then there is no need to worry about it either.
Worry can never help anything.* – THE 14TH DALAI LAMA

THIS CHAPTER IS POTENTIALLY a little gloomy but I want to
use it to help you understand that there is truth in the old
cliché that "things could be a lot worse".

Over the years, wisdom and experience has reminded me that
you never know what is around the corner in this life. This in
mind, I often call upon a smidgen of perspective to keep me on the

right path. Keeping things in perspective is a strategy I use to get on with my life and fight through the toughest times.

The more I live the more I understand that worry is a crazy, worthless pastime.

When I hear people complaining or worrying or taking a negative view of the world, I will say, or at least think, why worry so much, you could be dead tomorrow. This may sound like a blasé attitude but the reality is that this is the plain truth. While I don't necessarily live my life thinking that I may die tomorrow, I do use it as a reminder that every moment, every experience, and every day is special.

## ABSENT FRIENDS

In the five months since I started writing this book, three people I know have died in very, very sad circumstances. Two of them were close friends, the other was a young man whom I admired and respected.

When young English cricket star Ben Hollioake hugged his mum and dad, brother and sister goodbye at a restaurant, no one could ever have imagined that he was 10 minutes away from a fatal car accident. His death tore the heart out of everyone who loved and admired him.

During a eulogy for his brother, Adam Hollioake, a man of strong and respected character, said that for the first few days after Ben's death he couldn't find a single ounce of reason why his brother was no longer alive in this world. He was destroyed by the fact that his brother was gone and he was having trouble understanding why this beautiful life had ended so suddenly.

As the days slid by, Adam went on to describe how he thought the reason his brother had died right now, at the tender age of 24, was that  Ben was 100 per cent happy with his lot in life. Adam said he had never seen Ben so happy and that he was certain in his heart that he couldn't have been happier in this life.

While it is inconceivable to understand the pain that Adam and his closely-knit family felt at this time, he taught me a lesson during this eulogy that I hope I will never forget.

Ben Hollioake lived life to the fullest, cherishing every moment and not wasting his time or energy worrying too much about the irrelevant things in life.  In describing his brother's 100 per cent happiness, he reminded many of us of the importance of never taking this life for granted.

A friend of mine named Brett Birmingham died on Anzac Day at the age of 19.  He had lost his battle with Osteogenic Sarcoma, which is a cancer of the bone.  Brett had been introduced to the Western Australian cricket team 18 months before.  He loved cricket, he loved life and, although he had cancer, he would constantly blow me away with his incredibly positive and optimistic attitude.

Brett's sister, Alycia, summed up her younger brother's fight in her eulogy:

*Other than some Turkish blokes declaring war on Australia at Broken Hill during the first World War and firing at a train, there have been no wars fought within Australia.  Brett never left Australia, and seeing as he was born well after World War I, it could seem crazy to suggest that Brett was the leader of an army in the biggest war our family has ever seen.  Although Brett lost the war, he won many battles along the way. The battle of chemotherapy was won, because Brett was rarely sick, and if so, not very much. The battle of being able to drive his manual car even without much control of his right foot, Brett won. Being told that he was clear, even though short-lived, was a win for Brett and his army. All the battles Brett won did not win the war for him, but he pushed the enemy army back for two years and five months. Without that, we would not have had so many beautiful moments and times, and we would not have been able to express our love for Brett as we did, or as he did for us.*

*"I believe that the biggest battle Brett won was through his positive attitude, optimism, good humour and determination. Brett was not willing to concede defeat, and even to the very end, he did not concede defeat. Brett passed away on Anzac Day, but he had spent the day with thoughts of war, real historical useless wars. He showed his ring, from his great-grandfather, to the doctor, and asked us to hang his great-grandfather's war medals for him to see. Brett was, to me, a true soldier. One who personified what the Anzac spirit was about, and he taught me what real determination, optimism, good humour and love can do.*

*"Thank you, Brett, for fighting what would seem a futile war, because without it, we would not have had you. It was not in vain, and neither are you. We are all going to miss you, but we will never forget you.*

A week or so before he died, Brett rang me to tell me that he was about to die. Having seen him only a week before, I was surprised at how quickly the cancer had overtaken his body. That night, during the most surreal phone call of my life, he reminded me that there is always someone worse off in the world.

Brett's younger sister was right in everything she said, especially that he will be sadly missed.

Only recently, a scream rang through my house. Running into the kitchen I was horrified to see my wife sitting in the corner literally destroyed. The phone was lying by her side so I realised that something tragic had happened. It had. She had just learned that her best friend had died suddenly. At age 35, Nicky – beautiful, energetic and loving Nicky – had died while playing on the bed with her two beautiful kids, Jake and Page.

Without warning and, it seems, without reason she was gone. It just doesn't seem right. At just 35, and with hopes and dreams and loves, it is all over. Tragic. But yet another valuable lesson to us all.

You may ask why I am writing about this in a so-called cricket book? The reason is simple. I believe with all my heart that everything in life should be about living the moment and giving every moment your best shot. Whether that moment is watching a cricket ball, hugging your children, making your dinner or doing your job, it is about the moment.

The passing of Ben, Brett and Nicky are brutal reminders that life is short and that you just never know when your time is up. This is mind, we might as well give it our best shot while we can.

## LESSONS FROM THE KIDS

Some of the most valuable experiences in my life have come through my involvement with kids like Brett Birmingham, and specifically the Children's Leukaemia and Cancer Research Foundation of Western Australia.

Being asked to be patron of this foundation was an honour that has been far exceeded by the rewards and inspirations that I have gained since taking on the role. I have met some incredible young people who have invigorated my soul with their courage and tenacity to overcome their terrible diseases.

About two years ago I went to a celebration party at Princess Margaret Hospital in Perth. Mark had been told that he was clear of the cancer that had devastated his world. Everyone was over the moon, as his future looked far brighter than it had a few months before.

Three months later, Mark and his parents went for their standard three-month check-up. Everything was clear. The future was looking rosy.

Unfortunately, his standard six-month check-up told a different story. The tumours were back and so was his life of fighting cancer.

Happily, Mark soldiers on. His chemotherapy knocks him around and the long days away from his home on the farm are torturous, but still he keeps going back for more. His mum has been a trooper, looking after her youngest, like only a mum can. Mark flew to England and helped the team celebrate retaining the Ashes in 2001. My fingers are crossed that his next big celebration will be one of triumph over his cancer.

One thing I have noticed from my meetings with these young cancer patients is the pain in the eyes of the parents. Being a father of three, I simply cannot imagine the suffering and helplessness that the parents must feel.

## AND YOU THOUGHT YOU HAD IT TOUGH

When I consider some of the circumstances of people that I have met, I realise that I have never really had anything to worry about. It makes me smile, and at the same time shake my head, that when put into perspective, my problems have been minor. The privilege has been all mine in meeting some of the most courageous and inspiring people in the world.

Professional cricket has taken me to many points of the globe. From the streets of India, Soweto and Trenchtown in Jamaica, to the Khyber Pass bordering Pakistan and Afghanistan, to parts of Sri Lanka. My eyes have been opened to help me appreciate just how lucky I am to live in a country like Australia.

In their own way, these countries are magnificent places, but in the same breath, they have problems that have opened my mind to the real world.

We live in heaven on earth compared to some of places I have seen human beings living. The contrasts in our societies are so extreme that you really do have to see it to believe it.

Strength can be gained by understanding how lucky we really are, and while I know most of us take our resources, facilities and opportunities for granted, we should understand that we do live in the lucky land.

## VISTING INDIA

Since my first visit to India nine years ago, I have had some extraordinary experiences in this amazing country of mystique and extremes. I will never forget being invited to a function at the

Madras Rubber Factory on the first night of my first visit to India.

The MRF is a huge organisation in India; a very wealthy company which sponsors the fast bowlers' cricket academy in Madras, not unlike the Commonwealth Bank sponsoring the Australian Cricket Academy in Adelaide.

The night turned out to be unforgettable experience because for the first time in my life, my eyes were opened to a life of unimaginable extremes.

The cricket academy team that I was touring India with was treated to one of the grandest functions that I have ever seen. After being greeted by an official welcoming party, we were shown through to an amazing outdoor, second-storey setting of manicured lawns, water fountains, fishponds and palm trees.

We dined on fresh seafood, legs of roast lamb and beef, exotic fruits and drinks from the top shelf. We were even offered Cuban cigars and Moet Chandon champagne to top it all off. This was a feast and occasion fit for kings and I have to admit a great time was had by all.

While I have fond but vague memories of the feast, I will never forget what I saw that night after leaving the function. Just outside the doors of the MRF building and camped in their hundreds, were families sleeping on the streets with nothing. At first I thought it must have been the alcohol playing tricks on me, but I soon realised that this was the reality of life in India.

When I say nothing, I literally mean nothing. Apart from the clothes they were wearing on their backs, they had nothing more than a piece of cardboard or a tatty, dirty old blanket for which they could sleep on or under. I was dumbstruck by the fact that, just 10 metres away, I had been living it up in a world of pure affluence, and yet just outside, these people were living at the extreme opposite of the scale.

It was very sad for me to see. In fact, I felt ashamed to have so much, when so many others have so little.

Driving in the bus back to our hotel I saw not hundreds, but thousands of people; families living, sleeping and existing together on the concrete paths of the city. Their homes were the streets, they had no homes to go to, and they had no privacy or material possessions. As far as I could see, they had nothing except each other.

The saddest thing for me was not only did they have no material things, but also that the children wouldn't know about dreams and ambitions, about moving out of the life that they were born into. There is no way that the kids could have lived anything but day to day, gaining enough food to live until tomorrow. Their lives were purely about survival, hopefully begging enough coins from one day to the next so that they could buy something to eat, maybe something to keep them warm.

I learnt a lot from watching those poverty-stricken people and the way they live. Above all, I couldn't believe how happy they seemed. The children were always laughing and smiling, even though they didn't even have a pair of shoes on their feet. Their only form of income was through begging and, in a funny sort of way, they even made a game and a joke out of that dire predicament.

They will never have any education, except learning how to live a life of homeless survival on the streets. They will never see a hot bath or shower; they may have a wash in the filthy polluted river or waterholes once or twice a week, if that.

They will probably never taste fresh chocolate or warm bread. They will never feel the comfort or warmth of crisp sheets on a bed. In fact they may never feel the softness of a bed, full stop. Shampoo and soap would be as foreign as a trip to the cinema or local fun-park and a new pair of shoes would be a miracle gift from some generous passer-by.

To understand countries like India a little better, my diary entry the day before my last visit may give you a more clear insight.

## Going To India – February 19, 2001:

*Before arriving in India tonight we were briefed on many aspects of life in this part of the world. Of all the things we heard, an Indian friend of the team talked to us before the Allan Border Medal, giving us an insight into what we could expect. Only having been to India for a week, six years ago, I was shocked at what he had to say. I thought it might be of interest to share his experience and wisdom. A few of Darshak's views should be taken with a pinch of salt, as there may be a hint of sarcasm in some of what he says.*

*"Firstly, you should know a few facts:*

*"India or Bharat or Hindustan (land of the Hindus) is of course the world's second most populous country after China. The good news is that in about 20 years time it will be THE most populous.*

"Currently over a BILLION people live in India and it is conservatively estimated that we add one Australian population to our population every year.

"It is the country with the largest number of English speakers in the world. Remember, the Americans don't speak English.

"It may come as a surprise but India is one of the world's largest growers of food and is in fact a huge net exporter. The problem here is one that confronts a bald man every morning who is contemplating a shave - not production but distribution.

"India is the world's leading developer and exporter of computer software. E-commerce and IT are no longer buzzwords; they are now old hat. Other leading areas of trade dominance are diamond cutting and polishing, tea, floriculture, clothing and footwear.

"Over 80 per cent of Indians are Hindus, 14 per cent Muslim, two percent Sikhs, two per cent Christians and two per cent crooks.

"All of them are cricket followers, a lot of them will want to touch you, and many of them will want to feel you. They all want your autographs and if they have a camera, they will want your photo. They will spend hours just gazing at you. There could be stampedes while they are just following you. Last year, when a few of the guys came over to my place for dinner, there were well over 100 people waiting outside just to get a glimpse at their heroes – somehow word had got around. By midnight, the crowd had swelled to even more.

"For a lot of these people a meeting with you will be one of the high points of their lives – I guess that must be a pretty sobering or scary prospect – your kindness, patience and tolerance would be appreciated.

"If you value your personal space, have a long, contemplative walk one last time at Melbourne airport. For the next 54 days, you will find that personal space is a totally alien concept. You will not have much privacy I can assure you.

"The first thing that hits you when you arrive is the humidity followed by the unique sights, smells and sounds. Don't be afraid, just enjoy it all and relax.

"They say that there are more millionaires in Bombay than New York. It can't be that difficult as Bombay has some of the world's most expensive real estate. You will often see some of the poorest people in the world living in front of the richest.

"A land of amazing contrasts, a lot of my Aussie friends have had trouble coming to terms with India. I keep assuring them that no matter what their lot in life, they will rarely see an unhappy Indian cursing their own fate. Don't mistake poverty for unhappiness. There is no dole and yet they go about their rather bleak daily lives cheerfully and without complaints.

"If you ever wonder why they are so fatalistic, here is my theory: it is because of our belief in karma and reincarnation. We Hindus believe that God rewards us with human existence after about 33,000 previous lives in various shapes or forms. It is the ultimate payback from the Almighty. Only when you accumulate enough brownie points in your previous existence do you get to be born as a human being. Moreover, to be born, and strut around as, say, an elite sportsman, you guys must have surely done some good in your past lives.

"It has been inculcated in us that we must not waste our lives.

We must do good karma (deeds) whenever possible and only then will we achieve "moksha" or "nirvana" i.e: salvation and inner peace.

"Indians have a lot of respect for elders, authority and uniforms. They are extremely and obsessively family oriented. Very, very warm and hospitable. There is no black and white – only shades of grey and brown.

"There are two words that you will rarely hear in India – "please" and "thankyou". However, I assure you that it is not because of rudeness. Indians convey their requests and gratitude by the tone of their voice and use of phrases. Strange but true – so please don't be offended if someone says simply, "Can I have your autograph?"

"Don't be alarmed to see so many same sex Indians holding hands or with arms around each other's necks. It doesn't mean anything at all and it's just a manifestation of the touchy, feely people Indians are. Ironically, you will rarely see men and women showing any affection in public.

"Most Indians have great difficulty with the Australian accent. Steve Waugh, people find virtually incomprehensible. If you would like to make yourself understood, please take it easy. S-L-O-W. Please also try to avoid abbreviations and Australianisms — such as vegies for vegetables.

"Steve Waugh (after Sachin) is the most admired cricketer in India. In Calcutta, Tugga is God. In the rest of India, he is just slightly less divine.

"Sir Donald Bradman still gets 10 times more mail from India than any other country. He is of course bigger than God.

"*Please don't argue with any Indian about your Test or first-class record or statistics, or any highlights or lowlights of your cricketing life. They not only know it better than you but will probably carry written proof of it at all times.*

"*Of the current lot of Indian players, Sachin is the one who all Indians believe has been kissed by the Gods. It would be very unwise to do a touch-up job on him in India . . . I believe it would be extremely foolish knowing what I do about Sachin, India and Indians.*

"*Among the Aussies, the batsman everyone in India wants to watch is Mark Waugh. Michael Slater and Ricky Ponting have plenty of fans as well. I am only talking of cricketers who have previously toured India and played in Tests. Though I dare say you won't be hearing any 'Ooh...Ah...Glenn McGrath', I assure you that millions of fans will be watching him with interest. Shane Warne is a legend and Indian crowds desperately want to see him now he is back at his best. Adam Gilchrist is awaited with the anticipation of an exploding firecracker.*

"*One of the things that disappoint Indian crowds (and Indian cricketers) is the seeming hostility of the Australian cricketers toward them. It can easily lead to ugly situations. I am hoping that you will make a special effort to get along with the crowd and, in fact, get them on side. It should not be that difficult. In addition, I believe it will certainly help the team, not harm it, to have the crowds friendly – if at least not neutral.*

"*At this point, I would like to point out that for an Indian to spend a day at the cricket, there is an amazing logistics exercise. He has to get leave from work. Then he has to fight to get a ticket, spending virtually a whole day's wages on the price, apart from having to queue up for a few hours in the hot sun. Then, on match day, he has to spend at least three hours commuting in extremely over-crowded trains and buses. Then queue up for at least half an hour while the cops feels him up. They will confiscate newspapers, glass water bottles, radios and anything that remotely resembles a projectile.*

*"Then, at the ground, the loos stink and are filthy. He will be lucky if someone else is not already seated in his reserved seat. To evict that person would mean getting a policeman interested. That means a promise of 'baksheesh'. On most grounds, the spectators bake for most of the day. This despite the fact that they don't really need to work on their tans. Therefore, you can well imagine that the crowds are going to be fairly volatile and need to be occasionally kept in good humour!*

*"If you want to see the real India or meet some real Indians, the way to do it is to accept invitations to go out with them. Go out sight-seeing or shopping or visit their homes. I can promise you that it will be a deeply enriching experience. You will not find a more tolerant, hospitable and generous people anywhere in the world.*

*"I would like to take the liberty of reminding you about your personal legacy. You will all leave an impression on Indians. Make friends. Please think of life after cricket in the world's richest cricketing country."*

*So before a ball has been bowled we have some idea of what we are in for over the next seven weeks. The funny thing is, I wonder what the visitors are told before they set foot in Australia?*

*From Mumbai,*

**JL.**

My diary continues on life away from The Lucky Land ...

## A Sad Reality Check, February 21, 2001

*Arriving in most cities at 11 o'clock in the evening, you would expect to find a few cars and even fewer people occupying the streets. Not the case when we entered Mumbai last night. After a flight from Nagpur, the guys pushed through throngs of eager supporters and onto the team bus for an hour-long journey to our hotel in the heart of Mumbai. To my dismay, I was saddened at what my eyes could see from the coach window. Just out from the airport we drove past one of the biggest slums in Asia. Human beings living on dirt floors covered only by sheets of cloth or panels of tin. These makeshift houses would not even win second prize in the cubby houses the kids at home build to pass their time.*

*Further inland my heart felt strained as I saw thousands of people of all shapes, sizes and ages, sleeping on the footpaths. The lucky ones had a blanket, the others just a block of stone to use as a pillow. It was as if these poor people had walked until the point of exhaustion, and when they could finally walk no more, they simply found the nearest piece of vacant footpath and lay down to sleep.*

*Probably the saddest image was of a skeleton-thin lady cradling a baby that could not have been more than three months old. She was sitting on the side of a busy main road. Just sitting and staring into space. As I am the father of nearly three children, it was so hard to fathom the existence of this distressed mother. The expression on her face was one of total hopelessness. She just sat warming her child as the scrawny, hungry dogs tip-toed their way around the masses of homeless people looking for a feed of their own.*

*Here we were on the way to our five-star hotel, while other humans, with little else but the shirt on their backs, lay destitute in the middle of nowhere. At midnight, there were gatherings of young children sitting around like teenagers at a local hangout. The difference was that these groups of kids could only have been five or six years old. They seemed happy enough, but it just didn't seem right.*

*They say the crime rate in Mumbai is not that high and I am glad because I can't imagine what could happen to these children or these homeless souls if the atmosphere was more intense. Lying in my room, tucked up comfortably in my hotel bed, I almost felt guilty after witnessing the streets of Mumbai. Life is quickly shuffled into sharp perspective when you witness these unfamiliar scenes.*

*From Mumbai,*

**JL.**

And this . . .

## Feeling like Santa Claus! – March 3, 2001

*My heart bled for the street people when we arrived in Mumbai. I couldn't believe human beings had to live in such terribly poor conditions, when the opulence surrounding our every move is fit for kings. To try to help some of these street people, I started taking the complimentary fruit from my hotel room and distributing it every morning. Sitting on the team bus, I handed these makeshift breakfast hampers through the window to the throngs of beggars gathering outside.*

*My morning offerings have helped me befriend a family of four young street beggars who have started meeting the team daily for their early morning treats. For me it was a tiny gesture, but for them it was like Santa Claus had arrived with a sack full of Christmas presents.*

*We all appreciate the joy of a child's face when a brightly wrapped present is pushed in front of them on Christmas morning or on their birthday. Magnify that joy tenfold when you imagine how the faces of these four kids have come to life every morning and afternoon when the Australian cricket team bus turns up outside the cricket ground. Because of the surplus of extra food left over in the changing rooms at the end of a day's play, the morning ritual has extended to a dinnertime treat as well. Bags of biscuits, muffins, sugar, tea, bread and more fruit, have found their way into the hands of the four cutest looking kids you have ever seen. While they quite obviously have nothing materially, the smiles on their faces are as beautiful and priceless as the smile on any child's face.*

*After today's play, I gave my new little friends an Australian cricket team sponsor's cap. Maybe the kids will sell them to a cricket fanatic for their next meal, or maybe they might keep wearing them as a reminder of the Aussie team Santa Claus who visited their street one week in February 2001. Whatever way, it has given us a little joy to help lessen the hardship of seeing babies begging every day to keep their stomachs full. So sad, and while they probably know no different, it continues to break your heart.*

– JL

And more . . .

## A Breadcrumb In An Ant's Nest!

*If you have ever wondered what it feels like to be a breadcrumb in an ant's nest, just take a walk through one of the bustling streets in downtown Mumbai. Captain Steve Waugh, a demi-God in this part of the world, John Buchanan and myself, were invited to visit one of the communities in the red-light district of Mumbai to talk to the street children. What a humbling experience! Once again, these kids with no material possessions but the dirty and torn shirts on their backs or ankle-length dresses, couldn't get close enough to see and touch foreigners like ourselves. For half an hour we took questions from a translator while standing on a step of one of these squalid but infamous brothel rooms.*

*Within five minutes of arriving at our destination, the word had obviously got out that Tugga was in the area. Like bees to the proverbial honey pot, we were surrounded by hundreds of inquisitive faces searching for a glimpse of Steve Waugh and members of the Australian cricket team. The very fact Steve Waugh was walking through the streets was enough to have these Indian cricket fanatics shaking with excitement and disbelief. It was like a chapter in the bible, with followers of Jesus doing anything to get close to the miracle worker.*

*This was the real India for me. On the streets there were animals roaming, people sleeping and washing and rice boiling. The smells, the sights, the noises, are so different to home that I walked with my eyes opened like a child seeing his first circus. It was fascinating, sad, enchanting, profoundly confronting, complex and yet so simple. The way of life seems so simple and yet in this squalor, the questions of why seem to me so complex. But then, when there are so many people in such a relatively small area, the answers become obvious.*

*One thing that I noticed was the reaction of the women as we walked through the streets. Without fail every woman we saw turned their face from us and hid behind a scarf. When I enquired about this, I was told the reason for their reaction was that they wouldn't want to bring disgrace to their families by being photographed by one of the many photographers following our every move. Because we were in the poorest of areas, a red-light district, these women are considered by Indian society to be at the lowest echelon of the community. Hence the embarrassment of their predicament.*

*Equally as noticeable was the incredible knowledge in the game of cricket that even these people possessed. All of the children expressed that their greatest hero in this life was Sachin Tendulkar, and they knew everything about each member of the Australian team. There is no way any of these adults and children alike would own their own television set, or even radio, so how they acquire such a wisdom for the game is totally beyond comprehension.*

*Then again, I guess it is not that unbelievable when you consider the way these kids continue to smile and play, even though their living conditions are as unfortunate and dire as one could ever imagine.*

*This tour is turning into more than just a cricket tour for yours truly. It is becoming more of an eye-opener into how lucky the majority of us really are.*

## Memories from Mumbai

*My memories will remain happy ones of this complex city, although they will be memories of two worlds. One world is of material poverty, squalor and deprivation – the other of grand opulence as rich as any in the universe.*

*Arriving in Mumbai, I described the heartbreak of shoeless, homeless children, street sleepers and beggars. Asia's biggest slum, Dharavi, will be a lifelong reminder of an existence so foreign to that of which we are used to in the lucky land Down Under. A visit to the famous "cages" red-light district, at night and during the day, struck my heart chords like an electric shock. Especially when you could see the difficulties faced by the children who must know nothing but day-to-day survival. Maybe a good thing!*

*At the opposite side of the spectrum, we have been treated to service and facilities fit for a king. The Taj Hotel in the middle of the city has spectacular ocean views and service and infrastructure rivalling any hotel in the world. Where once touring India was a mystery of stomach bugs and sleepless nights, you now feel like you could be anywhere in the world as you enter the magnificent hotels like the Taj.*

*The cruelty of it all is that just outside the luxurious walls of my world is a humble ant's nest of human reality, so extreme in nature to the material social milieu, lived by such a minority of people in India today. While it would be easy to feel depressed and sorry for the poorer classes, the happiness displayed by these people is so very heartening and infectious. Materially many may have nothing, and yet spiritually it is hard to remember seeing a race of people sharing so many smiles. The whole society seems so ironic and yet is also seems to tick like clockwork.*

## Udayan And The Leprosy Colonies

*Visiting the living and schooling campus of Udayan – a girls home for children of leprosy colonies in Calcutta – in downtown Calcutta, was as heart-warming an experience as I have enjoyed for a long time. The drive to Udayan was an eye-opener in itself, with the squalor and poverty of every day life staring at us like a hungry, crying baby. Double, even triple, this regular poverty with the stigma and rejection of living in a leper colony, and you can start to get an indication of where these beautiful children we were visiting have come from.*

*The depths of despair are rapidly transformed into emotions of joy and promise as you watch these kids developing into polite, happy and hopeful children, who may one day have the opportunity to live and achieve their dreams. It was incredible watching these neatly dressed and smiling children show off their newly acquired skills learned at Udayan. A group of young girls between the ages of 10 and 15 (I am guessing the ages) were playing heavenly tunes on their violins. Heavenly, not only for the actual sounds, but more because two years ago these kids would never have even known what a violin looked like.*

*Following a concert by the violinists, a group of boys presented a range of yoga moves that made my body ache without even bending a limb. The skill and strength of these youngsters could have them competing in the Olympic gymnastics given the opportunity.*

*Udayan is all about opportunity. Taken away from the leper colonies (with the permission of their leprosy suffering parents) to pursue a brighter life, it is mind blowing witnessing the transformation of these wonderful young children. Every child in this world should have these opportunities. Simple opportunities like education,* clean clothes, healthy fresh food and a bed with a mattress and clean blanket or sheet. The harsh reality in parts of the world like here in Calcutta is that thousands, probably even hundreds of thousands of kids, don' t have these luxuries. Luxuries that seem like a part of every day life for people like you and me.

The saddest part of my visit today was the pride the school had in the donation of three hundred beds. It wasn't sad because of the pride, or of course the donation from a friend of Steve Waugh's in Sydney, but because these little children were experiencing a bed as a luxury. On the walls of the sleeping dormitory were pictures of teddy bears and animals, just like you would find in the room of my daughters at home in Perth. It seemed surreal walking through this newly constructed living quarters. Each night, 50 young girls set their heads down without their mummy or daddy to tuck them in at night. Obviously, they are better off and probably happier and safer living here, but it just doesn't seem fair to have people living away from their homes and their families because of a disease like leprosy.

The happiness and tenderness of the people we met was fantastic. Like so many charity workers, the strength, courage and foresight of the people running Udayan is inspirational. Having Steve Waugh as a figurehead of this worthy organisation helps to raise much needed funds for developing opportunities for these less fortunate children. For Steve, I am sure it is inspiring watching the progress of this wonderful organisation of which he is quite obviously a major contributor and role model.

From Calcutta,

Inspired!

**JL.**

Reading back through these Indian diaries, it is interesting to see me consistently mention how lucky we are in the world we live in. It is also interesting to note that the effect of touring India has had a permanent influence on how I view life.

Every time I find myself worrying about what I haven't got, I now smile and remember my little friends in downtown Mumbai. This very thought is a great remedy to the dangers of this material world.

I really think the challenge is to give life a real crack. Give it a red-hot go, get sharp, and get pumped! Start dancing, start smiling, start concentrating, focussing and moving in the direction that you want to go.

You have to do it for yourself because no one else will do it for you.

I remember Ric Charlesworth once saying that the only motivation of significance is the motivation that comes from within. If you don't feel the fire inside, then no one else can give it to you.

Nelson Mandela sat imprisoned in a tiny jail cell for 23 hours a day, for 27 years, on the famous Robbin Island. Visiting this island off Cape Town in South Africa was one of the most moving experiences of my life, especially standing in the cell where one of the most humble, yet most admired and respected men in the world lived for a greater part of his life. It was simply mind-blowing how this man survived and then re-entered the free world like he did.

A man by the name of Rory Stein, who is a great mate of the Australian cricket team, acted as Nelson Mandela's head security agent or bodyguard when he was freed from prison. Rory told me recently:

*"The old man (he uses this term with the greatest of reverence) is the most incredible and special man I have ever met. He is one of the few people I know who doesn't see the colour of another man's skin. He has qualities that I have never seen in a man before. He is simply an amazing person whom I love dearly."* As Rory admitted to me, this type of compliment would have once been impossible coming from his lips as he had been bought up under the apartheid system. *"JL, the old man has changed around my whole programming and understanding of life. It takes a pretty special human being to be able to do that."*

Having seen where Mr Mandela lived for so long made me truly understand the strength and determination of this man who came through unimaginable hardships to hold the highest office in his nation and help put an end to the apartheid system.

Helen Keller reached summit after summit in terms of achievement despite having her hearing and speech taken away from her. Infamous composer Beethoven followed the music in his mind, because of the deafness in his ears, to give the world the gift of beautiful music.

Genius Albert Einstein was accused at a young age of being useless and backward before achieving what he did throughout his life, and the inimitable Mother Theresa lived in one of the saddest places I have ever seen to leave a profound mark on the world. Her work in Calcutta, a place of extreme poverty and gloom, was as selfless an example of human life and labour that has existed. While I know there are many people who bring joy and hope like Mother Theresa, it was her who helped highlight the struggles to the more fortunate masses around the world.

It would be easy to write an entire book about people who have fought extreme odds to come up triumphant, but these are just a few examples to admire and use as an inspiration and guide.

At the end of the day, we can make the choice to turn our back on a life of despair and misery by striving one step at a time for our Olympic gold medal, whatever that may be.

Understanding that no one ever gets to the top without experiencing disappointments along the way makes the disappointments or plateaus easier to understand and overcome.

You have to get up and do it for yourself. Get strong; get powerful. Be bold. Back yourself to the limit. Keep it simple. Be humble but proud. Throw away the handcuffs of fear and limitation. Be tenacious. Accept things for what they are by trusting perspective. Don't fall for selective hearing. Be brutally honest. Eliminate the grey areas; real honesty is black or white. Be loyal; you are either loyal or you're not loyal, there is no middle ground with loyalty. Be creative. Don't hesitate. Be prepared; don't leave things to chance. Trust the instincts of your heart and stomach. Smile in the face of pressure. Be courageous. Show respect; and earn it. Enjoy tranquillity, peace and silence. Don't make excuses. Welcome adversity and learn from its lessons. Look after your mind, body and soul. Be kind, helpful, loving and honest. Enjoy other's successes. Never waver from your values and principles. Don't let your ego ruin you. Be single-minded and determined but never selfish or arrogant. Don't complain or whinge. Be positive and optimistic. Laugh. Don't be scared to show your emotions. Never get bored; there is no bigger insult that you can give yourself.

Cherish your friendships. Ask lots of questions. Be willing to listen. Never give up. Walk with your head high and your chest out. Tell people you love them; don't leave it until it is too late. Talk to yourself like the best coach would talk to you. Be inspired. Be happy. Don't worry; worry gets you nowhere. Aim high. Never look down. Control the controllables. Learn from the best. See the sunrise. Do right, not wrong. Don't be afraid. Be disciplined. Take your opportunities. Aim for a tight mind and a loose body. Go forward.

In a nutshell, be passionate about life and what you believe in. Revel in *The Power of Passion.*